THE HOUSE OF
LIBERTY

THE HOUSE OF LIBERTY
MASTERS OF STYLE & DECORATION

Edited by

STEPHEN CALLOWAY

*with 280 illustrations
including 100 in colour*

THAMES AND HUDSON

Half-title
The interior of Liberty's Tudor Shop, London.

Frontispiece
A Liberty oak carver, from a design by
C. F. A. Voysey, c. 1905.

Typeset by Footnote Graphics, Warminster, Wiltshire
Printed and bound in Singapore by C. S. Graphics

Contents

LIBERTY'S
MASTERS OF STYLE
& DECORATION

The House of Liberty occupies a unique place in the history of London's shops. Its reputation is certainly not based on longevity; many celebrated London firms can trace their origins to the eighteenth century or even go back as far as the seventeenth, and thus they were already old when Arthur Liberty first opened his doors in 1875. Nor yet is it simply a question of success; for the last century has undoubtedly seen the rise of greater commercial empires. What singles out the House of Liberty is the extraordinary degree to which the firm has always made itself synonymous with all that has been most stylish in fashion, dress and decoration.

A Liberty 'Hathaway' oak dining table with oak chairs (right) from a design by C. F. A. Voysey, c. 1905; in the background, a Liberty oak bureau and oak corner cupboard with lead-glazed door, both of similar date.

A selection of Art and Crafts copperware (below) by the Keswick School of Industrial Art, possibly sold by Liberty's c. 1900.

Introduction

A HUNDRED YEARS AGO it would have seemed unthinkable that the cultural history and artistic aspirations of a nation could be examined and written about in terms of the history of shopping. Many influential Victorian figures from Prince Albert and Henry Cole, the sponsors of the Great Exhibition, onwards were fascinated by the connections between Art and Commerce but, though they knew that industry and commerce could be enlightened and improved by contact with the world of art, they remained firmly convinced that Art ultimately belonged to a higher and more sacred plane of human thought and activity. Yet, little more than half a century later, the new art historians of the thirties began to discuss the works of even the greatest painters and sculptors not as examples of divine inspiration, nor yet as mere illustrations of current aesthetic theories such as Fry's 'significant form', but as objects ordered by patrons and paid for in documented financial transactions. By no means always a Marxist approach, such consideration of the position of the fine and decorative arts in what we now call the 'market-place' has become in recent years one of the most useful and sophisticated methodologies of the cultural historian.

The upper part of Regent Street in the eighteen-nineties, with Liberty's East India House on the right.

A Japanese metal charm necklace (above), *advertised in the 'Liberty Art (Dress), Fabrics and Personal Specialities' catalogue, 1886.*

An early Liberty import from Delhi: a pale grey merino stole (above right), *with cones and flowers embroidered in white floss silk, white silk fringes and tassel, c. 1880.*

Overleaf Furnishing fabric in designs by William Morris marketed by Liberty's: 'Honeysuckle' on the left and 'African Marigold' on the right.

Beginning perhaps in France, scholars came to realize how much could be discovered about the cities of the late nineteenth century by an examination of the ideals, merchandising practises and customers of *les grands magasins*. The proposition has now become generally accepted that a very great deal of helpful light can be thrown into otherwise poorly illuminated areas of the history of taste by the study of the history of a shop; the more so when the firm in question has, as in the case of Liberty, been established for rather more than a century, a period during which its activities have seldom seemed to be far from the cutting-edge of style and fashion.

In the early years the shop's position in terms of both image and influence was, it seems fair to say, more akin to that of a smart commercial art gallery rather than of a commercial retailer; the most obvious comparison perhaps being with that most influential phenomenon of the taste-broking world, The Fine Art Society (founded at about the same time as the House of Liberty, and still, happily, one of the chief ornaments of Bond Street). In the eighteen-seventies Arthur Liberty, already something of an expert on rare shawls and fabrics and porcelains from the East, became the friend of artists, aesthetes and designers such as Rossetti, Whistler and Godwin. He supplied them with ravishing silks and curiosities from India and especially the strange wares from Japan, for which the firm was rapidly establishing a vogue. At the same time, Liberty was imbibing their unconventional attitudes and tastes, together with their idiosyncratic ideas about decoration. He realized that he could retail the essential visual trimmings, if not the central underlying decadence, of this rich, sensual world of Bohemian aestheticism.

With the growth of what came to be called the Aesthetic Movement, the desire of middle-class women with a taste for decoration to live 'beautifully' and 'artistically' became intense. The flames which destroyed the old plush upholsterers' interiors of the mid-Victorian years were fanned by the popularity of Gilbert and Sullivan's *Patience* which cleverly parodied the aesthetic ideas and posturings of Oscar Wilde and his circle. To be artistic was all, and Liberty ensured that to shop at his emporium was to be artistic.

A good indication of the extent to which the shop and the Movement were identified in the public mind is to be found in the *Punch* cartoons of George du Maurier, who week after week chronicled in a wickedly amusing series of drawings the foibles of would-be aesthetes. Some of these are generalized comments on the aesthetic sensibility. In one, a soulful Pre-Raphaelite young woman scrutinizes a bluff dinner companion and demands 'Are you intense?', whilst in another, a newly married couple look longingly at a blue-and-white teapot and vow that they will try to 'live up to it'. But one of the most famous drawings in the series is also the most particularized in its actual use of the firm's name. In a frightful pun the pretensions of 'artistic' modern decorators are satirized with the heartfelt cry: 'Oh, Liberty, Liberty, how many crimes are committed in thy name!' Though Arthur Liberty's early reputation rested on his ability to select exactly the right Indian stuffs, Chinese porcelains and Japanese objects to appeal to the European taste for the exotic, his first ventures into commissioning designs and manufacturing goods for sale in the shop reveal the same astuteness in anticipating his market and an almost infallible eye for style. He clearly perceived the need to create pieces which would serve in the ordinary dining room or bedroom and yet still harmonize with his

An exhibition of Donegal carpets organized by Liberty's at the Grafton Gallery in 1903 (the carpet seen second from the left on the wall is illustrated on page 63); these Irish carpets formed an important element of Liberty's championing of Arts and Crafts design alongside the imported textiles from the East.

FELICITOUS QUOTATIONS.

Hostess (of Upper Tooting, showing new house to Friend). "WE'RE VERY PROUD OF THIS ROOM, MRS. HOMINY. OUR OWN LITTLE UPHOLSTERER DID IT UP JUST AS YOU SEE IT, AND ALL OUR FRIENDS THINK IT WAS *LIBERTY!*"
Visitor (sotto voce). "'OH, LIBERTY, LIBERTY, HOW MANY CRIMES ARE COMMITTED IN THY NAME!'"

A Punch *cartoon by George du Maurier, 20 October 1884, satirizing the Aesthetic Movement and the close association of Liberty's with its values.*

more exotic and decorative wares. Some of the first productions in this new area were close in style to the designs for 'Art Furniture' produced by E. W. Godwin and others in the newly fashionable Aesthetic Taste. Cleverly designated 'Anglo-Oriental' by the ever-astute Liberty, they included caned furniture, small tables of a more conventional European height and also wholly un-Oriental pieces such as fussy overmantels laden with shelves and brackets for 'artistic' arrangements of china. Some of these new lines were also offered in the early catalogues issued by Liberty, where it was made clear, in the same way as to customers at the store, that a service was available, whereby their requirements for artistic work made to fit specific spaces could be fulfilled. Even in those early years it appears that an in-house team was available to prepare drawings and to oversee the progress of commissions. The actual work of making these early Liberty pieces was given out to a considerable number of small contractors, such as the traditional chair-makers of High Wycombe and also to local Soho cabinet-making firms.

The success of these new areas of business seems to have been immediate and, as a result, Liberty was encouraged to develop the design and commissioning aspects of his activities and to move towards a new structure in his firm which would facilitate the exploitation of the public's avid interest in design in all its branches. Fairly rapidly, Liberty began to step up the processes of design and manufacture, in particular in the fields of fashionable dress for women, textiles for both dress and furnishing, silver and pewter wares for the table, larger pieces of ornamental furniture and, of course, in the lucrative area of small decorative items and costume jewellery. Liberty's success in all these undertakings was considerable, not only, it becomes apparent, because so many of the designs were very good

Previous double-page A room setting of Liberty furniture (left) *, including an oak refectory table, c. 1905, with copperware, including a firescreen, by the Keswick School of Industrial Art. Detail of a Liberty oak bureau, c. 1905, with a selection of Tudric pewterware* (right)*: a tall cylinder vase and two 'bomb' vases, designed by Archibald Knox, c. 1905* (above)*; a biscuit box, decorated with stylized leaves and flowers, designed by Archibald Knox, c. 1903, and two candlesticks, designed by Rex Silver, c. 1905* (below).

Liberty textiles and costumes of the mid nineteen-seventies (right)*: the 'Liberty in Cotton' exhibition of 1975.*

of their kind, but also because they satisfied a considerable public demand for artistic goods that were well made and readily available without recourse to the rarefied world of the craft exhibitions or the intimidating experience of attempting to commission designers or makers directly.

Then, as now, it was important to have the right chair or the accepted curtain treatment, whilst the tea or coffee pot of the moment made a clear statement about its owner's tastes and aspirations. There is, indeed, a curious parallel between the enthusiasm of artistically minded patrons in the eighteen-eighties and nineties for the work of new designers, and the obsessive concern for design which characterized the nineteen-eighties and gave rise to the extraordinary cult status which designers enjoyed.

From the end of the nineteenth century onwards a new phase of Liberty's can be seen to have opened. Successive stylistic phases embracing Art Nouveau- and Arts and Crafts-inspired merchandise met with immense success before the First World War. During the inter-war period a similar policy of careful commissioning of new designs was supplemented by the addition of well-chosen reproduction pieces that were calculated to appeal to a more middle-class clientele. Keenly aware of this shift in the market, all the heads of departments at the shop were exhorted to tailor their stock to appeal to the vast new constituency of Metroland. In most areas designs were 'updated' to include a high proportion of 'Olde English' elements, but of course the most significant and enduring monument to this major shift in the firm's orientation was the creation of the great 'Tudorbethan' building, which made so startling an impression among the conventional Neoclassical and Baroque blocks of the day which were being built along Regent Street.

In the years following the Second World War, Liberty's entered a period of relative stability without great excitements aesthetically. Not until the rather more innovative years of the late fifties and early sixties did things begin to look up. At that date the firm's glass and furniture departments began to look abroad and bring in interesting examples of the new Swedish furniture and adventurous glass from Venice and furnishings from Milan. By the latter part of the sixties, too, Liberty's had begun to investigate its own earlier history and played a vital role in the revival of interest in the designs of the Art Nouveau period. The shop's own centenary, which fell in 1975, encouraged a great deal of new and more serious research into the period and resulted in a highly popular exhibition at the Victoria and Albert Museum in that year.

The shop of the seventies and eighties and of the present day has remained one of the key retailers in London and abroad. Consistently interesting in its innovative approach to marketing, its history presents a unique opportunity to chart the changes in taste and style in the period since Arthur Lasenby Liberty first began in business in 1875. This book aims to follow those many changes in fashion by bringing together the work of a number of specialists in which each of the main phases of the Liberty story is examined in depth.

'The Plastics Age: from Modernity to Post-Modernity': a window display at the 1990 exhibition at Liberty's organized in association with a similar event at the Victoria and Albert Museum.

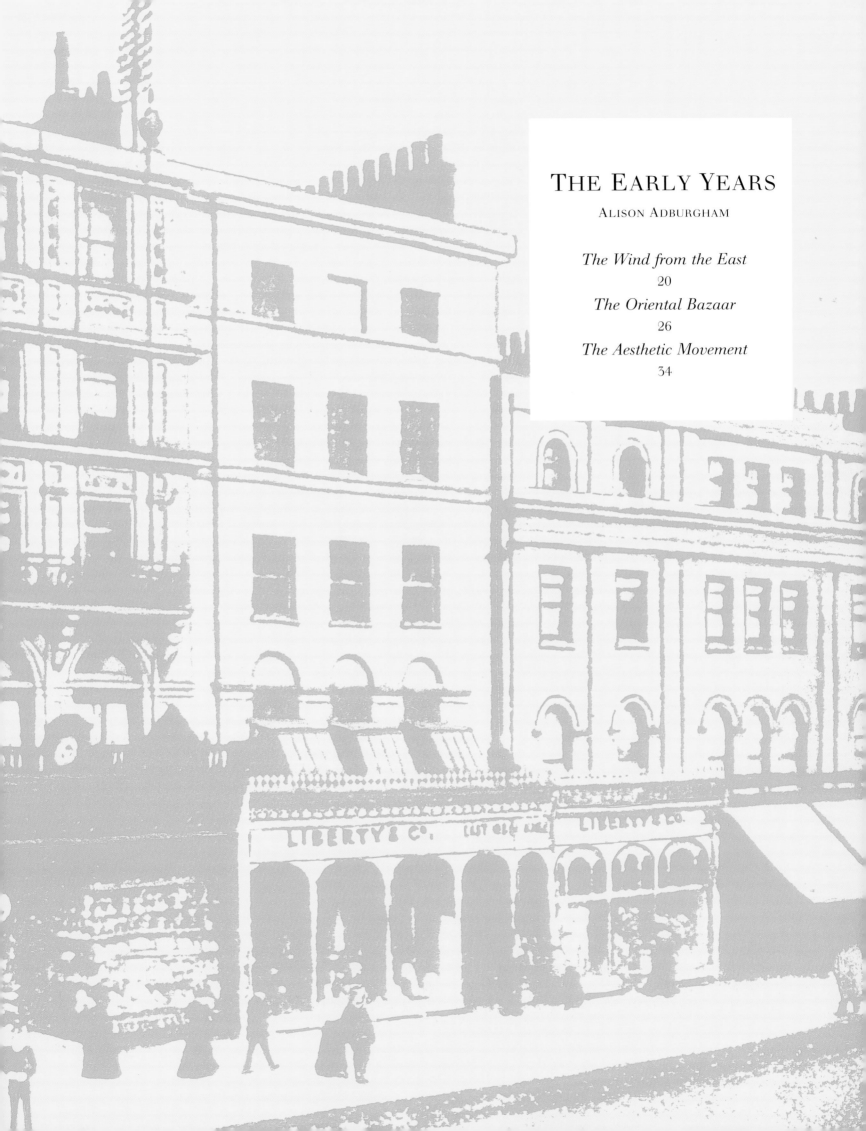

THE EARLY YEARS

ALISON ADBURGHAM

The Wind from the East

ARTHUR LASENBY LIBERTY'S arrival in this world was an unpropitious one; he was the eldest of the eight children of a hard-working draper in Chesham, Buckinghamshire. His mother, Rebecca, was the daughter of a farmer in the neighbourhood. When Arthur was eight years old, the family moved to Nottingham, where an uncle had a lace warehouse. Arthur was then sent to live with his aunt at High Wycombe, where he attended the small school of the elderly Miss Heath. Later, he was sent as a boarder to University School, Nottingham, where his best subjects were English, history and art; his hobbies were theatricals and scene-painting. Considered exceptionally intelligent, he was entered at the age of sixteen for a university scholarship, which he failed to win. He could not try again the following year, as his father had financial problems, forcing Arthur to leave school and take a job in his uncle's lace warehouse.

His attention, however, was fixed on London, the centre of the art world, where everything that he was interested in was happening. Another uncle, who had a wine warehouse in the City, offered to try and find his intelligent young nephew an opening; but the opening found initially seemed to shut the door on all Arthur's aspirations. He was apprenticed to Mr. John Weekes, a draper in Baker Street, serving the middle-aged, middle-class ladies of St. Marylebone. The year was 1859, the year when the crinoline was at its largest and when analine dyes were introduced – harsh, blatant, shrill magentas, emerald greens, purples. The fabrics were stiff and shiny: the more they rustled, the better they pleased. Corsetry was the mainstay of the business, haberdashery – pins, elastic and tape – the busiest department.

The long hours at the shop allowed Liberty no opportunity for visiting art galleries or museums, but he could save money for a very occasional theatre seat. Although Baker Street then, as now, was unexciting, Regent Street was not far away. In this most famous shopping street in the world,

Previous double-page Liberty's in Regent Street, London, in the late nineteenth century.

L. T. Piver, Perfumery and Gloves, 160 Regent Street and 10 Boulevard de Strasbourg, Paris; one of the prestigious establishments in 'the most famous shopping street in the world', from A Visit to Regent Street, *c. 1860, engraved and printed by Henry Vizetelly.*

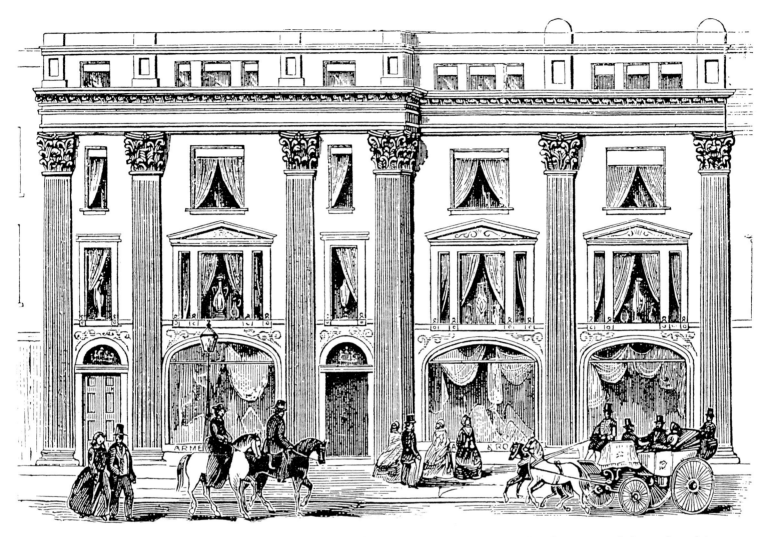

Farmer & Rogers' Great Shawl & Cloak Emporium, 171–5 Regent Street, as it would have been when Arthur Liberty joined the staff in 1862; from A Visit to Regent Street, *c. 1860, engraved and printed by Henry Vizetelly.*

designed by John Nash, one of England's most celebrated architects, no grocers were permitted, no ironmongers, no public houses, no butchers or bakers and no candlestick-makers. One of the largest and most fashionable shops for ladies was Farmer & Rogers' Great Shawl & Cloak Emporium, on the west side towards the top of Regent Street, opposite Piver's exclusive perfumery and Mappin Bros., famous jewellers and silversmiths. Farmer & Rogers' had taken over another prestigious business, that of J. & J. Holmes, specialists in Indian shawls and Oriental curiosities, by appointment to H.M. the Queen and several lesser Majesties. They imported cashmere shawls from France and India. Less costly were the large, square shawls from Paisley and Norwich, printed with Indian designs, which became known as 'paisley patterns'. Entranced by these rare delights in the windows of Farmer & Rogers', young Liberty somehow or other persuaded the firm to take him on. His apprenticeship at the Baker Street shop was ended by mutual consent – Mr. Weekes was probably only too glad to get rid of his reluctant apprentice.

Arthur Liberty's interest in design was much stimulated by the International Exhibition of 1862, held on the site in South Kensington where the

William Morris's 'Pomona' tapestry, 1885; the central figure is by Burne-Jones. Morris and the Pre-Raphaelites undoubtedly exercised a profound influence on the visual style of Liberty textiles and furniture of the Arts and Crafts period.

Japanese fukusa (opposite), *a buff-coloured silk gift cover woven with a pattern of flowers; the main design is a dragon amid clouds, embroidered with silver-gilt thread and silk cords. This example probably dates from the mid nineteenth century and is typical of such covers stocked by Liberty's in the early years of the shop.*

Natural History Museum was later built. This exhibition was not such a hugely popular and commercial success as the Great Exhibition of 1851; but for intellectuals, artists, designers and the like, it was significantly superior. For one thing, there was a section for Fine Arts as well as for Applied Art – the very word 'applied' was distasteful to sensitive souls. Walter Crane wrote of the exhibition much later in his *An Artist's Reminiscences*: 'There was a fine representative group of the Pre-Raphaelite Brotherhood's pictures, including some of Madox Brown's finest work. English decorative art, too, began to assert itself in this exhibition. There was a most interesting group of furniture and examples of interior decoration of all kinds shown by the Ecclesiological Society, among which, I think, there was early work of J. Seddon the architect, Pugin, William Burges, Philip Webb, William Morris and E. Burne-Jones.' This was the first time that work by Morris had been seen by the general public.

The young Arthur Liberty was fascinated by the section devoted to Japanese ceramics, prints, silks and wallpapers. This was the first time that imports from Japan had arrived in England in any significant quantity. For two and a half centuries Japan had been a closed society, access to her ports forbidden since 1624 to all but the Dutch, Japan's own shipping limited to small fishing vessels. After the revolution of 1848 a few contacts with other nations started. Then, in 1853, Commodore Perry sailed a

Another Japanese fukusa *in black velvet embroidered with silk cords, interpreting the story of Jo and Uba, mid nineteenth century, exhibited at the Liberty Centenary Exhibition in 1975 as an example of early stock.*

squadron of the United States fleet into the Bay of Yedi and intermittent contact began through American and British navy personnel. Walter Crane wrote that in his early work he found 'suggestive stimulus in the study of certain Japanese colour prints which a lieutenant in the Navy I met at Rode Hall, who recently visited Japan, presented me with. He did not seem to be aware of their artistic quality himself, but regarded them as mere curiosities . . . their vivid dramatic and decorative feeling struck me at once.'

In Paris, artistic antennae had first twitched to the wind from the East in 1856, when the painter and etcher Félix Bracquemond discovered some wood-block prints by Hokusai used as packing for some ceramics from China. James McNeil Whistler, then an American art student in Paris, saw them and was instantly enthralled. Madame de Soye conceived a new shop for the sale of Oriental *objets d'art* in the Rue de Rivoli, which she opened in 1858 and named 'La Porte Chinoise'. Baudelaire, the brothers de Goncourt, Manet, Fantin-Latour and Whistler were among those who made the new shop their meeting place, where the talk was of 'l'art pour l'art', which soon became in England 'art for art's sake': art had no story to tell, had no moral to preach, no religious faith to inspire, no social message, no reason to exist except to be beautiful. In 1858 Daniel Lee of Manchester produced a series of roller-printed cottons with designs originating from Japanese prints. In the same year, Japan signed a limited commercial treaty with Britain and America, and a variety of Japanese specialities began to reach the West. Soon the trickle had become a flood of delicious, decorative objects for the temptation of the intelligentsia. By the time of the 1862 Exhibition, the acquisitive collectors were joined by enterprising merchants and shop-keepers, alerted to the possibility of fresh fields of tempting merchandise to exploit.

The London apostles of art for art's sake found a meeting place when the Oriental Warehouse was opened at Farmer & Rogers' Great Shawl & Cloak Emporium in Regent Street, where Arthur Liberty had recently joined the staff. It had been partly his enthusiasm for the Japanese section at the 1862 Exhibition that had persuaded Farmer & Rogers' to buy up all that was available of the Japanese work when the exhibition closed, to form a basis for an Oriental Warehouse. Liberty and one other young salesman were appointed to run it; within two years Liberty was made manager. The right man had arrived at the right moment at the right place; the East was now firmly in vogue.

A portrait of Arthur Lasenby Liberty at Lee Manor, near Chesham, where he was the tenant from 1890 until 1902 when he bought the manor and gradually acquired 3,000 acres with farms, cottages, houses, and the Lee Gate Inn. This portrait is unsigned and undated, but would seem to present him in the character of country squire, a role which he took up from the turn of the century.

The Oriental Bazaar

An illustration from Walter Crane's Aladdin, or the Wonderful Lamp, *one of his Toy Books Shilling Series, 1874; Crane wrote in his* Reminiscences *that he was inspired by seeing early Japanese prints with their 'definite black outline and flat, brilliant as well as delicate, colours – their vivid, dramatic, and decorative feeling'.*

WITH THE OPENING of the Oriental Warehouse Arthur Liberty entered his own kingdom, surrounded by treasures, his customers as fascinating as his merchandise. For here came the apostles of art for art's sake to search among all kinds of Oriental curiosities – ginger jars decorated with prunus and blackthorn blossoms; tall vases which Whistler called 'Long Elizas' from their Dutch name 'Lange Lysen'. Rossetti, Godwin and Whistler came in friendly rivalry, seeking finds for their collections of Nankin blue-and-white porcelain. The most high-flung raptures of the artists were over the silk fabrics, so soft, so pliant, for the draping of their models.

Liberty not only served the artists but, so to speak, absorbed them, as they dawdled fascinated over fine hand-woven textiles, uttering audacious pronouncements upon life, death and destiny. He even dared to dress as they did (after shop hours of course): velvet jacket, low turned-down collar, loosely-knotted wide neck-tie. Some fifty years later he spoke of this time in an interview for the *Daily Chronicle*: 'Famous artists got the idea that I took a real interest in what we sold and my knowledge and appreciation of art were extended by prolonged visits to their studios, where I was always made welcome. The soft, delicate coloured fabrics of

ORIENTAL SILKS woven exclusively for LIBERTY & CO. Ltd.

"Liberty" Silks.

Hand-Block-Printed, in Varied Designs and colourings.
Dyed and Printed in England.   Woven in India.

THE PRINTED "LIBERTY" SILKS are woven in India, and imported in what is technically termed the "grey" state.

IN THE GREY STATE the Silks are Dyed (in England) and Printed by a special Hand-process, in which the latest Chemical and Scientific Knowledge is utilized to ensure the Stability of the Colouring Pigments applied.

THE CHARACTERISTIC AND BEAUTIFUL DESIGNS are the result of careful study and selection extending over a long series of years.

CONTEMPORARY DECORATIVE ARTISTS of acknowledged repute have been employed in the production of many of the Designs.

AMONG THE DESIGNS may be found reproductions of Ancient Indian, Persian, and other Classic Oriental Originals.   34 inches wide.

Price **28/6** per Piece of about 7 Yards.

Half-pieces cut without extra charge.

PATTERNS POST FREE.

LIBERTY & CO. LTD.]   5   [LONDON & PARIS.

An advertisement in the 'Silks, Eastern & Western' catalogue, c. 1896. The figurine of the lady by the fountain was drawn by J. Moyr Smith.

the East particularly attracted these artists because they could get nothing of European make that would drape properly and which was of sufficiently well-balanced colouring to satisfy the eye.'

Through the artists, Liberty began to meet actors and actresses. Artistic circles merged with stage circles. He also had a friendly sponsor in Arthur Lewis of Lewis & Allenby, Silk Mercers, at 195 Regent Street. Arthur Lewis had overcome some of the social disadvantage of being in retail trade, having travelled much on the Continent and being deeply interested in music, literature and art; he was one of the founders of the Arts Club in 1863. He had bought Moray Lodge in Kensington, whose grounds bordered on those of Holland House. Here he gave extravagant parties in rivalry to those of Mrs. Princeps, a leading hostess in the art world at nearby Little Holland House, who had made the painter G. F. Watts her living-in

A pair of bronze Japanese candlesticks (right), *supported on lions, with dragons encircling the stems, c. 1875, exhibited at the Liberty Centenary Exhibition as examples of the metalware stocked in the early years of the shop.*

A Japanese kimono (below), *dating from the second half of the nineteenth century, and made of silk damask, dyed blue, green and purple with a white reserve. It is embroidered with a design of clouds and birds in gold thread and coloured silks, and was sold at Liberty's, price £1. 15s., c. 1891.*

protégé. Arthur Lewis became engaged to Kate Terry, the leading actress of the day, who retired from the stage at his family's request. Her actress sister, Ellen Terry, had a brief marriage with G. F. Watts. Arthur Liberty, on the fringe of this world, also made a brief marriage, on 8 June 1865, to Martha Cotham.

Ellen Terry, after her separation from G. F. Watts, began living in Hertfordshire with the architect and designer Edward W. Godwin. He had been one of the first to collect Japanese prints, when he was a young architect in Bristol in the early eighteen-sixties, and wrote theatre criticisms for the local paper. It was his belief that all the visual arts should be united, and his criticisms were more about the costumes and stage décor than the acting. In 1874, when he and Ellen Terry moved to Taviton Street, Bloomsbury, the walls of their children's nursery were covered with Japanese prints. Whistler gave Ellen a blue-and-white Nankin dinner set, and later sent, she recalled in her *Memoirs*, 'to my little girl a tiny Japanese kimono when Liberty was hardly a name.' The actor Forbes-Robertson, who visited them when he was an art student, described their drawing room: 'The floor was covered with straw-coloured matting, and there was a dado of the same material. Above the dado were white walls, and the hangings were of cretonne, with a fine Japanese pattern in delicate greyblue. The chairs were of wickerwork, cushions like the hangings, and in the centre of the room was a full-sized cast of the Venus de Milo, before which was a small pedestal holding a censer from which rose, curling round the Venus, ribbons of blue smoke.'

Emma Louise Blackmore and Arthur Lasenby Liberty on their engagement in 1874, the year before Liberty left Farmer & Rogers' and opened his own shop at 218A Regent Street.

In 1874 Arthur Liberty, by this time divorced from Martha Cotham, became engaged to Emma Louise Blackmore. He was now thirty years old and for ten years had been manager of the Oriental Warehouse, the most profitable department of Farmer & Rogers' shop. He asked to be taken into partnership and was refused on the grounds that the business could not support another partner. Indignant, his artist friends urged him to start a shop of his own, promising to transfer their custom to him. He needed little encouragement, for by this time his ambition was strengthened by self-confidence. He firmly believed that he could transform the whole look of fashion, both in house decoration and costume. He dreamed of society ladies dressing more like the artists' models – discarding their corsets, bustles and padded shoulders and wearing soft, languid, flowing draperies in gentle, shadowy colours. A new look in fashion would be brought about by the *beau monde* dressing in Liberty fabrics!

The capital for the new venture came from Emma Louise Blackmore's father. He was of a Devonshire family from Littleham near Exmouth, but had moved to London and established a West End tailoring business in Brook Street. A correct Victorian, he needed a lot of coercing by his daughter to put up £1,000 and back a bill for Arthur Liberty with Henry Hill, a tailor in Bond Street, for another £1,000. The lease of a half-shop directly opposite Farmer & Rogers', No. 218A Regent Street, was taken. Liberty grandly named it East India House, and engaged two employees – Hannah Browning, a girl of sixteen, and Hara Kitsui, a Japanese boy – thinking he could not afford to employ a man. But on the early morning of

An illustration from Rossetti and His Circle *by Max Beerbohm, 1922 (right); Rossetti, having just had a consignment of 'stunning' fabrics from 'that new shop' in Regent Street, tries hard to prevail on his younger sister to accept at any rate one of these and have a dress made of it from designs to be furnished by himself: 'What is the use, Christina, of having a heart like a singing bird and a water-shoot and all the rest of it, if you insist on getting yourself up like a pew-opener?'*

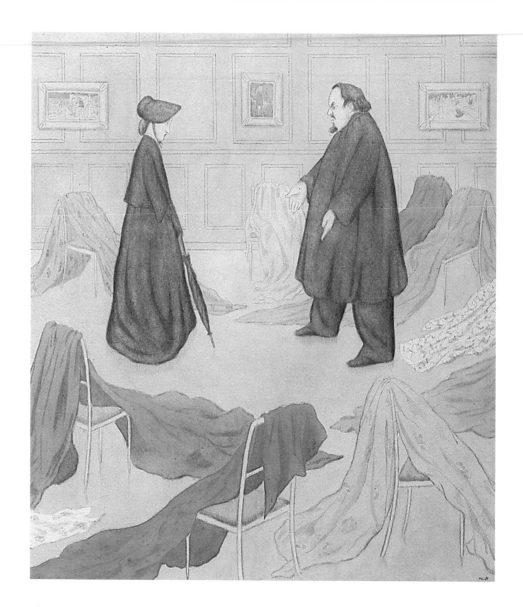

Japanese kimono (below) as sold at Liberty's in the late nineteenth century and worn by the assistants in the shop.

the opening day, 15 May 1875, he found William Judd from Farmer & Rogers' there saying he was resolved to follow Liberty.

Fifty years later William Judd spoke of that first morning to reporters when he had been invited to open the new Tudor building: 'I remember when there were only four of us – the Master, two others and myself. Now there's a thousand or more. We just sold coloured silks from the East – nothing else. The sort of thing that William Morris, Alma Tadema and Burne-Jones, and Rossetti used to come in and turn over and rave about.'

Farmer & Rogers' closed down soon after Liberty left. It transpired that their Oriental Warehouse had been carrying the whole business, shawls having gone out of fashion with the crinoline. At Liberty's the merchandise was not for very long restricted to silk fabrics. William Judd recalled that at about this time 'we got in touch with many well-known artists, and anything that was especially good and rare in embroidery or lacquer or cloisonné enamel, or Satsuma ware, I often had to take for them to see'. It

Edward William Godwin, 1833–86, was the son of a Bristol decorator, trained as an architect and practised in London from 1862. An early collector of Japanese prints, he lived with the actress Ellen Terry from 1867 to 1875, and designed stage costumes and scenery. He also designed houses for Whistler and Oscar Wilde, worked with Burges on the design for the New Law Courts, and published Temple Bar Illustrated *(1877), and* Artistic Conservatories & Horticulture Buildings *(1880). He was the director of Liberty's costume department from its inception in 1884.*

was only seventeen months after the original half-shop opened that E. W. Godwin wrote an article in *The Architect* (23 December 1876) telling how he had heard that a new importation of Japanese fans was about to be unpacked at Liberty's: 'There was quite a crowd when we arrived. A distinguished traveller had button-holed the obliging proprietor in one corner; a well-known baronet, waiting to do the same, was trifling with some feather dusting brushes; two architects of well-known names were posing an attendant in another corner with awkward questions; three distinguished painters with their wives blocked up the staircase; whilst a bevy of ladies filled up the floor space. Before I could catch the eye of the master of this enchanting cave, it was learned that the cases would not arrive till late in the evening. Almost in a moment the swarm of folk vanished, and I was free to pick my way from ground-floor to attics, for No. 218 Regent Street is from front to back and top to bottom literally crammed with objects of oriental manufacture . . . There are matting and mats, carpets and rugs for the floor; Japanese papers for the walls; curtain stuffs for windows and doors; folding screens, chairs, stools, and so forth.'

Godwin, however, detected a deterioration in the quality of many of the Japanese objects. In Japan, after the Royal Revolution of 1868, all trade restrictions had been lifted, and the trickle of Japanese exports gradually became a flood. Japanese warehouses sprang up in London, and some of the fast-expanding department stores also jumped on the bandwagon. The enterprising William Whiteley, known as 'The Universal Provider', had opened an Oriental department as early as 1874. Debenham & Freebody and Swan & Edgar were next and others followed. Such demand could not be met by the irregular output of Japanese craftsmen and artists, so exports were being bulked up with cheaply produced trash. The final word on the Japanese craze can be quoted from the contribution to a trade publication by a Miss Harrison, Lady's Underclothing and Outfitting Buyer of D. H. Evans: 'Japanese wraps and coats are very good sellers, and a smart line to sell at a cut-price.'

Even in the early days Arthur Liberty had foreseen a lowering of Japanese standards. In fabrics, the demand he himself had created was far exceeding the supply. He began to seek other sources in India, Java, Indo-China and Persia. He had also become aware that many of the Eastern fabrics were too delicate, or their dyes too fugitive, for the use to which they were being put by dressmakers and interior decorators. Another worry was that Eastern producers were beginning to change their subtle tints for the cruder colours they believed Westerners preferred. So he set about persuading English firms to experiment with Eastern dyeing techniques, and English textile manufacturers to adapt their machines to weaving processes that would produce fabrics similar to those of the East. Like William Morris, Liberty wanted to improve the nation's taste by giving ordinary people the chance to buy beautiful things. Unlike Morris, who had a revulsion to all things mechanical, he believed that machines

An advertisement from The Queen, *the Lady's Newspaper, 3 August 1878 (right); the headline 'SEASIDE COSTUMES' is misleading, since it seems to infer made-up clothes rather than fabrics for making them. Liberty's costume department did not open until 1884.*

could be brought to the service of art, could bring art to the people. Their co-operation he saw as essential, since hand-made things would always be too expensive for all but the well-off – as indeed, Morris's productions proved to be.

Liberty began his crusade by importing plain, undyed fabrics from the East and then getting Thomas Wardle, the dyer and printer of Leek in Staffordshire, to co-operate with him in the introduction of dyes which had until then been believed to be a closely guarded secret of the East. These delicate pastel tints they called 'Art Colours' and soon they became described all over the world as 'Liberty colours'. Liberty silks were soft and plain, without 'finish' or 'dressing', or any of the processes used to give 'body' or a meretricious silk surface to cheap fabrics. The irregularity of the hand-weaving, which gave them an accidental play of light, was another of their charms. The fabrics he imported were the soft woollens of Cashmere, the filmy gauzes of India, the fine light cottons familiar in

The carpet department at Liberty's (below), Chesham House, 142–4 Regent Street, acquired in 1885 and primarily devoted to carpets and furniture. The basement was called the 'Eastern Bazaar', with Japanese and Chinese antiques, porcelains, bronzes, lacquerware, screens, fans, and a hotch-potch of things described as 'decorative furnishing objects' and 'miscellaneous Eastern knick-knacks'.

tropical countries, the silks of China and Japan, mostly plain woven, but some with a small damask pattern. They included the tussore or 'wild silk' produced by the worm fed on the oak, as well as the true bombyx fed on the mulberry. Tussore silk in its natural colour had been fashionable for many years for dress and light furnishings, but no means had hitherto been found for its blanching and dyeing. Its use had also been handicapped by its narrow width. Liberty's representative in India now persuaded the weavers to use a wider loom, and new processes for dyeing it were evolved in England.

As he intended, Liberty's customers were no longer confined to the cognoscenti. A member of the staff at this time recalled forty years later: 'Our founder imported large quantities of Indian, Chinese, and Japanese silks to be dyed. They "caught on" with the public and literally *miles* of them were sold for draping purposes, often caught up and otherwise mingled with fans and hand-screens. In summer, the heavy poles and curtains were taken down and windows draped with silks in different shades of the same colour, hung in festoons. People found that an ugly Victorian room, with its gilt chimney glasses, walnut furniture of bastard French design, repp curtains and crochet antimacassars, which could boast nothing but an intense respectability, could be made comparatively interesting and brightened at a very small outlay, and East India House was besieged.'

With all this furore for his fabrics, Liberty was able, within eighteen months of the opening of his shop, not only to repay his father-in-law's loan but also to acquire the second half of the premises at 218 Regent Street. East India House had become an enterprise dedicated to leading the taste of the nation – it was no longer just an Oriental bazaar.

A design for a Saracen-style smoking-room from an undated Liberty 'Handbook of Sketches', c. 1890. The design studio at Chesham House served many rich clients for the then fashionable Moorish music-rooms, Arab halls and screened galleries. In 1887 Arthur Liberty and his wife travelled to North Africa to explore the Moorish scene for themselves and bring back new ideas.

The Aesthetic Movement

CULTS become movements in mysterious ways; to identify a precise starting date for the Aesthetic Movement is not possible. Nevertheless, the opening of the Grosvenor Gallery in Bond Street in July 1877 can be seen as the event which caused aestheticism to become talked about beyond the small introspective circles of artists and designers. The Grosvenor Gallery was intended to compete with the Royal Academy, which was felt by the Pre-Raphaelite artists to ignore the most significant work of the time. Burne-Jones took an active part in the founding of the Gallery, and the paintings exhibited in that first season included works by G. F. Watts, Madox Brown, Rossetti, Alfonse Legros, Holman Hunt and Whistler, whose *The Falling Rocket* was the target for venomous criticism by John Ruskin in his magazine *Fors Clavigera*. Ruskin's pen had the power to damage not only Whistler's reputation as an artist, but also his sales. Whistler brought a libel action against him, which he won; but it was only a moral victory; he was awarded a farthing damages and no costs.

Arthur Liberty sent him a letter of congratulation and sympathy, to which Whistler replied: 'Of course costs would have been more satisfactory to the minds of some – but to the world really it has been a great moral victory. And the first shot at the critic has at last been fired. You know I always win in the end.' In the meantime the costs made him bankrupt. He had to sell the White House designed for him by Godwin in Tite Street, Chelsea, and all its contents. Before he left it, Whistler climbed on a ladder and wrote over the doorway: 'Except the Lord build the house, their labour is but lost that build it. E. W. Godwin, F.S.A., built this one.'

Another of the founding directors of the Grosvenor Gallery was Sir Coutts Lindsay, and Lady Lindsay gave 'invitation only' receptions there on Sunday afternoons. Mrs J. Comyns-Carr, whose husband was also a director, wrote in her *Memoirs* that Lady Lindsay and her husband 'took a certain pride in being the first members of Society to bring the people of their own set into friendly contact with the distinguished folk of art and literature. In these fine rooms, hung with crimson damask, they certainly gathered together the élite of the great world as well as all the brilliance of a select Bohemia.' The artists' models in their soft, flowing gowns revealing un-corsetted, slim figures, were in contrast to the tight-laced, be-bustled society ladies.

Some of the more perceptive of these ladies would have sensed a wind of change in fashions soon to come. Indeed Mrs Comyns-Carr was boldly leading the aesthetic way, sliding around in soft, clinging attire. The Duchess of Rutland was one whose great beauty had always allowed her to ignore crinolines and bustles. Herself an artist, her portrait was painted by Watts and she sat for Millais as the nun in *St. Bartholomew's Day*. Her daughter, Lady Diana Cooper, remembered her as 'tall and frail with a complexion delicate as the palest anemone. Her hair was just auburn and she wore a cloudy fringe like Sarah Bernhardt ... flimsy open-necked shirt, free-wristed, with numberless little cream lace scarves draped round

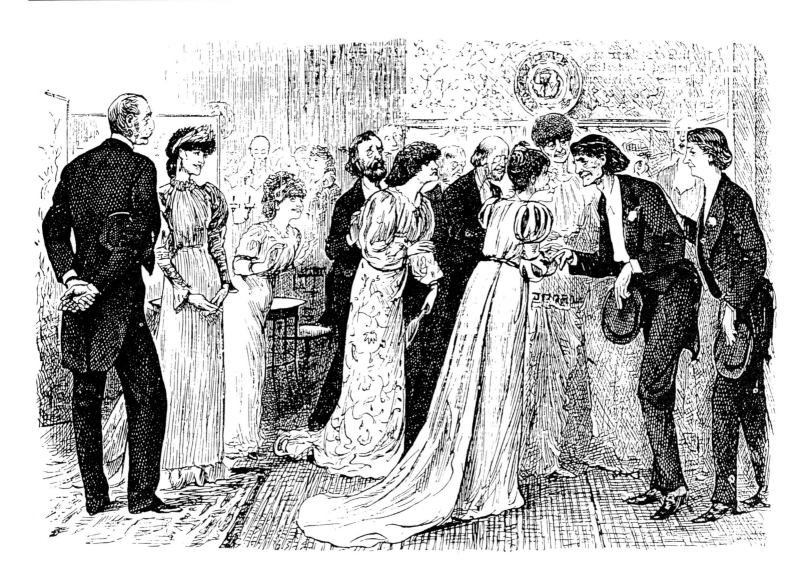

*'Nincompoopiana' – The Mutual Admiration
Society, by George du Maurier,* Punch,
*14 February 1880; du Maurier had begun his
brilliant mockery of the aesthetes in* Punch *in
1877, with such characters as Postlethwaite
and Maudle, Mrs Ponsonby de Tomkyns and
the Cimabue Browns of Passionate Brompton.*

*'Athena' from 'Liberty Art Costumes, Fabrics
and Personal Specialities', 1887 (opposite), in
Arabian cotton with silk himation; E. W.
Godwin, who directed the costume
department, favoured Grecian influences, as
did all true apostles of the Aesthetic
Movement.*

neck and elbows. Always a sprig of bay was pinned high up to her neck by
a green enamel tortoise.' Inspired by the Grosvenor Gallery receptions, a
new kind of customer – more wealthy – began coming to Liberty's in
search of aesthetic fabrics for dresses, furnishings and curtains; they often
insisted on consulting Mr Liberty himself as *the* expert of weft and weave
when making their choice. Never on Lady Lindsay's guest list, of course,
would there have been any of the *nouveaux riches*, who had risen to great
wealth through manufacturing industry and were cruelly immortalized in
Punch by George du Maurier in the character of Sir Georgius Midas.
Nevertheless, they had to be tolerated by practising artists since they were
the new patrons of the arts. Francis R. Leyland of Liverpool, self-made
ship-owner, could only be considered brash by the most biased. He spoke
French and Italian fluently, was much travelled and aimed to be a modern
Medici. When in 1876 he bought a house in Prince's Gate, Knightsbridge,
he hired Norman Shaw to direct a total rebuilding of the interior. Shaw
was one of the most fashionable architects of the day, and was responsible

for the planning of Bedford Park, the first 'garden city' intended to be a Utopia for aesthetes. Eighteen of the rooms in Leyland House were hung with paintings by Burne-Jones, Rossetti, Albert Moore, Ford Madox Brown, G. F. Watts and others of the Pre-Raphaelite Brotherhood; the dining-room was reserved for one picture, Whistler's *La Princesse du Pays de la Porcelaine*; but when Whistler saw it hung he declared it was ruined by the Spanish leather wall-covering, painted with red flowers, designed by Thomas Jeckyll. Leyland, still in Liverpool, gave Whistler a free hand to redecorate the room himself, and Whistler held open house there to all his friends while he worked on a striking design of peacocks. Arthur Liberty, one of those invited, said in an interview years later, 'Whistler always pretended that he valued my critical judgement, and certainly we had a feeling of sympathy on the Japanese impressionist side of things. I remember spending many hours with him when he was engaged on the famous peacock room, and it was a pleasant pose of his to suggest that I assisted him with advice. But no man, I suppose, was ever more independent of advice or less patient with it.'

On Leyland's part there was resentment at Whistler not only inviting his friends to the house, but also holding a press view and handing out publicity leaflets about his design with a general invitation to come along and see the work in progress. According to two of Whistler's American

A water-colour of James McNeill Whistler (above) *by the celebrated cartoonist SPY (Leslie Ward) for* Vanity Fair, *12 January 1878.*

AN IMPARTIAL STATEMENT IN BLACK AND WHITE.

ÆSTHETIC LADY AND WOMAN OF FASHION. | WOMAN OF FASHION AND ÆSTHETIC LADY.

'Aesthetic Lady and Woman of Fashion' by George du Maurier, Punch, *9 April 1881.*

A lithograph (opposite below) *by F. Hamilton Jackson (1881) of Bedford Park, West London, the first garden suburb, planned as a Utopia for aesthetes; begun in 1876, the first eighteen houses were designed by E. W. Godwin, then Norman Shaw was engaged to complete the project.*

biographers, these leaflets were also distributed at Liberty's and other fashionable shops. From then on the peacock feather became an emblem of aestheticism. The following year it was joined by the sunflower – Bruce Talbert's 'Sunflower' wallpaper having won a gold medal at the Paris International Exhibition of 1878. At this same Exhibition, Whistler and Godwin exhibited designs for a room, while Liberty fabrics, woven in India and printed by Wardle were shown in the British India Pavilion.

George du Maurier began his brilliant mockery of the aesthetes in the 15 April 1877 issue of *Punch*, in the year of the opening of the Grosvenor Gallery. It was widely believed that his model for Mrs Cimabue Brown of Passionate Brompton was Lady Lindsay, the wife of the Gallery's director. The following year, more grist to du Maurier's satiric mill arrived in London in the person of Oscar Wilde. Wilde had affected aesthetic attitudes at Oxford, with languid speech, 'poetic' clothes and an admiration for the works of Walter Pater. Now he welcomed himself rapturously into the artistic and literary coteries of London. For du Maurier he was a gift from the gods, a living embodiment of Postlethwaite and Maudle. He was a social 'lion' that Mrs Ponsonby de Tomkyns in her pursuit of 'cultchah' would wish to secure as a guest for her drawing room evenings. That same year, F. C. Burnard, the editor of *Punch*, wrote a comedy named *The Colonel*, in which the character of Lambert Stryke, played by Beerbohm Tree, was based on Wilde. It was the play in which the principal lady breathes the immortal words: 'There is so much to be learned from a tea-pot'. While *The Colonel* was still running, Gilbert and Sullivan's *Patience, or Bunthorne's Bride*, was produced at the Opéra Comique, the first performance being on 23 April 1881.

Liberty fabrics were used for the costumes in both *The Colonel* and *Patience*; many of those in *Patience* were designed by Gilbert himself. In the programme for the opera appeared an advertisement for Liberty 'Artistic Silks'. When the opera was moved to D'Oyly Carte's newly-built Savoy Theatre, Liberty's design team decorated a reception room festooned with silks for the Prince of Wales. This led to similar work at Covent Garden Opera House, the Haymarket Theatre, Drury Lane and the Lyceum. Liberty's boyhood dreams of becoming involved in the theatrical world were being realized in his forties, and he personally supervised every commission. When D'Oyly Carte was preparing *The Mikado*, Liberty envoys were sent to Japan to study the clothes worn there and to bring back exactly the right materials for the costumes and stage sets. Arthur Liberty himself always had a box for the first nights of Gilbert and Sullivan operas.

In *Patience*, the chorus of soulful maidens rebuffs the army officers in their bright uniforms, indicating that they would find them more attractive if they were dressed in 'a cobwebby grey velvet, with a tender bloom like cold gravy'; and colour is the main theme in the lyric:

> A Japanese young man,
> A blue-and-white young man,
> Francesca di Rimini, miminy, piminy,
> *Je-ne-sais-quoi* young man!
>
> A pallid and thin young man,
> A haggard and lank young man,
> A greenery-yallery, Grosvenor Gallery,
> Foot-in-the-grave young man!

Advertisement in a programme for The Mikado, 1885; *Arthur Liberty had sent envoys to Japan to select the correct fabrics for costumes and sets, all of which were supplied by Liberty's.*

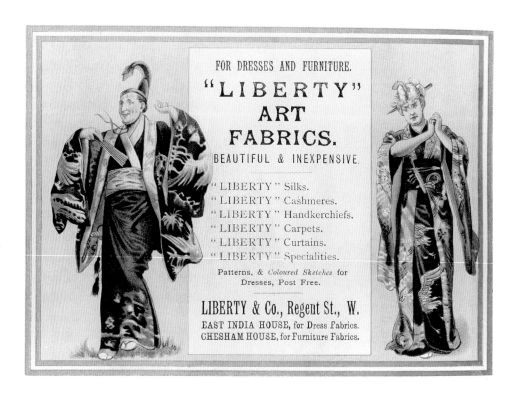

Yͤ Sovl Agonies in yͤ life of OSCAR WILDE. Illvstrated by Chas: Kendrick

Price

An American lampoon of Oscar Wilde published while he was making his lecture tour in the United States, 1882.

A description in *The Queen* magazine of the colours of Liberty Umritza Cashmere shows that they were in very truth greenery-yallery: 'There are tints that call to mind French and English mustards, sage-greens, willow greens, greens that look like curry and greens that are remarkable on lichen coloured walls, and also among marshy vegetation.'

When productions of *Patience* were running in New York and other American cities, Oscar Wilde made an eighteen-month lecture tour through the United States. One of his subjects was 'House Decoration', a splendid subject for giving publicity to Liberty fabrics. Indeed, Wilde's lectures can be said to have sown the seeds of the long love-affair between Americans and Liberty's of London. Two years later an American journalist wrote in the *British Mercantile Gazette* (January 1884) a long ecstatic account of a visit to Liberty's, ending: 'It is as inappropriate to regard Liberty's merely as a place of business as it would be to regard the public library at Boston merely as a storage house of books. Liberty & Co. is as much a feature of the metropolis as the National Gallery.'

In 1883, Wilde toured English provincial cities, lecturing on 'The House Beautiful'. This tour conveniently coincided with Liberty's winning a gold medal at the Amsterdam Exhibition for the newly launched furnishing fabrics. When a reporter some time later asked Arthur Liberty if he had influenced Oscar Wilde, he replied: 'Indeed, yes. My art fabrics were produced before he became a celebrity. I gave him his opportunity, and he helped me mightily with mine through the publicity he commanded.'

Other movements were stirring at this time, of which Arthur Liberty was almost certainly aware. A Rational Dress Society was formed in 1881; and the following year a Hygienic Wearing Apparel Exhibition was held in Kensington Town Hall 'to promote the adoption, according to individual taste and convenience, of a style of dress based upon considerations of health, comfort, and beauty.' Beauty? Well, the exhibit that attracted most interest was Lady Harberton's 'Dual Garmenture'; this was a divided skirt worn underneath an ordinary skirt of almost the same length, tantamount to a divided petticoat. It was of particular interest to the 'New Women' who were taking up tricycling. In 1885 Mrs Ada Ballin, a lecturer to the Health Society, published *The Science of Dress*, which became a bestseller. In it she warmly recommended Mrs Louisa Beck's 'Trouser Dress', available to order.

Although 'Rational Dress' and 'Aesthetic Dress' seem poles apart, they had two principles in common: corsets should be abandoned; all clothes should be loose and non-constrictive. Liberty fabrics were approved of by the dress reformers and won a silver medal at the Rational Dress Exhibition of 1883. They were commended for playing 'an essentially prominent part in connection with Rational and Healthy dress'. Their healthiness came from 'their purity, their natural dyes, their unadulteration by any "finish" or "dressing"; their freedom from any of the usual processes resorted to in order to impart a meretricious shine to worthless materials'.

Liberty tea-gowns worn in a typical Liberty furnished room, The Lady's World, *July 1887; it is noticeable that the loosely-draped Grecian lines favoured by the aesthetes were now being compromised by tight-waisting, which became fashionable in the eighteen-eighties.*

E. W. Godwin wrote a handbook for the International Health Society Exhibition of 1884, in which he said that some modification of Greek costume, whose principles he advocated, was perfectly applicable to the British climate if worn over 'a substratum of pure wool, such as supplied by Dr Jaeger under the modern German system'. He was referring to Dr Jaeger of Stuttgart's Sanitary Woollen Clothing, which had in 1883 become available in England and was the start of the 'Woollen Movement'. Many ladies of fashion began to patronize the Jaeger shop (then in Fore Street, City); and among the notable male customers were Oscar Wilde and Bernard Shaw. Jaeger's Sanitary Woollen Clothing would seem the very antithesis of Oscarism; but Wilde's wife was an active member of the Dress Reform Society and had persuaded him to give lectures on the subject.

E. W. Godwin, although remembered chiefly as a distinguished architect, fervently believed in the unity of all the arts. He was a founder member and honorary secretary of the Costume Society formed in 1882. When Arthur Liberty invited him to direct a costume department in his shop in 1884, they both visualized it as an almost missionary project, the aim being to establish the craft of dress-making upon some hygienic, intelligible and progressive basis; to initiate a renaissance that should commend itself artistically to leaders of art and fashion, and to challenge on its merits the heretofore all-powerful and autocratic fiat of Paris for 'change' and 'novelty'. This challenge was first mounted at the Paris Exposition Universelle in 1889 by showing aesthetic gowns, designed and made in the costume department. The following year Liberty entrenched himself in enemy territory, opening the Maison Liberty in the Avenue de l'Opéra. Already in France *any* softly draping silk was being called *soie Liberty*, and now the fashionable ladies of Paris flocked to buy the genuine fabrics and order aesthetic gowns. Later, a more extensive property was acquired in the Boulevard des Capucines, with several couture salons, a

Illustration from The Lady's World, *May 1887; Liberty's were now specializing in children's dresses in the Kate Greenaway style – Arthur Liberty was an admirer of her softly coloured drawings. Her many children's books, as well as* The Kate Greenaway Almanack, *engraved and printed by Edmund Evans, sold all over Britain, America, France and Germany, causing international demand for Liberty's hand-smocked children's dresses.*

The Maison Liberty, opened in 1890 at 38 Avenue de l'Opéra. Immediate success in fashionable circles allowed a move to grander premises at 3 Boulevard des Capucines, with spacious salons in the Empire style as in other Parisian couture houses. The shop survived through the First World War, and the nineteen-twenties brought great numbers of high-spending American visitors, including ready-to-wear garment manufacturers buying Liberty models for copying, until the Wall Street crash of 1929. New trade tarifs imposed in 1932 eventually caused the shop to close.

children's salon where Liberty smocks could be ordered, and a ground-floor boutique selling scarves, Indian bed-covers, shawls, cushions, and Oriental *objets d'art*. American visitors to Paris were always eager customers.

In London, the costume department was first accommodated in the Argyll Place building behind East India House, which Liberty had acquired in 1879 as a wholesale warehouse. This secluded positioning may have been because the Liberty staff were not very happy with the idea of a costume department. As Guy Bentley recalled later in the *Liberty Lamp* staff magazine in 1923: 'It was regarded by us all as a distinct break with the tradition of the shop, and many felt uneasy at the introduction of ladies' costumes, with its concomitants of millinery and other pieces of female adornment, into a business which was laying itself out for artistic decoration and the manufacture of articles and fabrics which would educate the public taste . . . Although these doubts have not even now entirely

An advertisement in The Art Journal Advertiser, *September 1880, the year following the launch of Umritza Cashmere. The spelling employed by Liberty's seems to have varied between 'Umritza' and 'Umritzur'.*

A New Material for Autumn and Winter Costumes.

UMRITZUR CASHMERE.

Manufactured specially for Messrs. LIBERTY & CO., from pure Indian Wool, and woven in this country, by which means the softness, lightness, and warmth of the Indian Cashmere is combined with the regular texture and durability of European fabrics.

As the present is only a sample delivery which cannot be repeated in time for the Winter Season, it is respectfully requested that all applications for patterns be made as early as possible.

IN ARTISTIC SHADES OF RED, BLUE, OLIVE, GREEN, GOLD, ETC.

Price 21s. and 25s. per piece of 9 yards, 27 inches wide.

PATTERNS POST FREE.

'Tanjore Lotus' (opposite), one of the Mysore silk range, dyed and printed for Liberty's in a range of nine colourings by Thomas Wardle of Leek, c. 1880.

Mysore silk designs (below) from an undated catalogue of 'Liberty Art Fabrics and Personal Specialities', c. 1887; Mysore silk was hand-woven in India, shipped in the raw state, then dyed and hand-block printed for Liberty's (some in colours, some in gold upon a cream background).

MOOLTAN MAY BLOSSOM.

RANGOON POPPY.

CHAMPA CHRYSANTHEMUM.

ALLAHABAD MARIGOLD.

POONAH THISTLE.

TANJORE LOTUS.

disappeared, subsequent events have much mollified them; and especially when it was found that from the very beginning "Liberty" Costumes were not to be influenced in the smallest degree by the ateliers of Paris. . . . The introduction of the department was made easier because from the earliest days of the Firm garments from the East had formed part of the stock — such as Japanese kimonos, antique Chinese and Japanese embroidered coats and robes, Turkish veilings and shoes. During the 1880s, we held annual exhibitions of embroideries, and the ladies of the Department used to don Circassian, Hindu, Japanese and Chinese attire. But the success of the new Department must be attributed to the Liberty fabrics ... the designs of the costumes showed the beauty of soft draping lines, and this influence extended to the present day and has greatly modified the canons of good taste both here and on the Continent.'

One of the most famous lines sold by Liberty at this time, Umritza Cashmere, was the result of long experimentation by Arthur Liberty with English weavers. He had realized that the deliciously soft hand-woven cashmere would not wear well, so had decided to introduce an English equivalent — a fabric with the softness of the Indian, but with a closer weave to give it longer life. Launched in 1879, Umritza Cashmere was a world-wide success. The English edition of *Le Follet* wrote: 'No material can be calculated so thoroughly to display the qualities of softness, suppleness, lightness, warm and graceful draping, as the Oriental fabrics sold by Messrs. Liberty. A recent introduction, Umritza Cashmere, possesses all the best qualities of the Indian make, combined with the durability and closeness of English manufactures. It is made in neutral tints and all the art colours, and the long hairs scattered over its surface give it a very foreign appearance and add to its attractions.' Other firms attempted imitations, but Liberty took this as a compliment: 'As *imitation* is judged to be the *sincerest flattery*, Liberty & Co. draw attention, with considerable pride, to the many subsequent and present attempts by other firms to copy their Umritza Cashmere.'

Some of the imported silks that Liberty had dyed in England with Oriental colours were now being printed with Oriental designs. Mysore silk, woven by hand in India and shipped in the raw state, just as it came

Print workers on the bridge over the River Wardle by Littler's hand-block printing works at Merton, Surrey. The date when Littler first printed for Liberty's is not known; but from written recollections by Liberty staff, it seems to have been within two years of the opening of Liberty's shop in 1875. By the eighteen-nineties they were taking up the whole of Littler's production, and in 1904 Liberty bought the works from the Littler family.

from the loom, was then dyed in England 'by a permanent process especially for Liberty & Co.'; it was then hand-printed by the wood-block process. Most of the designs were exact reproductions of old Indian prints, 'obtained under exceptional facilities'. These facilities included consultation with experts at the newly established Indian Museum in London. They were small floral designs, some printed in colours, some in gold, upon cream backgrounds, and were given evocative Eastern names.

Most Liberty fabric printing, formerly undertaken by Thomas Wardle of Leek, was now done at Littler's block-printing works on the site of the priory at Merton in Surrey, which had been established there by Edmund Littler at the beginning of the century and continued by his son and then his grandson. By the eighteen-nineties, Liberty was taking up the whole of Littler's production. In 1881, Morris had acquired Welch's calico printing works on the other side of the River Wardle, downstream from Littler. Wardle water was of the special quality needed for madder dyeing, and Liberty liked to say, 'We sent our dirty water down to Morris'. Liberty was later to buy the print works from Littler – in 1904.

Godwin died in 1886, but his association with Liberty had ensured the firm's close association with the values of aestheticism. His educational principles and theatrical interests, shared as they were by Arthur Liberty, were still apparent in Liberty's catalogue of 'Art Fabrics and Personal Specialities' for 1889: 'It is proposed to make a continued and systematic attempt to establish an Educational School of Personal Adornment, where shall be secured such forms, draperies, colours and ornaments as harmonise most perfectly with the natural characteristics of the wearer; and where shall be provided, for amateurs, artists and the stage, the most beautiful types of modern dresses, and the most reliable reproductions of ancient costumes, plain and rich.'

Arthur Liberty's flair for choosing brilliant, highly educated men for the most important and influential departments was evident in his choice of John Llewellyn to continue the work begun by Godwin. Llewellyn had formerly been an employee of Howell & James, the prestigious shop in Lower Regent Street. He began work for Liberty in 1889, soon displaying an invaluable gift of transmitting his enthusiasms to those who worked under him and endowing the salesmen with genuine appreciation of the fabrics they handled. He was responsible for the commission and purchase of designs, and for the liaison with Littler's hand-block printers at Merton. He also liaised with all the firms who undertook weaving, dyeing and machine printing for Liberty's. It was through Llewellyn that Alexander Morton used the Liberty shop as the first market-place for his famous 'fadeless' dyes. Llewellyn was indeed the right man to continue Liberty's determination to work in co-operation with industrialists and scientists, with his belief that the aesthetically pleasing could also be commercially viable. In 1891, Llewellyn was appointed head of the silks department, always the most important department in the firm, and under his direction many new fabrics were developed with British manufacturers.

These internal changes at Liberty's were paralleled by important shifts in the cultural climate. The Grosvenor Gallery closed in 1890, and its closure could be seen to signal the end of the Aesthetic Movement. Rossetti had died in 1882; Whistler left London the previous year to live in Paris. Morris designed his last print, 'Daffodils', in 1891 and died writing his last book in 1896. In Berlin, the Munch exhibition of 1892 heralded the approach of Art Nouveau; and in Paris, three years later, Bing opened his shop named 'L'Art Nouveau'. In 1894 the first issue of *The Yellow Book* quarterly brought a strong strain of eroticism to the graphic arts in the illustrations of Aubrey Beardsley. Oscar Wilde was in Reading Gaol and, with 'fin de siècle' the phrase on all fashionable lips, the Aesthetic Movement died of natural causes.

Arthur Liberty with William Street and J. W. Howe, who became directors of the firm in 1888. They are in the 'Trial Studio', where the brilliant young John Llewellyn, appointed director of the silks department in 1891, is showing them some fabric designs he has commissioned.

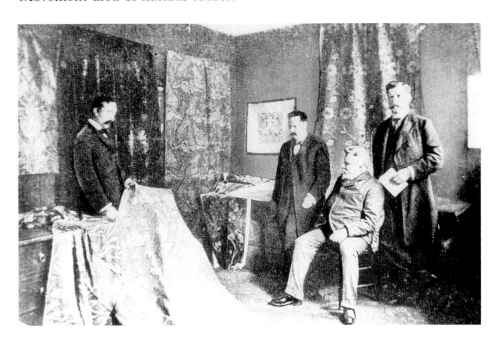

ARTS & CRAFTS AND ART NOUVEAU

Liberty's and International Art Nouveau

URING THE EIGHTEEN-NINETIES, Arthur Liberty was on good terms with almost all the important names in the English design world and was frequently referred to as an expert on the history of the decorative arts. He contributed, for example, essays on subjects such as the Spitalfields silk-weaving industry of the eighteenth century to *The Studio* magazine, and was certainly seen as one of the foremost taste-makers of the age. His emphatic championing of the Art Nouveau style, together with his espousal of as much of the look and philosophy of the emergent Arts and Crafts Movement as was compatible with the realities of commercial life in turn-of-the-century Regent Street, gave the shop a highly distinctive image. It is undoubtedly fair to say that no other shop of the period enjoyed such a high profile aesthetically whilst maintaining so healthy a turnover in trading terms.

This high profile of the shop was in part, at least, a conscious aim of the founder, who realized the importance of creating a 'look', and of ensuring that the look and the name were closely associated in the perception of the artistically-minded public. To this end, Liberty insisted that his own in-house designers remain anonymous, their names suppressed in favour of

Several of the designers used by Liberty's around 1900 are now seen to have been key figures in the development of international Arts and Crafts and Art Nouveau. Among them, Lindsay P. Butterfield was outstanding; this flower and leaf pattern (right) *by him was designed for block-printing on linen and manufactured by G. P. & J. Baker, 1903. The pattern was later printed with a solid background.*

An interior showing the work of C. R. Ashbee's Guild of Handicrafts (opposite) *at the eighth Viennese Secession exhibition, 1900; British design and its related organizations, including Liberty's, enjoyed a high reputation in all the artistic capitals of Europe.*

Previous double-page *Liberty's strongly promoted the idea of complete room settings in which furniture and decoration were conceived as a whole. The furnishing and decoration studio under Leonard F. Wyburd, would carry out complete commissions for private clients, as this drawing room arrangement.*

the all-important Liberty logo. As we now see it, several of Liberty's team have a claim to be regarded in their own right as key figures of British Art Nouveau. But it was not until very much later, indeed as late as the nineteen-sixties when design historians first began to take a new interest in the period, that any proper degree of recognition was at last accorded to such unsung geniuses as Lindsay P. Butterfield, the textile designer, or Archibald Knox, the creator of much of Liberty's celebrated Art Nouveau silver and pewterware. Only then, too, was any attempt made to place their work and the contribution of Liberty's as a whole in its proper context, in relation to contemporary achievements in other major centres such as Birmingham or more especially Glasgow in Britain, and Paris, Vienna and Darmstadt on the Continent.

By the mid eighteen-nineties an indigenous version of Continental avant-garde architectural and decorative styles was well-established in England. The style appealed to the young and the adventurous and, probably as much for this reason as for any other more rational one, it met with a degree of official disfavour in the Government Art Schools. Indeed, the authorities at the South Kensington Museum (now the Victoria and Albert Museum, the key institute in the propagation of principles of good design, as laid down by the great nineteenth-century pundits, Prince Albert, Sir Henry Cole and Richard Redgrave onwards) took it upon themselves to effectively banish from the sight of impressionable workmen and students the first representative collection of Continental furniture in the Art Nouveau style to arrive in England. There is evidence that this was done for fear of its deleterious effects on their aesthetic and moral senses; it is an extraordinary episode in the history of English taste.

Certainly the authorities were in some senses correct in detecting a nuance of anti-Establishment feeling among the adherents of the new style throughout Europe. But the ideals and character of the movement were very different from country to country. In France, where heavy, sensual, curvilinear forms predominated, Art Nouveau was rightly seen as a continuation of the luxuriousness of the Belle Epoque and justly associated with the attitudes and stylish poses of the *Décadents*. By contrast, in Germany and Austria the seminal expressions of the new style were lighter and simpler, generally austere and almost entirely rectilinear in character.

Even at home, the style was subject to considerable local variation. In Birmingham, where the School of Art was an important centre in the dissemination of ideas, Arts and Crafts forms and techniques were important in the formation of the styles of the young designers. Here, and indeed elsewhere, the influence of the writings and the artifacts of William Morris remained very strong, even after his death in 1896.

The other great creative centre in the United Kingdom was Glasgow, where a significant and quite distinct and independent style developed.

A silver panel on the front of a cabinet (right) *by Kolomon Moser, c. 1900, showing the remarkable affinity between Viennese design and the restrained version of Art Nouveau promoted by Liberty's in the firm's metalwork.*

One of the masters of Liberty design was undoubtedly Archibald Knox; his work, of which this silver and enamel casket (opposite) *is a supreme example, stands comparison with the best of contemporaneous European design.*

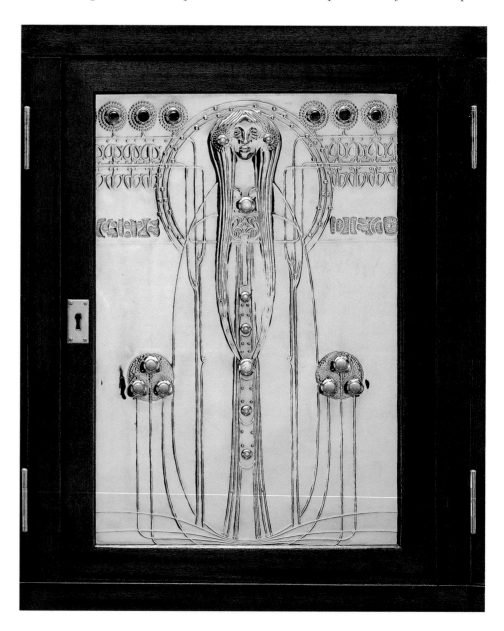

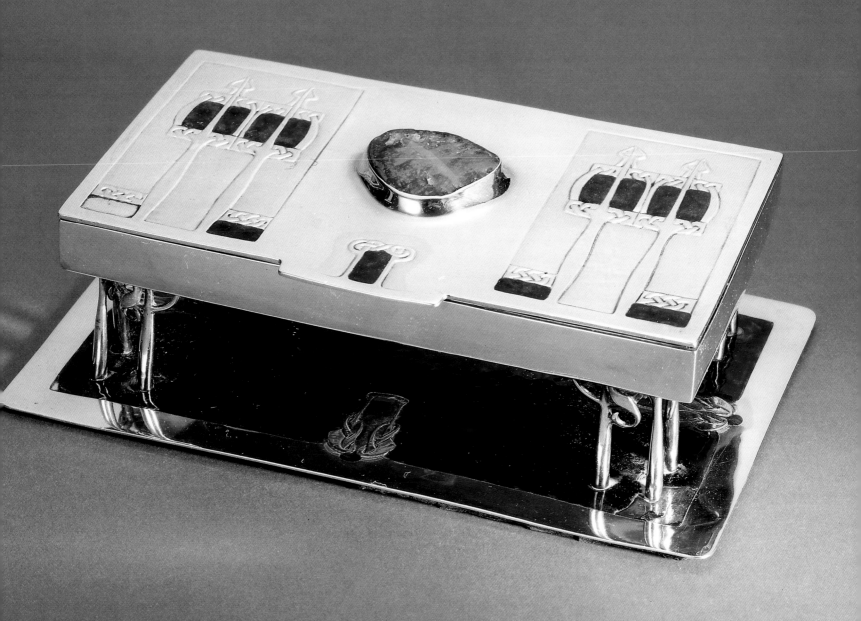

The main bedroom at Hill House, Helensburgh, designed by C. R. Mackintosh in 1905, a marvellous example of the ensemble approach to design which proved one of the most profound influences of British Art Nouveau on European styles.

Around the key figure of Charles Rennie Mackintosh a remarkable group, known as 'the Glasgow Boys', but including a number of very talented women too, forged a taut, extravagant rectilinear style more reminiscent of work in Germany and Austria. By an ironic, yet fascinating quirk of the internationalism of the worlds of art and architecture at this date, the work of the Glasgow group was better known and certainly more highly appreciated in Vienna and Darmstadt than at home.

The earliest significant champion of these anglicized versions of the Art Nouveau style was the influential art periodical, *The Studio*, founded in 1893, but there can be no doubt that Arthur Liberty's espousal of the style and his encouragement of several promising young designers who would become its luminaries, was a key to its wide success. Liberty was thus instrumental in the creation of many of the new movement's finest artifacts, including important furniture, classic fabrics and, perhaps most importantly, the jewellery and domestic metalwork in silver and pewter of Archibald Knox.

By this date Liberty was already in the position of being seen as a sort of contemporary, commercially-minded Maecenas. He was the closest English equivalent to the great French artistic entrepreneur, Bing, whose Maison de l'Art Nouveau had given the new style its name. In fact, to only a slightly lesser extent Liberty's name was associated in the popular imagination with the latest in furnishing trends; not least, it should be said because of his insistence, already referred to, that all his designers remain anonymous. Indeed, even today, 'Liberty Style' (or especially in its French and Italian forms: 'Style Liberty' and 'Stile Liberty') remains one of the most readily understood terms for the Art Nouveau style.

In spite of, or, it has been argued, because of its immense success, the Art Nouveau style was, in European cultural terms, a very short-lived phenomenon. Commentators and design historians from Pevsner onwards have consistently found in the movement the seeds of many of the crucial developments that would follow, and in particular identified a number of the starting points in the genesis of International Modernism. But as a visual style in its own right, Art Nouveau lasted only into the very first years of the new century; by 1905 it could no longer be said to be truly smart, and by the end of the Edwardian era it had a distinct feeling of having sunk to being merely suburban fashion.

An advertisement for Siegfried Bing's Maison de l'Art Nouveau, which had similar ideals to those of Liberty's in the promotion of the 'new art'; both shops were to lend their names to the new design styles appearing around 1900.

Textiles

AN IMPORTANT SHIFT of emphasis occurred at Liberty's in the eighteen-eighties. Although goods from the East continued to be imported in large quantities by the shop, this aspect of the business became less dominant, as an increasing amount of work by British designers was bought or commissioned specially for the company. This was especially true in the case of fabrics. Famed in the early days for its Oriental silks dyed in 'artistic' colours, embroideries and other textiles imported from Central Asia and the Far East, by the mid eighteen-nineties Liberty had become synonymous with the very best of new British design.

The timing was exactly right: a new, large and predominantly urban middle-class, with large disposable incomes, was beginning to take serious interest in the aesthetic of interior decoration. A plethora of household manuals and articles on the subject appeared at this period, offering advice on decorating schemes to those who had money but lacked confidence in their own taste. Liberty's were able to supply their furnishing needs with textiles and wallpapers of appropriately 'artistic' design and colouring. During the eighteen-seventies, manufacturers and retailers had quickly realized that 'art' might prove a profitable adjunct to manufacturing businesses. 'Art' manufactures were marketed as being free of the crude, commercial dyes and excessive ornamentation associated with High Victorian decorative art. By the eighteen-eighties the use of the term had degenerated to include parodies of fashionable designs or conventional goods in supposed 'art' colours. The leading exponents of 'art' manufactures, however, among whom Liberty was pre-eminent, were able successfully to combine commerce with the new style.

'Liberty Art Fabrics' became a byword throughout Europe for the best of avant-garde textile design at reasonable prices. In an interview with *The Citizen* (10 December 1898), after his appointment to the board, John Llewellyn echoed the new national self-confidence in design: '. . . just in the same way as there was a Louis XVI period, so we flatter ourselves that we have created a new "English" period. Years ago nothing but French designs would suit, now the English school is leading.'

From the late eighteen-eighties the fabric department at Liberty's began to draw on the talents of many of the period's most distinguished designers. As the company sought to establish a house style it was not their policy to name their designers, but they are known to have included C. F. A. Voysey, Lindsay Butterfield, Sidney Mawson, Joseph M. Doran, Jessie M. King, Harry Napper, Lewis F. Day, Allan Vigers, and others. The Silver Studio, founded in 1880, probably provided some of Liberty's first modern designs. One of Arthur Silver's own designs, 'Peacock Feather', printed by the Rossendale Printing Co. in Lancashire, was shown at the Manchester Royal Jubilee Exhibition in 1887 and, since being revived in 1975 for the Liberty centenary, has become almost a trademark for the company. A group of printed textiles, probably designed shortly before

Lindsay P. Butterfield, 'Hydrangea', c. 1896 (above), a roller-printed cretonne manufactured by G. P. & J. Baker; this design was clearly influenced by the restrained naturalism of William Morris.

Harry Napper, 'Magnolia Tree', 1906 (above right), a water-colour design for a roller-printed fabric manufactured by G. P. & J. Baker; the geometricized floral motifs and small squared-off leaves are typical of the styles of the early twentieth century.

A Silver Studio design, attributed to Arthur Silver (opposite), on roller-printed cotton, 1895; the Silver Studio daybook records that this design was sold to Richard Stanway, a furnisher and middleman, in January 1895.

Silver's death in 1896, has trees and foliage abstracted in the manner associated with Continental Art Nouveau and stylized roses very similar to those found in the work of Charles Rennie Mackintosh and the Glasgow School. In an interview with *The Studio* in 1894 Silver explained that the Silver Studio designs were intended to appeal to the broad swathe of the middle and lower middle-class – the same market, in fact, served by Liberty's and by some of the more enlightened manufacturers to whom they contracted work.

Two of the studio's most accomplished designers in the late nineteenth century were Harry Napper and John Illingworth Kay, both of whom sold designs to Liberty on a free-lance basis after leaving the studio, Napper in 1898 and Kay in 1900. Napper's idiosyncratic style, with its eccentric stylized flowers and a marked partiality for spiky leaves and thistles, is easy to recognize. His work also sold well on the Continent. From 1900 the Silver Studio was managed by Arthur Silver's son Rex, with help later from his younger brother, Harry.

Silver Studio, 'Gothic Thistle', 1896, block-printed cotton; design bought by Richard Stanway in November 1896 and subsequently sold to Liberty's. Although unattributed, the design exhibits many of the characteristics of Harry Napper's work.

Though primarily an architect, C. F. A. Voysey was one of the most prolific designers of the period and, arguably, one of the most distinguished and innovative of all British pattern designers. His work was always well represented at Liberty's, either through designs sold directly to the company or via the products of manufacturers to whom he was contracted or to whom he sold individual designs. His most characteristic textile designs of the eighteen-nineties use stylized birds, animals, trees, hearts, and flowers carried out in rather fresher colours than those fashionable in the two preceding decades. By 1900 he was using the same motifs, but on a slightly smaller scale and in comparative isolation on a plain ground. In an interview with *The Studio* in 1893 Voysey expressed his belief (shared by most of his contemporaries) that three-dimensional realism was unsuitable for decoration but, unlike many other designers, he did admit birds and animals as long as they were reduced to 'mere symbols'. His best designs show an economy of line and a sense of space which make them appear strikingly modern in comparison with William Morris's patterns and with other designers still working in this style.

One such was Lindsay Butterfield, another highly successful designer of repeating patterns for printed and woven fabrics. Many of his early designs, such as 'Hydrangea', printed by G. P & J. Baker for Liberty *c.* 1896, reveal the influence of William Morris in the crisply drawn and botanically accurate plants and flowers. In later designs, however, such as a block-printed linen of 1903, again produced by Baker's for Liberty, the flowers are more stylized and resemble some of Voysey's work. Walter Crane, a painter and book illustrator by training, was another versatile designer who produced some highly distinctive designs for printed and woven textiles, carpets and embroideries. His pictorial style was probably more suited to the latter, or to tapestry, than to repeating patterns where figurative designs work less well when draped in folds than floral or more abstract patterns. In contrast, Lewis F. Day, who maintained a highly public debate with Crane during the eighteen-nineties and the early years of this century about the nature of decorative art, objected to the use of birds, beasts and human figures in repeating patterns, although he paid Crane the compliment in *Nature in Ornament* (1892) of being one of the few designers equal to the task of manipulating them to ornamental purpose. Much more commercially aware than many of his contemporaries, Day produced designs for textiles of all kinds, although his style is so eclectic and sometimes derivative that it can be difficult to identify his hand.

From the mid eighteen-eighties to *c.* 1910 Liberty bought and commissioned designs for textiles by all of these designers and others in the Art Nouveau style. The term has come to embrace a wide variety of styles, but at the time was not applied to the majority of British textiles. It generally described the curvilinear designs of the French and Belgian designers as well as the work of the Glasgow and Vienna schools, characterized by an extreme stylization of natural forms. The relationship between Continental and Scottish Art Nouveau and its English counterpart is complex. While there are many similarities, the differences are equally marked. British decorative art of the eighteen-seventies and eighteen-eighties was highly influential in the development of European Art Nouveau, but the style was often derided by English designers. Crane, Voysey and Day were among those who scorned it, quite unable to see in it the extension of their own work and that of their contemporaries. One of the chief complaints of the English designers was that the Continental manifestation of the New Art lacked respect for the materials employed, a central tenet of the Arts and Crafts Movement.

Natural ornament is the basis of most Liberty 'Art' fabrics and it is the translation of nature, in one form or another, which provides the visual link between the British and Continental styles, if indeed British design of this period may be referred to as anything as homogeneous as a style. The more traditional English patterns, found in some designs by Butterfield and Sidney Mawson, continued to be based on the Morris format of naturalistic motifs confined within a formal framework. Repeating patterns for textiles of *c.* 1890–1910, however, tended to be more stylized and in the more modern work of designers like Voysey space became an integral element of the design, comparable to Charles Rennie Mackintosh's achievements in interior design. Whereas Morris, in the eighteen-seventies and eighteen-eighties had used curling leaves to form the framework for his patterns, this was now provided by the tall stems of plants, resulting in a much more linear style. The whiplash stems associated with Art Nouveau never really found favour in England. British Art Nouveau, for want of a better term, was characterized throughout the period by more rhythmic, linear stylization of natural forms.

Yet some British designers did respond to the new art and design on the Continent and, in the late eighteen-nineties, the work of Harry Napper and others took on strong geometric and curiously abstract qualities. By about 1900 other British designers were employing a very pared-down, controlled style, often with a squared-off format for their highly stylized floral motifs. Such designs influenced slightly later avant-garde pattern-making in Austria and Germany. All of these styles were well represented in Liberty's textiles during this period. In the decade leading up to the outbreak of the First World War, however, British textile design lost some of its energy and innovative edge, and products became rather predictable.

Liberty's registered designs bought from freelance designers, then commissioned printing or weaving firms to make up the fabrics which were sold in the shops. In other cases, however, they are known to have purchased finished products directly from a manufacturer, to be sold exclusively by Liberty's. In 1904 the company acquired the Littler Brothers print works at Merton Abbey and began to print their own designs, although they continued to use contract printers too.

Lindsay P. Butterfield, 'The Lomond', c. 1896; a silk and wool double-cloth manufactured by Alexander Morton & Co.; a good example of the linear style which characterized British Art Nouveau.

Silver Studio, roller-printed cotton, c. 1896, with a design of irises and leaves against interlaced whorls; it was printed in shades of blue.

Retailers like Liberty's and the manufacturers who supplied them publicly acknowledged the contribution made by William Morris in raising standards of design, but the emphasis on hand production at Morris & Co. was not a model they thought appropriate to follow. For some of the more domestic, middle-class items produced by Morris & Co., such as the wallpapers and many of the printed textiles, the machine would have been the more practical method of production and, indeed, Morris himself did not entirely eschew the machine for some products. Not only did it make good commercial sense to exploit the capabilities of the sophisticated machinery which was available by the end of the nineteenth century, but it enabled their products to reach a much wider public. In addition, standards of industrially produced goods had been rising throughout the second half of the century, and the manufacturers with whom Liberty did business were all of them sympathetic at least to the aesthetic ideals of the Arts and Crafts Movement, even if, as businessmen, they could not necessarily accept its ethical position.

From the mid eighteen-seventies there had been a revival in the use of printed cottons which lasted well into the twentieth century. Liberty's 1906 catalogue of furnishing fabrics included both cretonnes (the contemporary name for printed cottons) and printed linens, which were generally more expensive. The price of cretonnes ranged from 2s.3d. a yard for a more complicated design printed in several colours, such as 'The Melbury' by Sidney Mawson to 1s. a yard for 'The Milford', printed in only two colours and recommended for bedroom draperies and curtains rather than for one of the main reception rooms. Liberty's main suppliers of printed fabrics were Wardle & Co., Turnbull & Stockdale, G. P. & J. Baker and, after 1905–6, when Alexander Morton & Co. expanded to include printed textiles in their range, Morton Sundour Fabrics.

Sidney Mawson, 'The Melbury', c. 1906, a roller-printed cretonne manufactured by Turnbull & Stockdale; Liberty's 'Furnishing Fabrics' catalogue of 1906 recommended using the design for loose covers for furniture. This rather traditional pattern continued to find favour in England well into the twentieth century.

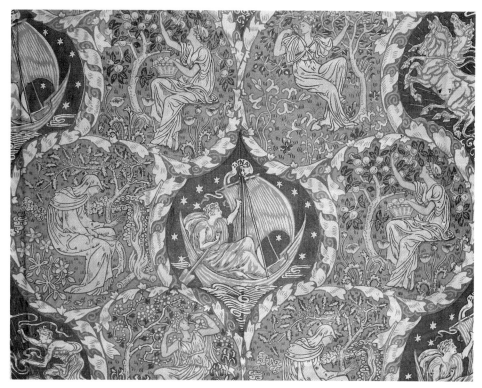

Walter Crane, 'The Four Seasons', 1893, roller-printed silk manufactured by Thomas Wardle & Co.; as a pattern designer Walter Crane diverged from the popularly held opinion that human figures were unsuitable as repeating patterns. His figurative style, which developed out of his early work as a book illustrator, was often loaded with symbolic content.

'Margate Sands', 1903 (below) *a water-colour design for a nursery cushion manufactured by G. P. & J. Baker; nursery cushion covers were block-printed on cotton or velveteen by Baker's at their Swaisland Print Works. Furnishing fabrics and wallpapers designed specifically for children began to be made commercially just before 1900.*

Thomas Wardle, a noted silk dyer and printer, whose works were at Leek in Staffordshire, was supplying Liberty's with dyed and printed Indian silk from the late eighteen-seventies. He went on to buy designs from many of the leading designers of the day – among them Crane, Butterfield, Voysey and Day – which he printed on to silk, wool, cotton and velveteen and sold mainly through Liberty's. Two of Wardle's finest printed fabrics, figurative designs by Crane ('Four Seasons') and Léon Victor Solon were both printed on silk and velveteen. They were shown by Wardle at the 1893 Arts and Crafts Exhibition. Printed velveteens were very popular during this period and were one of Wardle's specialities. He marketed them under his own label, 'Wardle Art Fabrics', in addition to those which he produced for Liberty's exclusively.

Turnbull & Stockdale in Lancashire were one of Liberty's main contract printers of cretonnes, which they produced both by block and engraved copper roller. Established in 1881, they employed Lewis F. Day as their Artistic Director. As well as the prestige and contacts which the partnership brought to the firm, he also produced many designs for them himself.

Like Thomas Wardle, G. P. & J. Baker printed textiles under their own name but also, as owners of the Swaisland Print Works, became contract printers to major retailers such as Liberty's, to which there are many references in the company's records. They printed on silk, cotton and linen designs by the Silver Studio, Voysey, Butterfield, Mawson, and George C. Haité, among others. Other items which Liberty bought from Baker's, in addition to fabric for curtains and upholstery, were printed silk bedcovers and cushion squares for nursery and other use. Printed on cotton or velveteen at, respectively 1s.9d. and 2s.11d. for a 24-inch square, these were advertised in a number of Liberty catalogues from *c.* 1902–3 and seem to have been a popular line. The nursery designs reflected a new interest at the period in decoration specifically for children. Those featured in the catalogues have nursery-rhyme subjects or scenes showing Dutch children and are related to similar wallpaper designs by the popular illustrators Cecil Aldin and William Kidd.

Liberty's sold a variety of woven fabrics in their furnishing department, ranging from light-weight silk damasks to the heavy-weight woollen cloths known as 'tapestries'. The latter were used both for upholstery and as wall-hangings or portières, while the lighter-weight fabrics were recommended for curtains, and, again, for upholstery. The shop was supplied by a number of specialist weaving firms established during the period. Arthur H. Lee and Sons, for instance, manufactured high-quality Jacquard-woven wool, silk and cotton furnishing fabrics at their factory in Warrington, Lancashire (and later at Birkenhead in Cheshire). Alexander Morton & Co., based at Darvel in Ayrshire, produced a wide range of woven fabrics for use as upholstery, curtains and carpeting, and Warner & Sons were silk weavers. All bought designs from the same group of free-lance designers who sold their work to the leading print firms – Voysey, Butterfield, Day and the rest. The business relationship with Alexander Morton, however, was probably the most advantageous for both partners. Liberty's were Morton's main English agents, while Morton produced a large number of fabrics and carpets exclusively for the shop.

Alexander Morton & Co. was established in 1867 as a manufacturer of leno (a type of gauze weave) in an area with an already important muslin industry. In 1881 the company expanded into lace curtain production and soon added chenille, both for curtains and carpet squares, three-ply carpeting and heavyweight woollen fabrics (tapestries) and, by the mid eighteen-nineties, double-cloths made from mixtures of silk and wool and cotton and wool. In 1900 all but the gauze weaving was moved to a new factory in Carlisle. The firm was run very much with the principles of Morris in mind, though on a sound industrial basis. A profit-sharing scheme for their workers was in practice in the eighteen-nineties, and their products were exhibited frequently at the Arts and Crafts exhibitions from 1896. Voysey had a contract with Morton's to supply ten designs a year, initially for a period of five years beginning in 1897, and double-cloths and woollen 'tapestries' which he designed for the company during the years around the turn of the century represent some of the most distinctive of all English woven textiles. Lindsay Butterfield signed a similar contract with Morton's in 1902.

Carpet manufacture flourished in the last quarter of the nineteenth century. In the eighteen-eighties the carpet industry introduced what were called 'art squares', carpet squares after contemporary designs and in artistic colours. They were produced in response to the fashion for Oriental

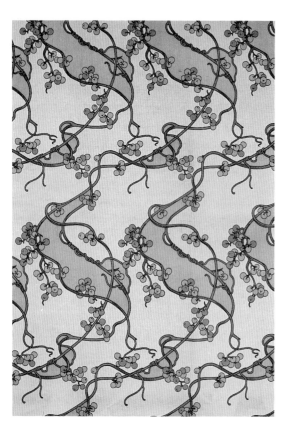

Roller-printed cotton, c. 1894, sold at Liberty's at 1s.4d. a yard; the sinuous shapes formed by the meandering stems anticipate the forms of Continental Art Nouveau around 1900.

Donegal carpets, early nineteen-hundreds, in hand-knotted wool, manufactured by Alexander Morton & Co.; the two carpets, left and centre, are examples of the Celtic style which began to enjoy a revival during the eighteen-nineties. Morton's began to produce carpets with Celtic designs in 1901.

carpets which many architects and designers used as floor coverings in their own homes. The principal suppliers of machine-woven Axminster carpets to Liberty's were James Templeton of Glasgow and Tomkinson & Adam of Kidderminster. Both firms bought designs from Voysey, the Silver Studio and others; in 1896 Voysey contracted with Tomkinson & Adam to produce ten designs a year for them. An article in *The Journal of Decorative Art* in 1888 stated that the company 'early joined in the protest which was made against the style of carpets in vogue twenty years ago . . . [they] have proved that they can supply high-class and artistic wares at a cost not exceeding the cheap and meretricious products which obtained a few years ago.'

In 1898 Alexander Morton & Co. set up a carpet-weaving workshop at Killybegs in County Donegal to produce hand-tufted carpets similar in feel and handle to Oriental rugs. It was a partly philanthropic venture in that it brought work to a depressed and over-populated area, and Morton was supported in the project by the Irish Congested Districts Board, a government agency set up in 1891 to revitalize such communities by encouraging investment in light industry. Voysey, who was already contracted to Morton's, designed a large number of Donegal carpets for the firm, invariably adapted from patterns that had been used for double cloth

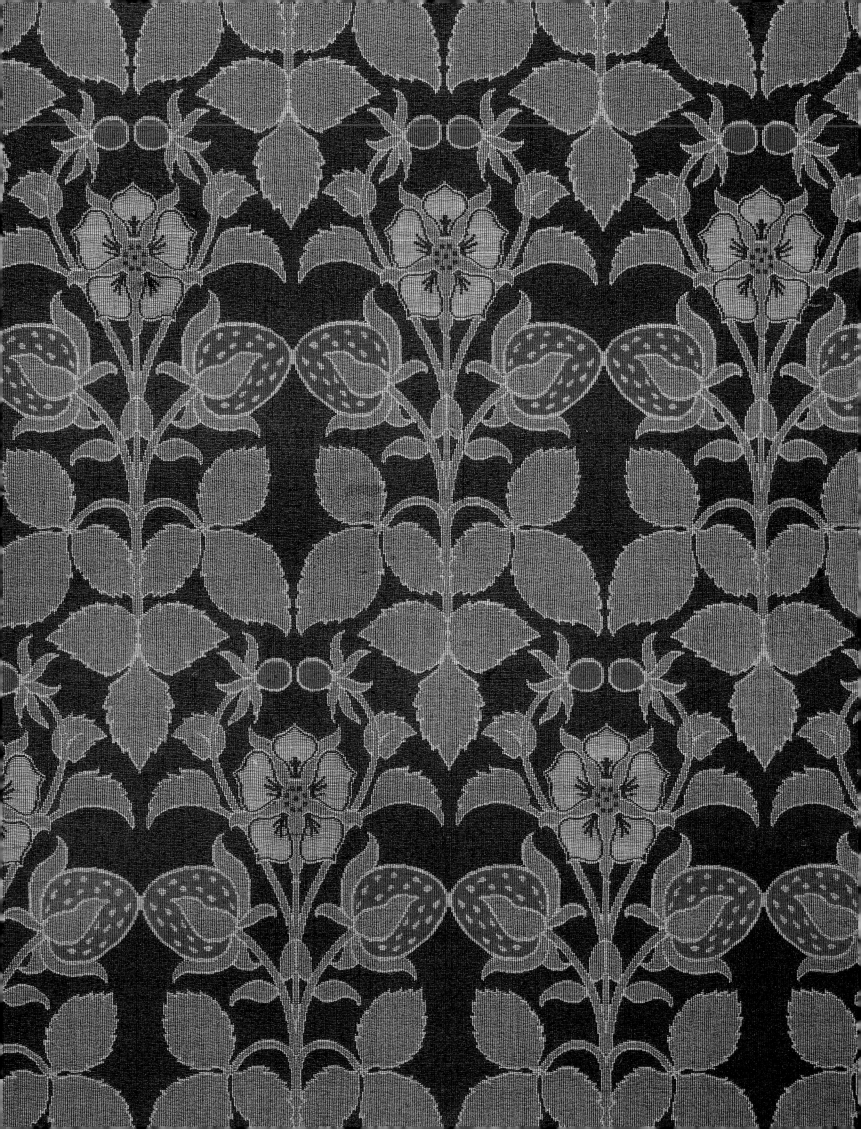

C. F. A. Voysey, 'The Lisburn', c. 1903 (above), a hand-knotted wool Donegal carpet manufactured by Alexander Morton & Co.; 'The Lisburn' was shown at Liberty's 'Irish Carpet Exhibition' at the Grafton Gallery in 1903.

C. F. A. Voysey, Jacquard-woven woollen double-cloth, c. 1900 (above right), manufactured by Alexander Morton & Co.; this design was first conceived as a wallpaper c. 1896, then sold subsequently to Morton's who produced it as both a double-cloth and a Madras muslin.

C. F. A. Voysey, 'The Strawberry', 1900 (opposite), wool and cotton tapestry manufactured by Alexander Morton & Co.; the two-dimensionality of the strawberry plants and the sense of space in this design make it appear strikingly modern in comparison with some of the more Morris-inspired work of other designers at this period.

or some other fabric. A design of stags and swans, with doves flying overhead, for example, was originally conceived as a wallpaper. Morton's then produced it as a double cloth and Madras muslin and later as a Donegal carpet, all of which were sold through Liberty's.

Liberty's contributed greatly to the promotion of Donegal carpets in the early years of this century, presumably to both their own and Morton's advantage. An exhibition of around seventeen carpets was organized by Liberty's at the Grafton Gallery in Bond Street from 7 to 13 March 1903. A catalogue of exhibits issued shortly afterwards suggests that about five or six might be attributed to Voysey, either on stylistic grounds or because they are patterns used in the manufacture of another product.

Morton's began to use Celtic designs for Donegal carpets in 1901, some adapted directly from the seventh-century *Book of Kells*, others designed by Archibald Knox. Some were included in another Grafton Gallery exhibition organized by Liberty's, entitled 'Modern Celtic Art', in 1904. The shop continued to promote Donegal carpets into the second half of the decade, even issuing a booklet on the project in 1907, entitled *Founding a National Industry*. Increasingly, however, the number of modern patterns gave way to neo-Georgian styles as Liberty's middle-class customers began to turn their backs on modernism. Donegal carpets were sold at a very competitive price in comparison with William Morris's hand-knotted

C. F. A. Voysey, 'Oswin', 1896, a silk and wool double-cloth manufactured by Alexander Morton & Co.

Hammersmith carpets, being well under half the price of the latter. Even cheaper, it would appear, were the hand-knotted carpets produced by an Austrian firm, J. Ginzkey of Maffersdorf, Bohemia, from whom Liberty also bought. Ginzkey's purchased designs from leading, contemporary European designers such as Josef Hoffmann and Alphonse Mucha, as well as some from Voysey.

By the mid to late eighteen-seventies art needlework was replacing in popularity the canvas-work embroidery known as Berlin woolwork which had virtually ousted all other forms of embroidery between 1840 and 1870. The art needlework movement, itself inspired by Gothic Revival ecclesiastical embroidery and the work of William Morris in the eighteen-sixties and eighteen-seventies, spawned a number of societies set up with the dual intention of raising standards and providing suitable work for needy women of different social classes. Some of these groups sold their work through Liberty's. Characterized principally by floral designs executed in crewel wools or silk, art embroidery was nevertheless applied to the same range of objects as Berlin woolwork – firescreens, cushions, tea cosies, blotters, photograph frames, and nightdress cases. The work could be purchased in a number of different forms, either as finished embroidery, in kit form complete with a piece of ready-printed fabric, embroidery wools or silks and needles, or simply as printed transfer designs to be ironed on to the fabric. Finished embroideries were commissioned from Ann Macbeth, who became head of the embroidery department at Glasgow School of Art in 1908, in the style which had become associated with Glasgow. Executed in floss silks or in appliqué, they included both floral and pictorial designs. Liberty, in common with much of the English design establishment, took a cautious attitude to the designs of the Glasgow School, although many of the embroidered items featured in the 'Yule-Tide Gifts' catalogues of 1900–10 and in the catalogues of transfer designs were clearly inspired by the Glasgow style.

Thomas Wardle provided Liberty's with silks, cottons and velveteens printed with outline patterns for embroidery, and the shop could also furnish the home embroiderer with specially dyed 'art' embroidery silks. In 1879 Wardle's wife Elizabeth set up the Leek Embroidery Society, which became noted for its embroideries worked on Wardle's printed and dyed tussore silks to designs clearly inspired by William Morris. The Society was particularly known for its ecclesiastical embroideries, but they did produce domestic pieces also, which Thomas Wardle, with his Liberty connection, almost certainly arranged to retail through the London shop.

'It is the particular claim of the firm', wrote *The Journal of Decorative Art* in 1888, covering Liberty & Co. in the fourth of its series on 'Famous Art Workers', 'that they have popularised forms of art which heretofore were known and attainable only by the wealthy and the great'. Arthur Lasenby Liberty was shrewd enough to see the commercial potential of the Arts and Crafts aesthetic. He linked the craftsman-designer to high-quality manufacture and, by making realistic use of industrialized methods and offering goods at competitive prices, made 'art' manufacture available to a far larger public than the hand-made goods of the pure craftworkers. The ethical basis for the Arts and Crafts Movement may have been largely ignored (although the company did support many of the philanthropic ventures initiated in the last quarter of the nineteenth century), but Liberty's can be seen as having fulfilled a useful, and even essential, entrepreneurial role in the Arts and Crafts Movement. The shops provided an important sales outlet for the products while, simultaneously, introducing the work of the leading craftsmen and designers to a wider public.

Liberty's excellent business organization was also a vital factor in promoting the reputation of British textiles on the Continent. The Paris shop, which opened in 1890 at 38 Avenue de l'Opéra, supplied the furnishing needs of fashionable Europeans. A number of European museums hold important collections of British textiles of this period, many of which were purchased from Liberty's Paris Shop. They include collections in Trondheim in Norway, in Krefeld and Stuttgart in Germany, and in Paris itself. In Italy, indeed, the term 'Stile Liberty' came to describe all decorative art in the style generally known as Art Nouveau.

Léon Victor Solon, allegorical design, 1893, a block-printed silk square manufactured by Thomas Wardle & Co.; Solon's only known textile design shows a masterful handling of human figures in pattern-making reminiscent of Walter Crane's work. Like Crane, Solon also designed ceramics.

Overleaf *Early twentieth-century textile design* (left): *a 1904 floral design with the original pattern sketch* (above left); *two natural flower designs dating from 1912, with woodblock impressions* (above right *and* below left); *the original artwork for 'Indian'* (below right), *signed by Lewis F. Day, a founding member of the Arts and Crafts Exhibition Society, in which Arthur Liberty was also involved. A pattern of 1912 by Linsday Philip Butterfield (page 67), a prolific contributor to Liberty's design repertoire; it is still in production today.*

Lindsay. P. Butterfield
1912
2912.

Costume

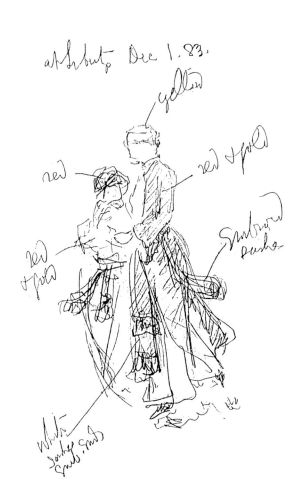

FROM ITS OPENING in 1884, Liberty's costume department maintained its sartorial identity, uninfluenced by the couturiers of Paris. Visitors to the department would select a style of costume, which was then run up in the workrooms in Liberty fabric. From 1894, catalogues for mail order were introduced, with sections for gowns, mantles and millinery, ranging from historically based costumes to the more conventional.

The *British and Mercantile Gazette* published this account of the department when it first opened: 'The reception room of itself is a study. To enter this room rests one instantly, it looks so sweet and quiet and full of harmony. Several young ladies spend their entire time in getting up new designs adapted from classic models. For the taste of today there must be a clinging underdress, fitted perfectly, of silk, velvet or cashmere. About this, soft drapings are arranged, suited to the figure of the wearer. The everlasting and monotonous rows of frills and pleats are thus done away with, and garments substituted which have a meaning and subtlety of their own.'

E. W. Godwin, the architect and aesthete appointed by Liberty to run the department from its beginning, believed it was possible to adapt historical prototypes to current dress without making the end result either 'eccentric or bizarre'. The art fabrics were indeed sometimes difficult to use, but a skilled in-house dressmaker could usually do any job quickly. For the fee of one guinea per hour, and a maximum of six hours a week, Godwin supervised the shop studio, receiving three per cent of the gross amount of all orders received through his personal introduction of clients. He arranged private views for likely customers, in which the employees of the embroidery department became mannequins, wearing gowns ranging from the classical to the medieval. The dressmaking department advertised its services, aimed at the leisured and artistic classes: 'An experienced dressmaker can wait upon ladies at their country residences with special selections of materials and sketches, for which no extra charge will be made. Instruction forms for self-measurement are also sent by post, but in the case of important orders we consider it most advisable that Measures and Instructions should be taken by a qualified Assistant.'

Working in soft and faded colours, Liberty deliberately rejected the bright aniline colours worn by the more conventional fashionable ladies of the day. In July 1884, the *Daily News* reported that the best-dressed woman now wore the soft colours favoured by Morris and Burne-Jones: 'The colours she wears delight the eye, there are no violent contrasts, no crude tints, all is soft and harmonious.' But while Morris promoted the idea of historical dress, Arthur Liberty combined the Oriental with Western models of the past to create commercially successful lines. The colours of the fabrics, combined with the quality of texture, were the essential ingredients of this success, as fashionable ladies sought to dress themselves in the classical drapery of the works of Albert Moore and G. F.

Watts. Both the latter and Oscar Wilde believed that true artistic dress was based on Greek costume.

The influence of Liberty's on mainstream fashion was huge, extending to both upper and middle classes by shrewdly offering information and services for those aspiring to the aesthetic condition. The departmental publication of *c.* 1887, 'Art Fabrics and Personal Specialities', was aimed not only at the artistic dresser but also at the dress trade. It proposed, too, a school of 'Personal Adornment' which would teach its pupils 'such forms, draperies, colours and ornaments as harmonise most perfectly with the natural characteristics of the wearer.' In the same publication, the firm claimed to have 'revolutionized the whole colour scheme, as now applies to articles of dress and wearing apparel in England and America and . . . the continent of Europe . . . and has been largely imitated. Mr Liberty has

'Sketch of a Fashion Parade', 1883, by E. W. Godwin (opposite), *costume adviser to Liberty's and a strong advocate of Japanese design.*

A Liberty 'medieval' wedding dress, c. 1894 (right), *in lustrous cream pongee, smocked in bands on the neck and yoke, 'ceintured' under the bust and with a mock-medieval 'girdle', both created by applied embroidery.*

Three plates from the 'Dress and Decoration' catalogue of 1905 of water-colours by A. E. Howarth: the 'Josephine' evening dress (below) in Empire style; the dress is made of silk crêpe (or satin) and finished with hand embroidery and beads; the 'Henrietta' Charles II home gown (opposite left) of flowered Tyrian silk, with high-waisted bodice of velveteen and fichu and sleeves in crêpe; 'Helen' Empire tea gown (opposite right) of flowered crêpe-de-chine (or gauze).

the satisfaction in the reflection that it was through his personal instrumentality that the extensive and beneficial revolution has taken place.'

In 1888, *Woman's World*, edited by Oscar Wilde, published an article called 'Shopping in London'. It was a review of 'types' and their favourite shops. When it came to Liberty's, the fashionable young woman was firmly associated with the name: 'Liberty's is the chosen resort of the artistic shopper. Note this lady robed in Liberty silk of sad coloured green, with rather more than a suspicion of yellow in ribbons, sash and hat (suggestive of a badly-made salad) who talks learnedly to her young friend – clothed in russet brown, with salmon-pink reliefs showing in quaint slashings in unexpected places – of the value of tone, of negatives and positives, of delicious half-tones, and charming introductions of colour, fingering the while the art stuffs and faded silks shown her with a certain amount of reverence expressive of the artistic yearning of her soul.'

By 1890, Liberty catalogues were featuring different historical styles adapted for the day. 'Athene' was a gown in 'Arabian cotton with silk Himation' for four and a half guineas; the waist is unconstricted by a corset. Other styles on offer were 'Greta', with artistic smocking and medieval embroidery, 'Marianne', with flowing lines in cashmere and brocade for nine guineas or Venetian silk and velvet for eighteen guineas. 'Valeria' has a medieval flavour with embroidery at the neck, and, as recommended by the Rational Dress Society, the weight falls from the shoulders, not the waist.

Many of the gowns produced by the shop were beginning to look comparatively conventional by 1895. A catalogue from that year divides 'Picturesque' – aesthetic – from the rest. This section of the catalogue was continued in subsequent years, and the best examples are to be found in 'Dress and Decoration' from 1905.

Aesthetic dress soon had much influence in Britain, and it could not be ignored by the Parisian ateliers. Liberty and Godwin had intended to challenge the dominance of Paris in fashion, and to a certain extent, they succeeded. The Maison Worth dressed such clients as the Duchesse de la Torre and Princess Viggo in gowns reminiscent of Liberty's. 'Soie Liberty' became a generic term meaning softly draped 'art' fabrics and, in 1889, the firm showed aesthetic gowns made by the costume department at the Exposition Universelle. The enthusiastic response to the models must have contributed to the decision to open a branch in Paris in 1890.

As well as being a profound influence on Liberty's graphic style of the period, Kate Greenaway was also the inspiration for Liberty's children's clothes. Admired by Arthur Liberty and John Ruskin, her illustrations, based on the styles of the early nineteenth century, soon found their way into the wardrobes of many a child with an artistic mother. This development was another example of aesthetic considerations coming before the puritanism implicit in the attitudes of the dress reformers. Lady Harberton, leading light of the Rational Dress Society, roundly condemned Kate

V Is Vera—the sweetest of tiny wee tots,
Is longing for fun, and wants lots and lots.

An illustration from 'The Children's Frock Party' catalogue of 1906.

A cream linen overdress, c. 1900, with a formal trailing poppy design on a light ground; the panniered effect is created by swagging, with rudimentary boning.

Greenaway, for dressing 'the children of her fancy in pretty garments totally unsuited to the practical need and comforts of boys and girls.' Nevertheless, the Greenaway–Liberty style had become all the rage among children in London and Paris by the early eighteen-nineties. There is even a charming picture of the seven-year-old Queen Mother in a 'Queen Mab' smocked frock from Liberty.

Embroidery was a major feature of Arts and Crafts dress from the early days to the outbreak of the First World War. It associated dress with hand- rather than machine-work, and could thus be considered more 'artistic'. All Walter Crane's clothes for girls featured it, and the embroidered dresses sold at Liberty's often had an Oriental touch. As the textures of chiffon and heavy velvets became ultra-fashionable in the nineties and Belle Epoque, embroidered decoration served as a remaining link to the earlier attitudes of the Arts and Crafts Movement. It was also a relatively inexpensive way of decorating dress.

In 1894, students at the Glasgow School of Art held an exhibition which featured the decorative style that was to be known as Art Nouveau. The curvilinear, organic designs were ideal for the embroiderer, and Jessie Newbery, who worked in this medium set out her creed clearly: 'I like the opposition of straight lines to curve; of horizontal to vertical; of purple to green, of green to blue ... I specially aim at beautifully shaped spaces and try to make them as important as the patterns ...'

The 'Dress and Decoration' catalogue of 1905 illustrates perfectly the influence of Art Nouveau on Liberty's approach to costume design. Stand- ing in a room decorated in the Nouveau style was a sequence of female figures dressed in gowns in some way linked to a period in history: 'Hera' is a Greek evening gown; 'Jacqueline' a fifteenth-century indoor gown; 'Iseult' a fourteenth-century French evening gown reminiscent of those illustrated in *Les Très Riches Heures du Duc de Berry*. Two Empire- inspired gowns are especially notable in that they influenced Paul Poiret's first collection. 'All that is good in current art is the outcome of the experiments and efforts of past centuries,' reads the catalogue, 'Messrs Liberty ... offer suggestions based upon a close and intimate study of the history of costume and a definite knowledge of modern requirements ...'

The dresses shown in the 1905 catalogue were perhaps the closest Liberty's ever came to high fashion, 'and could have been worn in any London drawing-room without provoking a smile or a raised eyebrow.' This was regarded as an optimistic sign for the twentieth century: 'The question of dress has to a large degree become one of individual settle- ment ... while conforming to the prevailing mode, [one can] reserve the right to adapt it to particular tastes and requirements. This is a feature of the new century ... women's dress is more graceful, more refined and more suited to its requirements than in any previous age.'

In response to the prevailing styles of the Edwardian era, Liberty's now began to sell the frothy chiffon confections so closely identified with the

Heavy pink 'Orion' satin coat, c. 1905 (above), *cut asymmetrically in 'Directoire' style, but with flat-cut, two-piece 'Oriental' sleeves, with a white collar and turned-back cuffs, embroidered with a pink floral design. A theatrical brocade and velvet 'Tudor' coat and underdress, c. 1905 (above right), green and cream over green and gold edged with green plush; puffed satin inserts near the wrist imitate slashing, while smocking is used to create sleeve puffs.*

Belle Epoque, along with large 'picture' hats to perch on the massive coiffures. Silk underwear had made its debut in the shop in 1901 and, in 1903, Paul Poiret set up his own fashion house and used Liberty fabrics. An account published in *The Queen* in 1910 shows that he used Liberty silks with a proper regard for the traditions of the shop: 'One very pretty girl had on a pink mauve turban and a gown in which the lower half of the skirt was in old rose Liberty, and the upper half in mauve *mousseline de soie*, slightly gathered both in the high waist and the knees. The corsage was pure Madame Recamier style.' As the author of 'Dress and Decoration' had written just five years before: 'All that is good in current art is the outcome of the experiments and efforts of the past centuries . . .'

Furniture

IN 1880 LIBERTY'S was restructured into a series of departments, each responsible for the design, manufacture, and sale of a type of merchandise, although in practice much of the first two functions was subcontracted. Furniture was the responsibility of 'D' department, although at that time only a few designs were available, mainly imported from Cairo. In 1883, with the move to Chesham House, came a new manager, a Mr Robinson and, most importantly, the foundation of a furnishing and decoration studio under the designer Leonard Wyburd.

By 1886 the increasing number of decorating orders was such that the paper hangings section of the shop was also transferred to 'D'. In 1887 the cabinet works of James Thallon was taken over, giving the department full control of a large part of its production. Thallon was retained as manager, a post he was to hold until 1898, when he was succeeded by his son Thomas.

Robinson resigned in 1891 and the department was then placed under the dual control of Wyburd and P. Campbell. Wyburd and his junior assistant, E. P. Roberts, took the roles of artists and organizers, while Campbell became the department's main salesman. In this role he later claimed to have covered over 250,000 miles for the firm over thirty-eight years, obtaining and supervising contracts in Paris, Venice, Genoa, Milan, Vienna, Budapest, and Mulhouse, a graphic indication of the international nature of the firm's business. The cabinet works was moved to Highgate, north London, in 1912.

Chesham House, 140–150 Regent Street, acquired by Arthur Liberty in 1883; it was used mainly for the sale of furniture and carpets, while the basement housed the 'Eastern Bazaar'.

A Liberty hall compendium in the firm's much-loved 'Mock-Tudor' style, c. 1895; this piece incorporates a tile panel by William De Morgan.

Campbell, in an article in *Liberty Lamp*, the house magazine, July 1927, recalled that the style of furniture which was to become known as 'Art Nouveau' was originated by Wyburd and Robinson, so giving a date of between 1883 and 1891 to this change in direction. Little is known of Robinson and Wyburd is only slightly better documented.

Leonard Wyburd was the son of Francis John Wyburd (*b.* 1826), a painter of literary, genre and historical themes, who had studied at the Royal Academy schools. Wyburd's father exhibited widely and over a long career; between 1846 and 1889 he showed thirty-four paintings, several of which had Orientalist themes. To complete the artistic family his mother also exhibited at the Royal Institute. From the eighteen-eighties, Leonard Wyburd exhibited at a variety of venues, at first from his parents' house in Bryanston Street and later from his own house in Cambridge Street, London. His most famous painting is probably *The Studio*, which was exhibited at the Royal Academy in 1886 and shows an archetypally 'artistic' interior, cluttered with antiques and curios, such as might be collected by a gentleman with antiquarian tastes. Standing next to an open door giving a view through to a similarly crowded room is a small side table of Middle Eastern origin, on which is standing brassware from a similar source. The history of 'D' department in *Liberty Lamp* confirms this interest, describing Wyburd as '...a versatile and accomplished artist, who had made

An Ancient Egyptian stool (above) *in the British Museum, drawn by J. Moyr-Smith and published in* Building News, *17 December 1875; this stool is a probable inspiration for the 'Thebes' stools* (above right)*, one of Liberty's great furniture successes, appearing in two versions after the design was first registered in 1884. Another possible influence was this chair* (below)*, designed by Ford Madox Brown for Holman Hunt in 1857.*

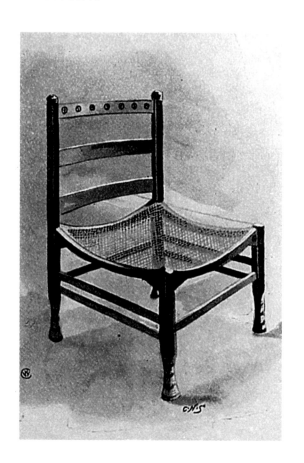

a profound study of Arabian design.' Beyond this, tantalisingly little is known of him. It was also company policy to maintain the anonymity of its designers, whether their work was manufactured by Liberty's or not.

Under Wyburd's influence Liberty furniture was to evolve rapidly. Among the first pieces produced after the creation of the furnishing and decorative studio were two stools based on ancient Egyptian prototypes. The designs for these were consecutively registered with the Patent Office in 1884, and they appeared in Liberty catalogues from that year. Although the first had four legs and the second only three, they were both known as 'Thebes' stools. The four-legged version had a leather seat held in place with leather thongs, and was available in walnut, mahogany, or oak. It was sometimes sold with a matching cushion. The stool's parentage can perhaps be traced to an 'Egyptian chair' designed almost thirty years before by the pre-Raphaelite painter, Ford Madox Brown, for William Holman Hunt. This chair was later depicted in a painting by Millais, so its design achieved wide circulation.

The three-legged stool was closely based on an example in the collections of the British Museum, and was described in museum catalogues as '. . . a reproduction of an ancient Egyptian model'. It was advertised as available in mahogany or oak, but examples are to be found made of various woods, including beech, and stained appropriately. It is not clear who manufactured the stools for Liberty, but it seems likely that William Birch Ltd of High Wycomb or B. North & Sons supplied them. A very similar stool appears in North's catalogue for 1915. Originally priced at 17s. 6d., they remained in production at least until the First World War. In about 1904 a small plant stand or occasional table was produced as a direct derivative of the stool. It was sold as the 'Wylye' and made from oak. Because the legs were lengthened to give it greater height, a small triangular shelf was inserted for greater strength.

The stools proved popular throughout Europe. Eleven years later they were included in the opening display at Siegfried Bing's L'Art Nouveau, the shop that was to give its name to the style. The Trondheim Museum bought several pieces of Liberty furniture from Bing, including a three-legged 'Thebes' stool in 1896. Other European museums which purchased Liberty furniture included Hamburg and Vienna, an indication of the international regard in which the furniture was held. Further proof of the popularity of the 'Thebes' stool is provided by the use of copies of the three-legged version in the Villa Karma (1904–6), in Vienna, designed by Adolf Loos. These were made in Vienna of walnut, stained red, by Loos's favourite cabinet maker, Josef Veillich, and in some contemporary publications claimed as Loos's own design.

An oak chair designed by Richard Riemerschmid, with carved decoration in low relief on the front sides of the seat frame and leather seat fixed with brass-headed nails, 1899; as well as stocking the Riemerschmid chairs, the shop also produced a very similar chair in the Liberty workshops, with champfered decoration on the side supports and legs.

Liberty's close affiliation to Arts and Crafts ideals is evident in the sturdy, simple design of this carver (right) and armchair (far right).

A Liberty side chair (c. 1905) in a restrained Art Nouveau style showing, unusually, a certain French influence in its predominantly British form.

The stools were essentially products of a design studio established at the height of the Aesthetic Movement in Britain. Towards the end of the century Liberty's began to evolve a style of furniture that was to become internationally recognizable as Liberty's own. This was a combination of commercial Art Nouveau, of the kind known to the contemporary press as 'quaint', the design vocabulary of the British Arts and Crafts Movement, and a rugged, rural style, supposedly derived from traditional British forms. Bringing these together created a series of powerful and evocative pieces that were to prove of great and enduring appeal.

Although often referred to as being in the Arts and Crafts style, Liberty furniture does not fit in the mainstream work of that movement. One of the key concepts of the Arts and Crafts Movement was that of the figure of the artist-craftsman, recreating the supposedly medieval ideal of the designer also being the maker. This situation never really applied at Liberty's, the firm being structured according to conventional business models of the late nineteenth century, whereby a furnisher would either employ his own designers or subcontract, the work again being sub-contracted to a series of manufacturers. There were many such firms in London, ranging enormously in size and in degree of mechanization. Traditionally they were located either in Shoreditch, north of the City of London, or in and around Soho, conveniently near the furnishing retailers in Tottenham Court Road and Oxford Street. It was one such firm which Liberty's took over in 1887.

The other term often used to describe Liberty furniture of this period is 'Art Nouveau'. This usage is also problematic, especially since in Italy Art Nouveau is known as 'Stile Liberty'. Of course no Liberty furniture is Art Nouveau in the narrower, more specific use of the term. There are none of the sinuous line and vegetal forms that typify French or Belgian Art Nouveau furniture, and there are certainly no echoes of the Rococo which are found in the work of, for example, Louis Majorelle. 'Stile Liberty' would appear to refer more to Liberty's textile production rather than the furniture. In its wider sense, describing the pan-European 'art revival' of the eighteen-nineties and early nineteen-hundreds, the term Art Nouveau can be applied to some Liberty furniture, although this always remained distinctly British. On the subject of some of the wilder French and Belgian furniture, with its extravagant, circular motifs, Arthur Liberty was generally scathing.

The third strand of influence on Liberty furniture of this period was the English rural tradition of solid, simply made pieces, which had evolved over centuries of craftsmanship rather than being the result of self-conscious design. Indeed, the echo of an older tradition in the furniture formed part of the appeal for the purchaser. In 1854 John Ruskin had attacked Holman Hunt's painting *The Awakening Conscience* partly on the grounds of the newness of the furniture shown in the painting. Ruskin

A typical interior from Liberty's own interior decoration service, 1897; this setting was displayed in the Regent Street shop.

believed that a home needed a generally old atmosphere in its decoration, to provide it with a depth of emotional resonance. The idea had rapidly gained wider currency, and was for many people still a factor in the choice of furnishings. Liberty furniture therefore combined several potent resonances which ensured its wide popularity. It brought all the appeal of the Arts and Crafts Movement, but without the high cost of craft production. It was 'artistic', but had its roots in the English tradition of old workmanship, and it was sold by a shop with exactly the right image of being slightly exotic to be of interest to those looking for something stylish rather than simple reproduction.

The major printed source of information about Liberty furniture is the series of catalogues the firm produced throughout the latter part of the nineteenth century and the pre-First World War years. These not only illustrate the range and variety of furniture sold, but also give some insight into the firm's retailing methods and pricing policy.

In 1889, the 'Handbook of Sketches' catalogue shows complete interiors, including an Arabian morning room, a room in the Jacobean style, and the interior of a house in what has been called 'Surrey Vernacular', a style almost identical to the work of the young Edwin Lutyens. Although this interior is shown as being furnished with reproductions, it also includes a kettle stand by W. A. S. Benson, an eminently 'artistic' touch. The catalogue is also something of a manifesto. It includes long quotations from Viollet-le-Duc, advocating fitness for purpose and the merits of simplicity in furnishings, not '. . . false taste and false luxury', which are seen as 'cheap splendours'. This is followed by a series of quotations from Ruskin on the use of colour in the home. Of the furniture illustrated, the 'Lochleven' sideboard is one of the most typical Liberty products of its type. It is a large and solid piece, made of oak, which the catalogue

An oak armchair, designed by E. G. Punnett and made by William Birch in High Wycombe, 1901.

The 'Valkyrie' piano, possibly designed by Leonard F. Wyburd, and made by J. J. Hopkinson for Liberty's in 1902.

A bedroom designed for Liberty's by George Walton, a member of the Glasgow School; this setting, c. 1900, shows the distinct influence of Scottish Art Nouveau in the design of the curtains.

describes as '... rendered the colour and finish of old work'. The strapwork hinges are of hammered iron, and the cupboard door is glazed with leaded glass, in a pattern of 'bulls-eyes'. The whole composition is carefully asymmetric. This sold for £24 and is shown with matching Jacobean-style chairs. The 'Lochleven' proved popular throughout Europe, and an example was purchased by the Österreichisches Museum für angewandte Kunst in Vienna. Many of the chairs described in the catalogue are clearly related to those produced by Morris & Co. or to the simple country furniture which delighted those interested in Arts and Crafts. Bedroom furniture tended to be simpler in design, and made from pitch pine which could be stained to suit clients' wishes. This catalogue was reissued in 1895, almost unaltered, indicating that its first issue had engendered a satisfactory amount of business.

As the eighteen-nineties progressed, more country furniture began to feature in the catalogues, such as the bobbin-turned 'Norfolk' chair, which was rush-seated and available in black, walnut or vermilion finishes. Two other recurring lines were bamboo furniture and cabinets featuring ceramic tiles by William De Morgan. In the 'Yule Tide Gifts' catalogue for 1892 a chair with a back composed of splayed ribs is shown. This is described as,

A Liberty oak carver, from a design by C. F. A. Voysey, and oak cupboard, c. 1905; the branched candlestick is probably by Archibald Knox, c. 1905 (above).

'A quaint chair, strong and light, made of walnut, seat upholstered and covered with tapestry'. This was called the 'Antwerpen' and sold for 15s., although this had gone up to 25s. by the following Christmas. A similar chair had, however, featured in the *Cabinet Maker and Art Furnisher* some three years previously, sold by another retailer, and described as an 'old fashioned type of kitchen chair refined up to the form of a "gossip" chair painted in artistic green with a prettily upholstered seat'.

Another distinctive feature of Liberty furniture became apparent during this period – that of applying mottoes or apposite quotations to furniture; this practice also had its roots in the British Arts and Crafts Movement. Early examples can be seen in the work of companies like Morris & Co. Some of the mottoes chosen by Liberty's were especially appropriate to the function of the piece. In 1895 a pair of oak sconce brackets went on sale for 35s., complete with Celtic dragon motifs and hammered copper reflectors, and bearing the inscription, 'Let the Tapers Burn Unwaveringly'. The 'Kenwald' photograph bracket held both photographs and books, and proclaimed, 'Choose an author as you choose a friend'. A writing desk was inscribed, 'Reading makyth a full man Writing an exact man', and a smoker's cabinet bore the words, 'The man who smokes thinks like a sage and acts like a Samaritan'. By 1897, however, this 'quaint' furniture was having to compete with antiques, such as 'Chippendale' chairs at 25 gns. a pair, 'Spanish' and 'Flemish' chests and cabinets, and 'Venetian' chairs at 10 gns. each. This eclecticism in design was to continue until the Liberty cabinet works closed in 1940; from the Edwardian years, however, emphasis on reproduction styles increased.

This dressing table and washstand were designed by Leonard F. Wyburd for manufacture in the Liberty workshops, c. 1899; the dressing table has inlaid pewter motifs above a swivel mirror, slatted sides and hinged side flaps; the washstand has a woven straw back panel, stencilled and bound and thonged in leather.

A room setting (opposite), including a pair of Arts and Crafts mahogany tub chairs, probably sold by Liberty's c. 1900, and Liberty corner cupboard.

Perhaps the apogee of the quaint oak style came with the 1899 'Yule Tide Gifts' catalogue, where a double page was given over to an illustration of the 'Athelstan' and 'Ethelbert' chairs and the 'Suffolke' stand. These are shown in a heavy black and white illustration, like a woodcut, complete with border and a distinctive quaint lettering style. The furniture is described as 'Quaint & Comfortable Soundly Constructed', and 'Substantially Made in Solid Oak Colour and Finish Like Old Work'.

At about the turn of the century Liberty's published 'A Book of Sketches', showing suggestions for complete interiors. It also advertised the firm's interior design services, offering completely new plans or the possibility of modifying existing ones. By this time, Liberty furniture was totally eclectic in style. An entrance hall and staircase is shown in the 'Jacobean' style, complete with a helmet on the table. Over a fashionable inglenook is the motto, 'Welcome ever smiles and farewell goes out sighing'. There are rooms in the 'Elizabethan', 'English Renaissance', 'Domestic Gothic' and somewhat modified 'Tudor' styles. There is a 'Cromwellian' dining room and, for the dining room of large dimensions, there is 'German Gothic'. Reception rooms are shown in the 'Adams' style, while for the breakfast room there is the 'Dutch' style with a stained glass sunrise. All these are in addition to the usual Liberty collection of 'Middle Eastern' rooms and 'Italian Renaissance' pieces. In the middle of this tour through styles and centuries is a room labelled 'Recent Developments' which is in a modified Arts and Crafts style of the sort made internationally popular by the architect M. H. Baillie Scott. This room is described as commending 'itself to those who want to avoid the common place'.

A corner of a morning room, designed and executed by Liberty's, reproduced in The Studio Yearbook *for 1906.*

A settle, c. 1905, covered in 'Stag' design fabric by C. F. A. Voysey.

Baillie Scott's influence could also be found in the 'Yule Tide Gifts' catalogue of 1900 which shows a chair with a matching round back and foot rails. Called the 'Stanmore', it was made of oak, stained brown, with a tapestry cushion on the seat. It was priced at £2. 19s. 6d., and a child's version was also available. The chair is based on one shown in a tapestry designed by Edward Burne-Jones and made by Morris & Co. for Stanmore Hall, Uxbridge, in 1894. The design was then turned into furniture by Baillie Scott in 1897 for the Grand Duke of Hesse at his palace in Darmstadt. Liberty's was not the only firm to make a version of the chair. A very thin and rather downmarket variant known as the 'Teenaty' was illustrated in the *Cabinet Maker* of January 1905 as being made by Goodearl Brothers.

After the turn of the century the trend was firmly towards simpler, plainer pieces, which shared the catalogues with more and more reproductions. In 1906 these simpler pieces are described as being 'for Town Houses, Flats, and weekend cottages', and 'Designed to combine Utility and good taste with Modest Cost'. They no longer bore names taken from British history; when they did have names these were from the places where Liberty customers might live, such as 'Shiplake', 'Weybridge' and 'Twyford'. While a few classic lines, such as the three-legged 'Thebes' stool, continued, more accurate reproductions of eighteenth-century styles begin to proliferate in the catalogues. By the time the 'Yule Tide Gifts' catalogue of 1910 was published there was just one page of modern furniture competing with the reproductions which by now encompassed all the major periods of English furniture history.

A Liberty interior reproduced in The Studio Yearbook *for 1910.*

Metalwork

A display of Keswick and Newlyn Arts and Crafts copperware, possibly sold by Liberty's c. 1900.

A display of Liberty Tudric pewterware, c. 1900–1908 (opposite), *including designs by Archibald Knox, D. Veasey and Oliver Baker (clockwise from the top): Tudric pewter candlestick, designed by Knox; Tudric pewter loving cup with a motto, 'For old times sake', designed by Veasey; Tudric pewter rosebowl, designed by Knox; Tudric pewter biscuit barrel with handles, attributed to Knox; Tudric pewter cake basket, designed by Knox, with central enamel reserve; Tudric pewter belt, designed by Knox; Tudric pewter bowl, designed by Knox; Tudric pewter dish, designed by Knox; Tudric pewter vase, designed by Knox; Tudric pewter 'bomb' vase, designed by Knox; Tudric pewter vase, with glass cabochon; Tudric pewter rosebowl, designed by Veasey with the motto, 'The musk of the rose is blown and the woodbine spices are wafted abroad'; Tudric pewter tankard, designed by Oliver Baker.*

THE LIBERTY METALWORK VENTURE was the initiative of the founder of the firm, Arthur Lasenby Liberty, and his talented director, John Llewellyn. The evocative titles used by the firm, 'Cymric' in the case of their range of silver and jewellery launched in 1899, 'Tudric' for their associated range of pewter which started production in 1902, are thought to have had their origin in Llewellyn's Welsh ancestry. This is a pleasant and sentimental explanation which, however, does little to illuminate the diverse influences on a range of metalwork which made a substantial contribution to the English decorative arts at the turn of this century.

Liberty metalwork first of all must be seen within the context of the British Arts and Crafts Movement and an immediate and important influence was the work of Charles Robert Ashbee, the founder of the Guild of Handicraft; Liberty's range of silver owed a considerable debt to the pioneering work of Ashbee's Guild. The characteristics in common were large expanses of plain silver, concentrated ornament, clusters of coloured stones and enamel work and the use of planished rather than highly polished silver surfaces. Aymer Vallance, writing for *The Studio*, drily

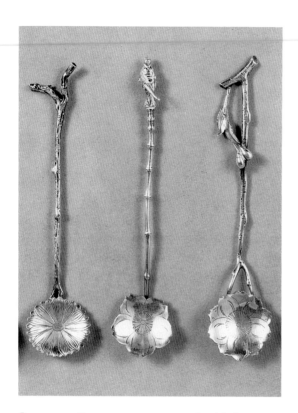

Japanese silver spoons, engraved with human and plant motifs, imported c. 1893 and bearing the marker's mark 'S M' and the Liberty mark 'L Y & Co.'.

commented in his review of the Cymric range in 1901 that 'the Guild of Handicraft had for some years been producing work with not dissimilar properties.' Comparison of Cymric silver and jewellery alongside the work of the Guild of Handicraft, however, always shows distinctive differences. The Cymric style was a rich blend of Arts and Crafts influences and Continental Art Nouveau with a style all of its own. Liberty himself expressed cautious admiration for Art Nouveau until the movement reached its zenith at the Paris Exhibition of 1900. Thereafter, his public statements tended to conform more closely to the prevailing academic distaste for it. On the whole, there was something rather too florid about Art Nouveau for it to appeal comfortably to English taste. In the case of the English, the role of the craftsman had moral and social overtones altogether lacking in Art Nouveau. Within this framework, Liberty's metalwork venture neatly straddles both movements but if it had a tendency to lean either way, its origins were more firmly rooted in the English Arts and Crafts, not only in its designs but also in the circumstances of its manufacture.

However, if the dignity and the identity of the craftsman was one of the core elements of the English Arts and Crafts philosophy, this was not a principle that was ever acknowledged by Liberty's. Identifying the contributing designers of Liberty creations and in some cases the manufacturers has always proved to be a frustrating task, since the firm seldom acknowledged the source of its work. When Liberty's entered metalwork in the exhibitions of the Arts and Crafts Society, the designer and executant of each piece had to be identified, since this was one of the conditions of eligibility. But the amount exhibited included only a small proportion of their output and the majority of it remained anonymous.

Various reasons have been advanced for this. Liberty's always retained the right to modify the designs at the production stage to make them more commercially viable if necessary. Thus, the design was not necessarily one individual's conception. After all, the customers continued to patronise the shop because they felt comfortable with the overall image of the style promoted there. It was the Liberty name which was more persuasive in making their decision to purchase, rather than the individual designer or manufacturer which the majority of customers would probably not have had sufficient confidence to select for themselves.

The first maker's mark for Liberty, 'L Y & Co', was registered by Arthur Lasenby Liberty at Goldsmith's Hall on 8 February 1894; coincidentally, the same year that Liberty's was registered as a limited liability company. At this time, the shop was described as 'wholesale and retail drapers, furnishers, estate agents etc.' and 'jewellers, goldsmiths and silversmiths, dealers in gold, silver, precious stones, curios and articles of vertu'. But despite this claim, the registration of a maker's mark in 1894 did not signify any immediate intention of entering into silver and jewellery production. The primary need for a mark was because of the shop's activities as an importer of foreign, and particularly Japanese silverware. Legisla-

Japanese silver teapots, embossed, chased and engraved with chrysanthemum and leaf motifs, made by Konoike of Yokohama; they bear import marks for 1896–97 and the maker's mark of Liberty & Co.

CYMRIC

tion introduced in 1842 and further modified in 1867, stipulated that all 'gold and silver plate imported from foreign parts … shall be assayed, stamped and marked by an Assay Office in the United Kingdom …'. There is a silver teapot in the collections of the Victoria and Albert Museum, made and signed by Konoike of Yokohama with the London maker's mark of Liberty and Company and the import marks for 1896–97.

In May 1899, Liberty's registered a further three variants of their London mark, just prior to the official launch of their Cymric silver the following month. The new variants suggest that there must have been a last minute rush to have the Cymric wares fully hallmarked in accordance with the requirements of the hallmarking laws. For the following two years the London mark continued to be used on Liberty silver but towards the end of 1901, their Birmingham mark began to appear on Cymric silver with increasing frequency. Liberty's had registered their mark with the Birmingham Assay Office on 26 September 1899. The signatures on the application were those of two partners in the firm, J. W. Howe and W. Street. The third signature was that of William Rabone Haseler who described himself as 'Managing Director' and was a director of the firm of W. H. Haseler, goldsmiths and jewellers at 8 Hylton Street, Birmingham.

Haseler's quickly established themselves as the major and then the sole suppliers of Cymric silver. The relationship between the two firms was formally recognized on 17 May 1901 when a joint company under the name Liberty and Co. (Cymric) Ltd was created, although Haseler's description of his role on the hallmark application indicates that a joint venture was probably the intention from the very beginning. The start-up

A Cymric silver casket (right) set with turquoise, designed by Archibald Knox, c. 1903.

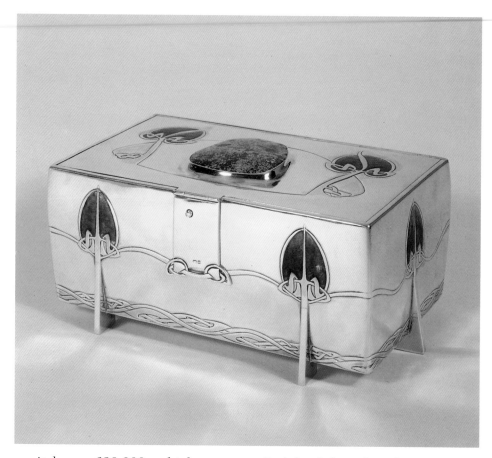

A Cymric silver tankard (below), gilt inside, with a broad frieze of interlacing ornament set with turquoises; the high-domed cover is set with turquoise matrix and hinged to the handle below a flaring thumbpiece. This piece was probably designed by Archibald Knox, c. 1902.

capital was £20,000, which was supplied by Liberty's, who in return received Haseler's lease on the factory in Hylton Street along with the plant and tools. It was only in 1903 that this new company registered its own mark, though, in fact, it was rarely used; the majority of Liberty silver continued to carry the mark registered in 1899.

Haseler's initial designs for the Cymric scheme appear to have originated in Birmingham. Oliver Baker, a friend of William Haseler's, was a landscape painter and etcher with a studio in Edgbaston. Baker records in his diary for 11 May 1898 that it was over an informal discussion with Haseler that they evolved the idea of designing and producing an 'artistic' line of silverware. Undeterred by his complete lack of experience in any field of the decorative arts, he started immediately on a series of designs which initially ran into some difficulty. In September of that same year, Baker enrolled at the Birmingham School of Art in a class for 'Designs executed in the materials for which they are intended'. By early 1899, Baker had developed sufficient proficiency for Haseler's to put some of his designs into production on a trial basis. When Haseler met Liberty in London later in September of that same year, Liberty's director, John Llewellyn, chose some of Baker's designs for inclusion in the newly launched Cymric range. Baker's contribution was a distinctive form of boldly scrolling strapwork, possibly ultimately derived from Renaissance ironwork, which gave his work a strong character. It was this bold use of

Cymric silver frames (right), *designed by Archibald Knox, c. 1903.*

A Cymric silver clock (below), *probably designed by Rex Silver, 1903; the numerals are enamelled in green and blue, and the silver hands end in red enamelled hearts.*

ornament, with an understated reference to Continental Art Nouveau, which set the tone for the Cymric scheme, although in the hands of others it was to be considerably refined.

Other contributors to Cymric designs from Birmingham included Bernard Cuzner (1877–1956), a young graduate from the Vittoria Street School who started his career working for Haseler's in the early years of the century. He designed and produced a range of jewellery and silverware which was in the best traditions of the British Arts and Crafts. One rose bowl with four curving legs on a ring foot of 1905, produced under the Cymric scheme, can be definitely attributed to him. It proved enduringly popular. Another notable contributor was Arthur Gaskin, appointed head of the Vittoria Street School in 1902, who along with his wife is known to have worked for Liberty's until they had established themselves as silver and jewellery designers in their own right. Liberty's later stocked their work independently of their own line. But while the design input from Birmingham was initially very important, after 1900 Liberty's increasingly began to rely on the Silver Studio, based in Hammersmith, London, to supply designs for their metalwork production.

The Silver Studio was immensely important to the development of Liberty's and its house style. Founded by Arthur Silver in 1880, it flourished as an independent design studio until its closure in 1963 when Rex Silver, the son of the founder, retired. Arthur Silver was fortunate in

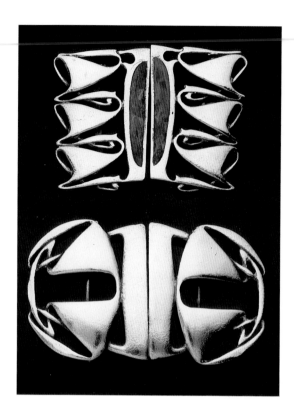

Two Cymric silver waist clasps, possibly designed by Archibald Knox, c. 1901.

being apprenticed in 1873 to H. W. Batley, a talented and progressive designer of furniture, textiles and wallpapers. Batley was fluent in working in a number of styles and, during the eighteen-seventies, often incorporated Japanese motifs in his furniture designs in particular. It is thought that it was Batley who cultivated Silver's interest in Japanese art; he was certainly responsible for instilling in him a sound practical knowledge of the technicalities involved in designing for specific materials. Silver owed much to Batley, but he had an original talent of his own and it was shortly after the birth of his eldest child, Rex, that he decided to exploit it fully and establish his own design studio. It flourished from the start and, under Arthur Silver's direction, was responsible for some of the most graceful and innovative textile designs ever produced on Liberty's behalf. The Studio contribution to the Liberty metalwork venture, which began shortly after the scheme was established, was also of major importance. Its success was assured after Silver recruited a brilliant young designer, Archibald Knox, in 1898, the same year that the Cymric scheme was initiated.

Knox was the son of a marine engineer from Cronkborne on the Isle of Man. From 1878 until 1884, he studied at the Douglas School of Art where he subsequently taught. It was here too that he made the acquaintance of the architect Hugh Baillie Scott, with whom he briefly collaborated. In 1897, Knox moved to London, first obtaining a teaching post at Redhill in Surrey, and in the following year starting work for the Silver Studio. It remains uncertain just how Knox came to be introduced to Rex Silver who had only recently taken over the direction of the Silver Studio after his father's premature death in 1896. One possibility is that he was introduced by Baillie Scott who had designed textiles for Liberty in 1893. Equally possible is that he was introduced by Christopher Dresser whose son was an apprentice at the Studio. Dresser, one of the most accomplished designers of his day, had been a friend of Arthur Liberty since their first meeting in 1878 and had supplied a number of textile designs to the firm in 1882. Liberty's also stocked some of Dresser's textile designs produced by other firms and carried some of his avant-garde metalwork designs. It is widely believed, although impossible to confirm, that Knox worked briefly in Dresser's design studio on coming to London, which would explain how they first met. If Knox's introduction to the Silver Studio was by way of Dresser and Liberty, the latter may well have recommended Knox to sell his work through the Studio because the Studio was already familiar with preparing designs to Liberty's specifications. Another possible route may well have been directly through Harry Napper, design manager of the Studio in October 1898, when preparations started on the first batch of metalwork designs for Liberty's. Napper belonged to both the Arts and Crafts Exhibition Society and the Art-Workers' Guild and could well have made Knox's acquaintance at one of the many meetings held by either body.

Knox started designing silver and jewellery for the Cymric scheme in 1899 and continued to do so until 1911, although many of his designs continued to be manufactured through to the nineteen-twenties. His most prolific period was between 1903 and 1905. While positive identification of his work is difficult because of Liberty's policy of complete anonymity, there are characteristics, such as the stylized interlaced embossing, reminiscent of Celtic scrollwork, which make an attribution to Knox probable. It is thought that the Celtic element was Knox's personal contribution to the Cymric scheme.

The problem of attributing with any certainty Knox's designs is not only complicated by Liberty's policy of anonymity, but further exacerbated by the same practice being adopted by the Silver Studio itself. Arthur Silver and his son Rex never credited individual designers in any public mention of the Studio's work. Any publicity was inevitably credited to the head of the Studio and, furthermore, in an interview towards the end of his long life, Rex Silver maintained that he was responsible for all the metalwork designs that were produced in his studio for Liberty's.

This claim cannot of course be sustained. The only design that can now be positively attributed to him is a pair of candlesticks, named 'Conister', which were illustrated in a number of *The Studio* in 1900 and credited to him. Even then, this may have been in his capacity as head of the Studio, although the editorial board of the magazine were usually very particular in crediting the exact executant of the design and indeed became so irritated with Silver's insistence on only citing the head of the Studio, that they deliberately omitted his name from *The Designers' Yearbook* of 1909.

A pair of silver candlesticks, the 'Conister', designed by Rex Silver, 1899/1900; they have applied struts on the columns, which separate into stylized leaf forms below wavy drip pans. The nozzles are detachable.

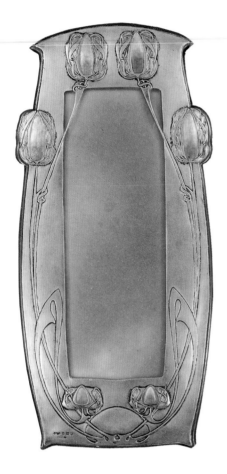

A Cymric silver and enamel mirror frame (above), *probably designed by Archibald Knox, c. 1902, incorporating decoration derived from Celtic motifs.*

A silver enamel spoon and a napkin ring (right), *both designed by Archibald Knox, c. 1903. Both pieces are chased and ornamented with peacock, green and orange enamels.*

A Liberty Tudric pewter tea-set (opposite), *designed by Archibald Knox, c. 1902, comprising teapot, hot-water jug, sugar bowl and milk jug; the tray is probably not a Knox design.*

Another designer who contributed to the Silver Studio production of Liberty metalwork designs was John Illingworth Kay, who was associated with the Studio between 1892 and 1900 and designed not just metalwork but book covers, wallpapers and textiles. Kay's real vocation was as a water-colour artist. He left the Studio in 1900 to manage the stencilling department of the wallpaper firm of Essex and Co., which he left in turn in 1922 to take up a part-time teaching post at the Central School of Arts and Crafts.

Harry Napper was also a prominent water-colour artist who joined the Studio in, it is thought, 1893. On the death of Arthur Silver in 1896, he became head of the Studio's design production department for two years after which he left to work for the Studio on a freelance basis and continued to do so for many years. Another contributor to the scheme was Harry Silver, the brother of Rex. He successfully incorporated Knox's Celtic motifs into his work which now makes the task of distinguishing the work of the two of them extremely difficult indeed.

It should, of course, be remembered that Rex Silver was ultimately responsible for all the Studio output, which meant that he often, if not always, made some contribution to the final design. He suggested, supervised, criticized and occasionally amended all the designs which emanated from his Studio and this could include, particularly if it were for an important customer such as Liberty, selecting the source material. If one is to be accurate in ascribing the artistic responsibility for the Silver Studio designs supplied to Liberty's, it must be described as a partnership between Rex Silver and the designers he employed. In particular, the partnership between himself and Archibald Knox produced some of the most inspired and exhilarating work for the Cymric and Tudric ranges.

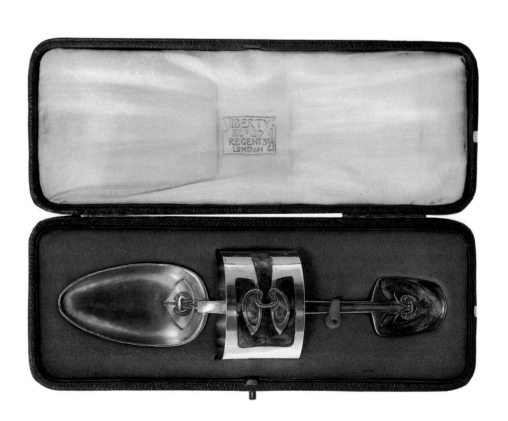

Liberty's introduction of their own range of pewter revived the status of an industry which had sunk perilously low. For most of the nineteenth century, the British pewter industry was virtually synonymous with the Sheffield Britannia Metal industry. Britannia metal, an alloy which consists of fifty parts tin to three or four parts antimony and one part copper, began to be manufactured in Sheffield in 1770 by two men called Hancock and Jessop; the city remained the principal source of Britannia metal products for the next fifty years. Until the advent of electroplating, this industry was always considered the poor relation of the Sheffield trades. Its softness did not make it very durable. These qualities prescribed certain attitudes within the industry and the public who bought the products. Cheap, flimsy, imitative and expendable described the trade. It was not an industry whose practices either encouraged or even required innovations and investment in new design. When electroplating got underway after 1840, the Britannia metal industry saw it had little to lose by subscribing to the Elkington patents and Britannia metal became, along with nickel silver, one of the standard base metals in this booming new industry. Again it was being principally used to imitate another material. The silverplated surface of Britannia metal, or for that matter nickel silver products, imitated the fashionable dictates of the sterling silversmiths.

It was against this background that, in 1899, Arthur Lasenby Liberty began importing pewter from Germany for sale in his Regent Street shop. His principal suppliers were J. P. Kayser Sohn of Krefeld-Bockum (founded 1885), Walter Scherf's Osiris-Metallwarenfabrik für Kleinkunst of Nurenberg (founded 1899), the Orivit-Metallwarenfabrik in Cologne (founded 1894) and Ludwig Lichtinger Werkstätte of Munich. An interest in manufacturing pewter, as a material worthy of interest in its own right, had started in France almost a decade previously and had subsequently spread to Germany. It was the facility with which pewter could be cast that particularly favoured the material as a medium for the new Continental style, Art Nouveau. Its importation into London by Liberty met with considerable commercial success and it was this which was primarily responsible for Liberty's deciding to introduce a pewter range of their own commissioning.

Liberty's decision to sponsor a range of pewter is fortunately well documented. On 17 May 1904, Arthur Liberty presented a paper to the Royal Society of Arts titled 'Pewter and the Revival of its Use'. In this, he traced the decline of the English industry and its subsequent, recent revival. The talk was illustrated with contemporary examples of German manufacture by the firms listed above and, not surprisingly, Liberty drew particular attention to his own range which had begun production under the brand name 'Tudric' in 1901. By contrast to the Continental ware with 'the fantastic motif which it pleases our Continental friends to worship as l'art nouveau', he stressed that the Tudric range was decorated simply with modifications of Celtic forms, augmented with floral and plant motifs.

A pewter bowl (above), *designed by Rex Silver, 1903; it is decorated with a band of stylized flowers, while the two handles extend beneath the bowl to form the feet. A Tudric pewter mount for glass* (above right)*; it was probably designed by Archibald Knox, c. 1904–5.*

Liberty was being ingenious rather than ingenuous, for this neatly overlooked that contribution that Art Nouveau had made to the revival of pewter and the success of German pewter in the style at Liberty's, which had encouraged him to introduce the Tudric range in the first instance. Moreover, besides the sources acknowledged by Liberty, whether Celtic or naturalistic, the designs produced in pewter, as for those in silver and jewellery, show a distinct Art Nouveau influence. Liberty was at least gracious enough to observe: 'Alongside the foolish and undesirable, it must in justice be admitted that the Germans have recently produced many original and pleasing designs in pewter.' But he was anxious, as always, to emphasize the superiority of his own products: 'The German alloys have, however, in my opinion, the disadvantage of being more brittle than those used in this country and I refer particularly to those by the Company with which my own name is associated. The alloys used by it are, as before mentioned, the results of careful trials made by my friend, Mr Haseler, a Partner in, and Director of Liberty & Co.'s works at Birmingham. His endeavour has been to produce a metal similar, as far as possible, to the best of old English pewter and in point of solidity, the new alloy is, I believe, unequalled.'

The alloy that was finally chosen after these investigations was a composition of 90 per cent tin, 8 per cent copper and 2 per cent antimony, but these words, in passing, refer to one of the rather extraordinary aspects of the Tudric venture. Haseler's, who were again chosen as manufacturers

A small pewter cake tray, probably designed by Archibald Knox, c. 1904; it is decorated with stylized leaves and flowers.

for the new range, clearly had no previous experience of pewter smithing at all. Moreover, Liberty admitted in the same lecture that his firm's decision to start manufacturing a range of pewter arose from the early success of the Cymric scheme. Liberty was at pains, however, to stress that while he believed some of the same motifs could be incorporated into a range of pewter ware, the pewter surface was most emphatically not intended to imitate that of silver and simply serve as a poorer substitute. Those involved in the production of the Tudric range, not least of all himself, the Silver Studio who produced the designs and Haseler's who manufactured them, were fully aware of one of the principal tenets of the Arts and Crafts philosophy: the suitability of the material to the chosen form. The range which evolved over the next few years displays some similarity to the austere style and an identity all of its own.

Like the Cymric venture, the designs were the responsibility of the Silver Studio and were probably largely conceived by Archibald Knox. As for the silver and jewellery, it is impossible to identify who was responsible for what, but the most successful designs in the Liberty catalogue for 1904 show an assurance in the overall form and a tautness and economy in the applied decoration which makes an attribution to Knox fairly safe. Glass, either used as liners for butter dishes or as beakers in an elegant holder first issued in 1905, was supplied by James Powell & Sons of Whitefriars, London. Colour was occasionally, if sparingly used in the form of applied, turquoise enamel, usually to highlight stylized, floral motifs. A rather more ambitious use of enamel was a range of cigarette boxes designed by Fleetwood Charles Varley, a minor water-colour painter who had previously been associated with Ashbee's Guild of Handicraft between 1900 and 1907. He did a series of small, sometimes distinctly whimsical, land and seascapes which were used to decorate not only the lids of pewter but also silver boxes in a manner very similar to his previous work for the Guild.

Unlike Cymric silver and jewellery, none of the Tudric range was produced entirely by hand, but sometimes machine stamped or, more usually, cast in iron moulds. It is a tribute to Haseler's expertise that the firm mastered the technicalities of pewter casting quickly and efficiently, for the surfaces of Tudric ware show no trace of any blemish, caused by trapped air bubbles, which can so easily occur in inexperienced hands. Haseler's had little room for manoeuvre for the products had to be cheap enough to appeal to a less affluent market against stiff competition from the Germans. The immediate and popular success of Tudric pewter demonstrates that once again all those involved were capable of producing Arts and Crafts metalwork on competitive terms.

Again, the most innovative period and peak of production for the Tudric range occurred between its introduction in 1901 and the First World War. After Knox had left the firm in 1912, fewer new designs were issued although the range continued to be in production until the nineteen-thirties. Even by the time of Knox's departure, Rex Silver had begun to perceive that changing fashions once again favoured a more historicist approach. There were a few new designs produced during the twenties which, if they can be related to any identifiable taste, conform to the Tudorbethan approach, best exemplified by Liberty's new shop in Great Marlborough Street. The designs have some charm and elegance but are at best only a pale reflection of the verve and originality characteristic of the metalwork production of the early years. The fact that the best of the pre-war designs continued to be manufactured, long after they had ceased to be the epitome of fashion, shows a decline in confidence. The Cymric scheme was finally wound up in 1927. The production of Tudric pewter continued for a few more years, but finally ceased abruptly when Haseler's handed over all but four of their iron moulds to the Government at the outbreak of war in 1939.

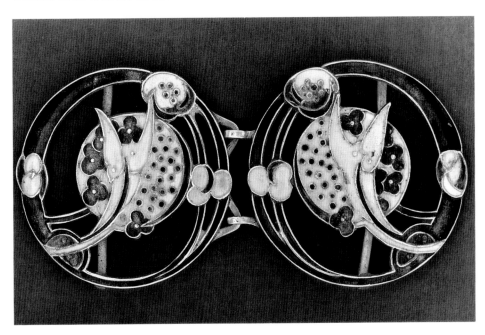

A silver and enamel waist clasp, 1906, designed by Jessie M. King, who also designed textiles for Liberty's.

Ceramics

WHEN ARTHUR LASENBY LIBERTY opened his shop on Regent Street in 1875, London society was in the grip of what had become known as 'chinamania'. One form the derangement took was the obsessive collecting of antique porcelain. Much of the search for ceramic treasure was concentrated on Oriental pottery and porcelain, particularly Chinese blue-and-white, the appreciation of which had spread from a small circle of artists and connoisseurs during the eighteen-sixties to affect most members of polite society in the course of the following two decades.

The craze for china-painting was another form of 'chinamania', and one which made an important contribution to the development of the Arts and Crafts Movement. In 1871, Minton's had started their Art-Pottery Studio in Kensington Gore, London, and fashionable young ladies had flocked there to receive tuition in pottery decoration and to have their work fired by professional kiln-workers. When the buildings were destroyed by fire in 1875, Howell & James, a firm of silk mercers, wine merchants and house-furnishers, stepped into the breach. They opened a new department at their Lower Regent Street premises where Miss Florence Judd, an instructress from Minton's Studio, could continue to hold her classes, and they provided facilities for firing the students' work. George Ensworth, who joined the staff of Liberty in 1878, later recalled 'taking a plaque painted by Miss Octavia Liberty to Messrs. Howell & James to be fired. The subject was, I think, Daffodils.' Octavia (a sister of Arthur Lasenby) entered her work in exhibitions of paintings on china which Howell & James held each summer from 1876, and in 1880 she won the prize offered by the women's magazine *The Queen*, for a plaque that she had painted with marsh marigolds.

During the period from 1875 to about 1885, Howell & James dominated the art pottery market in London. They stocked the products of several of the more prominent manufacturers and held special exhibitions of work from less well-known studios, such as Sir Edmund Elton's Sunflower Pottery and the Cincinnati Pottery Club. Until about 1883, however, Liberty's kept clear of the modern British pottery trade; instead, they aimed to satisfy the cravings of the bric-à-brac hunters, particularly those in search of Oriental pottery and porcelain. Their stock included the work, both antique and modern, of Chinese, Japanese, Indian and North African potters. At first, the selection offered seems to have been limited and unremarkable. By 1881, however, there was a wide range of Oriental ceramics available at the shop. Most important, in relation to the evolution of Art Nouveau and the Arts and Crafts Movement, was the Japanese pottery, both old and new, which was on sale. A Liberty catalogue issued in 1881 lists most of the leading Japanese potteries and particularly draws the customer's attention to the 'works of famous artists', including Ninsei and Makudzu. Ninsei represented the past; the seventeenth-century potter had done much to liberate Japanese ceramics from the dominating

Japanese porcelain of the Satsuma type (right) *was illustrated in Liberty catalogues from the early eighteen-eighties. This style of painted enamel decoration proved very popular all over Europe and among its derivatives were the porcelain produced by the Danish firm Bing & Grondahl and some of the wares created by William Moorcroft for James Macintyre & Co.*

Liberty's imported pottery from several Eastern manufacturing centres, including Bombay. This earthenware vase (opposite) *was made at the School of Art there, c. 1880, and is decorated with floral motifs and abstract patterns inspired by Persian art.*

influence of Chinese wares. Makudzu was a contemporary hero; in 1878 his work had been shown at the Paris Exhibition where it had won much praise and admiration. One aspect of Japanese art which particularly appealed to Westerners was its living tradition. It was widely felt that industrialization had cut off the European art and crafts from the work of the great masters of the past. The popularity in the West of modern as well as antique Japanese artefacts was gratifying to dealers such as Liberty who could always obtain more when their stocks ran out, although the complaint was often heard that standards of Japanese craftsmanship were declining as a result of over-production.

Liberty's had started stocking the wares of the Bretby Art Pottery almost as soon as it had been established in 1883 by Henry Tooth and William Ault near Burton-on-Trent (Derbyshire). Tooth had been manager of the Linthorpe Art Pottery in Middlesbrough which, from 1879, had been producing earthenware strongly influenced by contemporary Japanese ceramics. The designer, Dr Christopher Dresser, who had been art director at Linthorpe, had visited Japan in 1876–77 where he had been particularly impressed by the work of Makudzu and the Awaji potters. Some of the Linthorpe glazes, in which two or three colours flow into each other, and the irregular shapes of many pieces produced by the pottery, reflect Dresser's admiration for Japanese ceramics. Linthorpe pottery was sold at the Art Furnishers' Alliance, a Bond Street emporium which opened in

1880 with Dresser as Art Manager. Arthur Lasenby Liberty was one of the principal shareholders in the Alliance, and when it went into liquidation in May 1883, he took over the retailing of some of its lines. Liberty was probably more interested in retailing the Bretby wares, made under Tooth's supervision and closely related in style to Linthorpe pottery designed by Dresser. Several Bretby models, featuring either irregular, dimpled shapes or strong, clean geometrical forms, appear to have been designed by Dresser but rely heavily on Japanese originals. Later Bretby wares sold by Liberty's included vessels simulating beaten copper or wood; these too were derived from Japanese ceramics. Others were in a style inspired by Egyptian art which Dresser had also frequently adopted.

By 1888, Liberty's had started selling Burmantofts Faience. It was advertised that year in their 'Yule-Tide Gifts' catalogue. This pottery, made in Leeds, was similar in style to Bretby and Linthorpe wares. It had been exhibited by Howell & James in 1881, and probably became available to Liberty's a few years later as Howell & James's commercial position began to weaken.

The London agency for C. H. Brannam's slip-decorated earthenware also passed to Liberty's in the late eighteen-eighties. Charles Hubert Brannam began making art pottery at Barnstaple, Devon, in 1879 and the following year Howell & James started retailing the ware. It does not seem to be known for certain exactly when Liberty's first sold Brannam's pottery, but its first mention in a Liberty catalogue was not until 'Yule-Tide

The style of the decoration on these Barum-ware vases (below) *reflects a taste created by the Arts and Crafts Movement, and their colour scheme – blue and brown on a green ground – was first made popular by designers such as C. F. A. Voysey and M. H. Baillie Scott. The vases, manufactured c. 1905 by C. H. Brannam, are impressed 'Made for Liberty & Co'.*

The fish-head spout is a traditional feature of north Devon pottery, but the fish painted in slip on the side of this Brannam jug (below right) *were inspired by the carp depicted in Japanese woodblock prints. The jug was made c. 1900.*

A group of pottery manufactured by C. H. Brannam between 1880 and 1910 reveals the different sources from which the Devon firm derived the shapes and decoration of their wares. Although an Oriental flavour predominates, as might be expected from a firm supplying Liberty's, ornament from the Italian Renaissance is also evident.

Gifts' of 1894, where it is described as a 'new and effective highly-glazed pottery'. Until about that time, Barum-ware (as it was designated from 1885) had been decorated with designs of flowers, birds and insects drawn in the Japanese manner and incised through a layer of slip of different colour to that covering the body of the vessel. However, early in the eighteen-nineties, the decoration changed. The designs, mostly of fish and flowers treated in a loose, swirling style that presaged Art Nouveau, were modelled in low relief with slip applied to the vessel's surface. The shapes, which had previously been quite restrained, now became 'novel and quaint', as the 1894 catalogue described them, meaning elaborately con-

103

trived and often adorned with handles, either twisted or in the form of dragons or fish. After 1900, some of the Barum-ware sold at Liberty's was decorated with Celtic motifs, in conformity with the shop's house style of that period. Another, more sober form in which the pottery appeared, from about 1905, was characterized by traditional shapes decorated with plain glazes which were generally blue, green or yellow.

A second West Country maker whose wares were retailed by Liberty's was the Royal Aller Vale Art Pottery. The shop had probably been encouraged to start stocking this ware by the patronage bestowed on the pottery in 1889 by H.R.H. the Princess Louise, a distinction which Liberty's did not fail to mention in their promotional material. The Aller Vale ware sold by Liberty's was decorated with a pattern of foliate scrolls in applied slip which, according to an 1892 catalogue, 'aims at reproducing . . . the effect of Old Rhodian Ware'. The description goes on to suggest a didactic, paternalistic attitude towards the labouring classes which was an important ingredient of the ethos underlying the Arts and Crafts Movement: 'The Ware is almost entirely produced by young lads under the direction of Masters, who have made a thorough study of the Old Moorish and Mediterranean Potteries.' A modified form of the same sentiment appears in the promotional material for the wares made by the Della Robbia Pottery of Birkenhead. A Liberty catalogue issued in 1896 declared: 'The Founders of the "Della Robbia Pottery" aim . . . by encouraging "handwork" to secure freedom of touch and the charm of individuality. The designs . . . are executed by Young Apprentices, and are in the main of *their own device* . . . Girls are employed for the painting process . . . As a stimulus for superior work, a certain Small Sum is offered in prizes, in addition to the weekly wage.'

The Della Robbia Pottery had been founded in 1894 by the painter Harold Rathbone and the sculptor Conrad Dressler. The earthenware produced was decorated with carved, incised and painted designs derived – as the name implies – from the *maiolica* of the Italian Renaissance. The same source had inspired another type of pottery sold at Liberty's, the tinglazed ware made by the Italian firm of Cantagalli. Probably as a result of links between this firm and the English potter William De Morgan, whose ill health forced him to spend his winters in Florence, where the Cantagalli pottery was situated, examples of their wares were displayed at the Arts and Crafts Exhibition Society 1889. The Society's shows were held at the New Gallery in Regent Street, just a few doors down from Liberty's and the shop's buyers would certainly have taken a close interest in the exhibits. Sometimes Liberty's used the event to promote lines which they already stocked, but they also found new suppliers among the exhibitors. The Aller Vale Pottery, for example, had shown its wares at the New Gallery in 1889 and 1890, shortly before Liberty's began to stock the work.

The situation that prevailed at the Aller Vale and Della Robbia potteries, where the pots were designed by experienced artists and decorated by

A vase made at the Della Robbia Pottery in Birkenhead displays the hand-made look which became popular in Britain at the turn of the century, and which Liberty's promoted by retailing the products of the small workshops that sprang up all over the country at this time.

The green glaze covering this bowl and vase, made by A. Harris & Son, Farnham (Surrey), blended with most decorative schemes, and 'green-ware', as it was called, soon became one of Liberty's best-selling pottery lines after its introduction in the early eighteen-nineties.

young workers in the position of students or apprentices, suited Liberty's who always endeavoured to offer their customers attractive goods at low prices. The painted pottery which the shop imported from India was produced in comparable circumstances. It was made and decorated by students at the Bombay School of Art working under the supervision of the British instructors. When Liberty's started stocking the wares towards the end of the eighteen-eighties, the Persian style of decoration traditionally associated with Sind pottery had recently been abandoned, and new designs featuring patterns of birds, animals and flowers adapted from the paintings at the Ajanta cave-temples, had been introduced.

By 1890, the pottery of Absolon Harris at Wrecclesham, near Farnham (Surrey), was producing horticultural and domestic wares, and a few green-glazed pots which were imitations of medieval pieces. In that year, W. H. Allen, the newly-appointed headmaster of Farnham School of Art, began designing shapes for Harris. The new art pottery was covered with the green glaze, and it soon proved hugely popular with an element of the middle-class public which had developed a taste for peasant crafts, from Honiton lace to Windsor chairs. Farnham green-ware was stocked by Liberty's from the early eighteen-nineties until well into the twentieth century. The designs were for the most part based on pots in the Victoria and Albert Museum which Allen believed had been made in the Farnham area during the sixteenth century. There were vases, jugs and bowls with one side in the form of an owl's face, a design which evidently sold well, as they were also manufactured for Liberty's by Brannam. A green-ware

About 1905, Liberty's issued a 'Garden Pottery' catalogue. The wares shown were manufactured at the Compton Pottery in Surrey and the examples illustrated here were designed by Mary Watts (left), *the founder of the pottery, and Archibald Knox* (right).

model of a pig was also popular; some pots were decorated with incised ornament executed by students at the Farnham School of Art. One reason for the success of the ware was that, in the words of an 1898 Liberty catalogue, 'soft rich shades of green will harmonise with almost any scheme of decoration'.

Not far from Wrecclesham is the village of Compton in Surrey, where the renowned painter George Frederick Watts settled down with his second wife, Mary, to spend his declining years. Towards the end of the eighteen-nineties, Mary Watts organized a pottery class for the local inhabitants, and they started making ornamental garden wares in a porous terracotta. Mrs Watts had been brought up in Scotland and from an early age had been deeply interested in Celtic art. She designed the 'entrelac' patterns in the style of Celtic ornament with which the Compton terra-cotta ware was press-moulded. Liberty's added this range of garden pottery, which included pots, sun-dials, fountains and benches, to their other goods decorated with Celtic designs. In 1904, the shop held an exhibition at the Grafton Gallery in London entitled 'Modern Celtic Art', where Cymric silver, Tudric pewter, jewellery, Donegal carpets and Compton pottery were displayed together. To Archibald Knox, who was responsible for many of the metalwork and jewellery designs, can be attributed the ornament on one or two of the Compton pieces, but Mrs Watts herself designed most of them. Conformity of style across different media also determined the design of a stoneware vase and a candlestick made for Liberty's by Doulton of Lambeth, London. These pieces were decorated with patterns of stylized honesty, a motif that occurs on Liberty furniture and on some items of Tudric pewter. The tall, square-sectioned vase, with a spread foot, echoes forms found as legs or shelf supports on Liberty furniture.

In 1899, the buyers from Liberty's at last turned their attention towards the manufacturers in Staffordshire, the centre of the British ceramics industry. Up to that time, most of the firms which had supplied the store with ceramics had been small art potteries or country potteries, for which an order from Liberty's was a significant boost to turnover. It is a measure of the growth in the shop's buying strength that Staffordshire firms were now prepared to turn out wares in the style that Liberty's wanted, a style much more advanced in artistic terms than any that had been adopted in the Potteries for twenty years.

Two factories started making wares which suited Liberty's: Wileman & Co. of the Foley Potteries, Longton, and James Macintyre & Co. of the Washington Works, Burslem. Wileman's had recently taken on a new art-director, Frederick Rhead, whose brother George Woolliscroft Rhead had designed the cover of Liberty's 'Yule-Tide Gifts' catalogue of 1893. At the Foley Potteries, Frederick Rhead introduced new lines decorated with ornamental designs which combined elements of Italian *maiolica* and contemporary painted ceramics from the Netherlands. Wileman's new

'Florian Ware', designed by William Moorcroft and manufactured by James Macintyre & Co, was shown in Liberty's 1901 'Yule-Tide Gifts' catalogue. The caption writer claimed that, while some of the pieces were 'reminiscent of Pompeian models, others are adapted from the Italian and contemporary schools', thus seeking to appeal both to customers who desired something modern and to others whose taste was a little more staid.

wares were displayed at Liberty's in 1899. The designers included both Frederick Rhead's brothers, George Woolliscroft and Louis, and Mrs Waterhouse, wife of the architect Alfred Waterhouse. She ran the Yattendon metalwork class whose copper wares were also available from Liberty's. Another example of this cross-fertilization between Liberty suppliers was a Donegal rug called 'The Pelican' which was woven by Alexander Morton & Co. to a design by Mrs Watts. Wileman's new range of art pottery included 'Intarsio' ware which was decorated with ornamental designs hand-painted on transfer-printed outlines, and 'Spano-Lustra', 'Urbato', 'Primitif' and 'Pastello', all given various forms of slip decoration. In 1898, Liberty's had sold some German pottery with raised slip decoration, designed by Max Läuger and made by the Majolika-Manufaktur at Karlsruhe. Subsequently, Wardle & Co, a small pottery in Hanley, Staffordshire, which appointed Frederick Hürten Rhead (one of Frederick Rhead's sons) as art director in 1899, produced for Liberty's a range of vases called 'Hadcote' which were decorated with a pattern of flowers in raised slip, similar to Läuger's work. But the best-selling line was made by James Macintyre & Co. and designed by William Moorcroft.

Florian Ware (English).

An exceedingly decorative English Pottery. The designs are delicately treated, and are in cream colour relieved with olive green. The elegant forms in many specimens are reminiscent of Pompeian models, others are adapted from the later Italian and contemporary schools.

Many other Specimens in Stock.

No. 1. Vase.

Diameter, 3¼ inches.	Price 6/–
,,	5½ ,,	,,	13/6
,,	7½ ,,	,,	25/–

No. 2. Vase.

			Price
Diameter, 3 inches.	Price 3/6
,,	4 ,,	,,	5/6
,,	5 ,,	,,	7/6

No. 3. Vase.

Diameter, 5½ inches.	Price 8/6
,,	6½ ,,	,,	10/6
,,	7½ ,,	,,	11/6
,,	8½ ,,	,,	13/6

No. 4. Tea Jar.

Price
Height, 5½ ins. ... 9/6

Tobacco Jar
with two lids.
Height, 5½ ins. ... 10/6

No. 5. Vase.

Price.
Height, 6 inches ... 7/9
,, 12 ,, ...15/9

No. 6. Flower Pot.

Price
Diameter, 3 inches ... 4/9
,, 4½ ,, ...11/9
,, 7½ ,, ...27/6

No. 7. Vase.

Price.
Height, 3¼ inches. Price 4/9
,, 5 ,, ,, 8/6
,, 8 ,, ,, 18/6

No. 8. Flower Pot.

Price.
Diameter, 3 inches 4/6
,, 5½ ,, 10/6
,, 6½ ,, 14/6

No. 9. Vase.

Price.
Height, 6 inches 6/–
,, 12 ,, 15/9

The Specimens illustrated are shewn on small Blackwood Stands which are not included for the prices mentioned.

A 'Hazledene' stoneware vase (above) *with decoration of trees in a landscape in blue-green and yellow, produced by William Moorcroft at James Macintyre & Co., c. 1902. Peacock feathers* (above centre) *and tulips* (above right) *are featured on these 'Florian Ware' vases, c. 1899 and c. 1900, respectively. All pieces made by Macintyre's, and later by Moorcroft when his firm took over production, were thrown on the wheel and decorated by hand. The ornament was applied in raised lines of slip which prevented the different colours running together.*

'Florian Ware' was introduced by Macintyre's in 1898 and it was being sold by Liberty's within a year. William Moorcroft had been responsible for its development, both artistic and technical, and he supervised every stage in the production of the ware. The decoration combines features of the English Arts and Crafts style as it had evolved from the work of William Morris, with some of the characteristics of Continental Art Nouveau. Moorcroft had visited Paris before embarking on his career in the ceramics industry, and he had probably observed and noted such products as the porcelain designed by Georges de Feure and Edward Colonna which Siegfried Bing sold at his Paris shop, La Maison de l'Art Nouveau; its swirling floral ornament is a likely source of some of Moorcroft's early designs. Liberty's retailed 'Florian' under the name 'Burslem Ware', and the shop subsequently stocked several other Moorcroft designs including 'Hazledene' (trees in a landscape), 'Claremont' (toadstools), 'Flamminian' (monochrome-glazed with one small circular motif of stylized leaves) and 'Murena' (pomegranates); there were several other designs which achieved more modest commercial success. The classical shapes which characterized 'Florian Ware' eventually gave way to more rounded forms with strong, clear contours.

When Macintyre's decided in 1913 to abandon the production of art pottery and concentrate on electrical insulators, Moorcroft opened his own factory at Cobridge, Staffordshire, where he continued to produce the same kinds of wares. He had become friendly with the Liberty family, particularly with Aylwin Lasenby, A. L. Liberty's cousin, and the shop bought considerable quantities of pottery from his new works. One of Moorcroft's most successful lines was introduced almost as soon as the Cobridge factory had been opened – a range of tableware covered in a blue glaze speckled with black. The shapes were simple and functional and in appearance the ware was not far removed from the porcelain tableware decorated with Jugendstil ornament which a few years earlier Liberty's had been buying from the German firm of Ferdinand Selle.

If Moorcroft's modern, utilitarian tableware was one indication of changing attitudes and tastes, the decorated pottery imported from the Netherlands and sold by Liberty's under the name 'Breda-ware' was another. It was manufactured by more than one Dutch pottery and was painted in bright colours with patterns which often incorporated geometrical motifs, such as zigzags and chequers. It owed at least some of its inspiration to the innovative theatre design of the Ballets Russes which was breaking new ground in the decorative arts all over Europe and sowing the seeds of Art Deco, the style which was to dominate the nineteen-twenties and nineteen-thirties.

Breda-ware was made exclusively for Liberty's by several potteries in the Netherlands. It was decorated in a variety of patterns and its strong colours and bold outlines gave a clear indication of the direction in which European style was moving about 1910. On these examples, geometrical patterns and spiral motifs reflect advanced taste in Austria and Germany at the time, which made an important contribution to the Art Deco of the nineteen-twenties.

Glass

ARTHUR LASENBY LIBERTY must have felt somewhat nonplussed about what glassware – if any – he should stock during the early years of his shop. He was, after all, trying to establish a reputation for merchandise which reflected modern artistic taste and, as Charles L. Eastlake observed in his *Hints on Household Taste*, the British had developed a blind spot in the matter of glass. 'The same national peculiarity', Eastlake had written in 1868, 'which makes us fastidious to secure spotless purity in our table-linen and a mirror-like smoothness for our French-polished wood, leads us also to require that every article of glass that we use shall be absolutely free from flaws or blemishes of every kind. Now it is easy to see that a demand for this sort of perfection, although it may tend to make admirable housemaids and laundresses, does not do much to promote the interests of art.'

A delight in 'flaws or blemishes' had been expressed by Ruskin and echoed by Morris. They had created a body of opinion which gladly accepted Eastlake's injunctions and which found that the Oriental goods offered by Liberty often displayed imperfections and irregularities enhancing their aesthetic attractions. Whether it was the accidental imprecision of glazes covering certain types of pottery, or the deliberately asymmetrical compositions of decoration found in metalwork and lacquer, Japanese goods provided welcome relief from the mechanical exactitude and classical balance which characterized the products of Western industry. But Liberty's problem was that Japan did not produce any glass, flawed or otherwise. He would, no doubt, have been quite prepared to sell glass made in Britain, had there been any that conformed to the tenets of Japanese art, but again he was frustrated. Although two firms of glassmakers, Stevens & Williams and Thomas Webb, began about 1878 to produce rock crystal glass cut, engraved and etched with naturalistic decoration in the popular Japanesque style, its Orientalism was superficial. Not only in technique but in appearance it belonged to the category of typical Victorian glassware, all sparkle and yet ponderous.

Frustrated by a lack of suitable products manufactured in Britain, Liberty turned to France, and the shop introduced glass from the Paris studio of François-Eugène Rousseau. At the 1878 Exposition Universelle, held in Paris, Rousseau exhibited a collection of glass decorated with cameo-carving, engraving or enamelling which attracted much critical acclaim. Alfred Darcel, for instance, writing in *Le Temps*, praised Rousseau's work, pointing out that, although the technique of cameo-carving was usually associated with Chinese glass, the style of Rousseau's exhibits was distinctly Japanese. Darcel observed that Rousseau had introduced into the field of glass the kind of decoration that the Japanese applied 'to pottery in enamels, to wood in lacquer, and to bronze in precious metals'. As well as carrying decoration inspired by Japanese art, Rousseau's glass was streaked with clouds of internal colours and bubbles, capturing precisely the haphazard effects so characteristic of craftwork from Japan.

Rousseau's glass must have looked well in Liberty's 'Eastern Bazaar', but each piece was a work of art and very expensive. Rousseau did not himself make the glass vessels that he designed. They were handmade in the workshops of the Appert brothers in Clichy, Paris, and then decorated in Rousseau's studio. As well as employing a group of highly talented craftsmen including the engravers Eugène Michel and Alphonse-Georges Reyen, Rousseau was continually experimenting with innovative techniques of decoration. He regularly consulted the Apperts who helped him achieve new effects.

Liberty's interest in Rousseau's glass would certainly have been aroused by the pieces shown at the 1878 exhibition in Paris but, because of the high cost, it is possible that none of it was purchased for retail through the Regent Street shop until after 1885 when Rousseau retired and his workshops were taken over by a more commercially minded director. Ernest-Baptiste Léveillé, who had worked for Rousseau as an artistic and business assistant, continued to produce glass to Rousseau's designs or in very much the same style, but it was now turned out in much greater quantities. Furthermore, at an exhibition held in Paris the previous year, entitled 'Pierre, Bois, Terre, Verre' ('Stone, Wood, Clay, Glass'), Rousseau had introduced a crackled ware which, decorated with clouds of colour and flecks of gold within the glass, had an even more Oriental appearance than the earlier work. Under Léveillé's regime, such pieces often had far less elaborate carving and engraving than had been normal while Rousseau had been in charge, and more of these could be produced at lower cost.

Léveillé's new glass, in fact, was quite similar in appearance to Clutha glass, another line which was sold by Liberty's. Any account of Liberty's connection with Clutha glass is vitiated by a lack of information and con-

Dr Christopher Dresser, who designed this Clutha glass vase (opposite) *made by James Couper & Sons about 1895, always wanted the nature of the material to dictate the form of the object. Dresser and Arthur Lasenby Liberty were close friends and shared a great admiration for Japanese decorative arts.*

Clutha glass was decorated internally with air bubbles, flakes of gold or silver, and sometimes ribbons of white enamel. Liberty's made a selling point of the flaws and irregularities which appeared in the glass, features that appealed to a public conditioned by Ruskin's and Morris's claim that imperfection was an important ingredient of true beauty. These examples (right) *were possibly designed by Dresser and made by James Couper & Sons, Glasgow, c. 1900.*

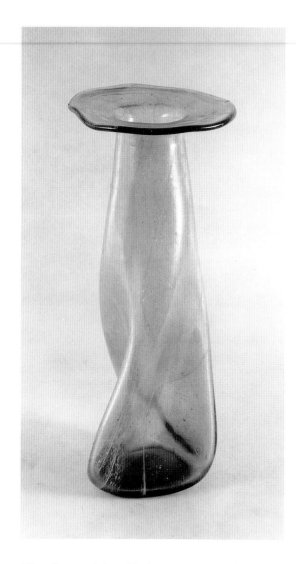

The shape of this Clutha glass vase (above) indicates the consideration that Dresser gave to the processes of manufacture as well as to the material of the object. The form of a blown-glass vessel depends on its manipulation round the axis of the blowpipe, and this apparently complicated shape can be achieved quite simply by an experienced glass-blower.

Some Clutha bowls were designed to fit into Tudric pewter stands (right). The pale colours of the glass are complemented by the dull sheen of the pewter and, with the glass appearing through the ornamental shapes pierced in the pewter, the two elements become visually fused.

tradictory evidence. Since most of the glass was designed by Christopher Dresser, it is reasonable to suppose that his daughter Nellie would have been right when she asserted that he designed a few pieces for Liberty in 1882. This nearly matches the theory that, when the Art Furnishers' Alliance went into liquidation in 1883, this line of glass, among others, was taken over by Arthur Lasenby Liberty who was a major shareholder in the Bond Street shop set up by Dresser and his partners. A catalogue entitled 'Eastern and Western Ware', issued by Liberty in 1896, however, describes Clutha glass as 'one among recent successful developments of British Art-Industries'. This could hardly apply to a product which had been available from the shop for over ten years.

What may have happened is that either the glass had been too advanced for English taste in 1883 and had been withdrawn when the public ignored it, or the manufacturers, James Couper & Sons of Glasgow, had been too busy with their regular lines to produce the small amounts of Clutha that would have been required by Liberty's in the early eighteen-eighties. This glass first appeared in a Liberty catalogue when it was described as 'Decorative, Quaint, Original, Artistic' in 'Yule-Tide Gifts' for 1895. Such a re-introduction of the glass, if that is what it was, might well have been instigated by the realization that much of Léveillé's glass at this date was similar in appearance, and that Clutha had the advantage of its interesting shapes designed by Dresser which by the mid-eighteen-nineties would have been judged more acceptable.

The origins of Clutha glass lay, according to the catalogue issued by Liberty's in 1896, in the 'intelligent observation of the pleasing colour effect of the accidental irregularities (in the form of air bubbles and flaws), occurring in the routine process of standard crystal-glass manufacture'. In

the eighteen-sixties, James Couper & Sons had been producing coloured glass for stained-glass window makers, of which there were several in Glasgow. Called 'St Mungo' glass by the manufacturers, Dresser's attention had probably been drawn to it by one of his assistants, John Moyr Smith, who had used it in at least one of the Glasgow interiors which he had designed before coming south. Dresser himself may well have employed it in stained-glass windows he had incorporated in decorative schemes at Allangate Mansion, about 1870, and Bushloe House, Leicester, in 1879–80.

Clutha vessels were made in the subdued, delicate colours which Dresser recommended for stained-glass, such as amber, olive, russet or pink, and, like Rousseau's and Léveillé's glass, it often had two or more tints fused together in one piece. Also like the French glass, Clutha was often enriched with flakes of gold, silver or white enamel. Sometimes the white enamel was hooked and pulled into loose patterns of festoons, reminiscent of the decoration on some of Tiffany's glass; more often coloured bands flowed at random through the material. 'Irregularities', according to the Liberty catalogue of 1896, were 'multiplied and designedly produced'. The description goes on to invoke the authority of a style of modern art which appealed to most of Liberty's customers: 'The effect is a rich translucent substance interspersed with air bubbles and brilliant flakings and whorls forming a very "Kosmos" of impressionist designs.' Although the stylistic analysis was wildly wrong, the description accurately reflects the sort of advanced artistic taste disseminated in the pages of *The Studio* during the nineties.

Dresser's shapes for Clutha were well adapted to the blower's art and to the properties of the material. Globular or conical bodies ascend through long thin necks into wide flared rims; small angular handles are applied to bulbous, flattened shapes; cylinders are twisted into spirals; mouths curve and spread like flowerheads; rims rise and fall; necks are pinched and bent at an angle. In contravention of almost universal practice in the British glass industry at that time, vessels were free-blown, the blower being merely guided by Dresser's design and never using a mould. The only applied decoration was in the form of glass thread, usually coiled round a neck, an indication of the revival of Venetian glass during the eighteen-sixties and eighteen-seventies which had been greeted with enthusiasm by the propagandists of the Aesthetic Movement.

Towards the end of the eighteen-nineties, the Scottish architect and designer George Walton created a range of new shapes for Clutha. Walton's designs are less exotic than Dresser's, and they were generally made in pale green glass often flecked with gold and white enamel. Walton also designed furniture sold by Liberty's, so the shop may well have recommended him to Couper's. On the other hand, as a Glasgow-based designer who frequently included stained-glass in his decorative schemes, he would already have been well known to Couper's. Clearly at Liberty's

Archibald Knox designed this green glass claret jug with silver mounts (right) which was made in 1903. The interlacing pattern on the collar is typical of Knox's very individual interpretation of Celtic ornament, and the extended thumb-piece is equally characteristic of the Manx designer. The Tudric pewter mount on this green glass jug (far right) was manufactured by W. H. Haseler of Birmingham. James Powell & Sons made the jug at their Whitefriars glass works in London. The piece dates from c. 1905.

instigation, some Clutha vessels were designed to fit into Tudric pewter holders; these were presumably designed by Archibald Knox, who created the holders.

Clutha glass disappears from the Liberty catalogues early in the twentieth century and is soon replaced by a comparable make, the iridescent glass manufactured by Loetz. The 'Yule-Tide Gifts' catalogue issued in 1903 proclaimed 'A New Lustrous Glass, Glinting and glowing with opalesque radiance in rich metallic colourings'. The Bohemian glasshouse of Johann Loetz Witwe, founded in 1836, had developed a wide

The blue enamel decorating the Tudric pewter mount, together with the green of the glass bowl made by Powell's, create in this piece the colour combination most frequently encountered among the products of the Arts and Crafts Movement. This piece was probably designed by Archibald Knox, c. 1904–6.

Liberty's catered for the widespread popularity of iridescent glass at the turn of the century by offering examples manufactured by the Bohemian firm of Johann Loetz Witwe (above and above right). Some of the shapes used by Loetz were inspired by Christopher Dresser's designs for Clutha glass. The decoration was close to the work of Louis Comfort Tiffany, but Loetz glass was significantly cheaper than the American artist's product.

range of differently coloured iridescent glass during the eighteen-nineties which was shown in 1898 at an exhibition held in Vienna. The iridescent decoration, achieved through the application of metal oxides in controlled atmospheric conditions, is very different to the sort of internal decoration used for Clutha glass, but some of the Loetz shapes are close to Dresser's designs. Recent research in the Loetz archives has brought to light drawings made from photographs of Clutha glass reproduced in *The Studio*, illustrating an 1899 article about Dresser's work. Twisted cylindrical forms, heavily dented bodies and openings frequently shaped as schematic flowerheads, appear to have been quotations from Dresser's Clutha repertoire. The painter and craftswoman Maria Kirschner, who was engaged by Loetz as a designer in 1903 (the year the glasshouse started supplying Liberty's), put angular handles on many of her vases and bowls, reminiscent of the handles which Dresser had given to some Clutha jugs.

Kirschner's models were made in semi-opaque iridescent glass, usually gold or pale purple, without any of the decorative patterns with which Loetz pieces were normally embellished. The two principal styles of decoration were called 'Papillon' and 'Phenomenon', and both exploited the charm of random haphazard effects which had characterized Clutha glass. 'Papillon' was dappled with small, tightly clustered patches of iridescence, and 'Phenomenon' bore ribbons of iridescence loosely arranged in feathery

The 'Mediaeval Decorative Glass' shown in this illustration from a Liberty catalogue issued about 1900 was manufactured by James Powell & Sons. The shapes are derived from glassware made between 1400 and 1700 at various European locations.

patterns or running round the vessel in irregular waves of zigzags. Much of the decoration was unashamedly derived from the iridescent glass made by Louis Comfort Tiffany, and a strong selling point in favour of the Bohemian product was that it was much cheaper. The creation of each piece of the American glass was supervised by Tiffany himself, whereas Loetz glass, if not mass-produced, was certainly made in quantities much larger than would have allowed such individual treatment. With Tiffany's glass on sale in the American firm's London shop at 221 Regent Street, it was a shrewd move by Liberty's to have on offer a much cheaper variant just along the street.

The popularity of iridescence as a form of decoration on glass had grown during the last quarter of the nineteenth century as increasing archaeological activity had unearthed huge quantities of ancient glass, much of which was covered with an iridescent bloom. It had not been generally apprehended that this was due to a chemical reaction between the glass and the soil in which it had been buried for centuries, so manufacturers had often given their iridescent glass a name which had a classical allusion. For example, Tiffany produced a line called 'Cypriote',

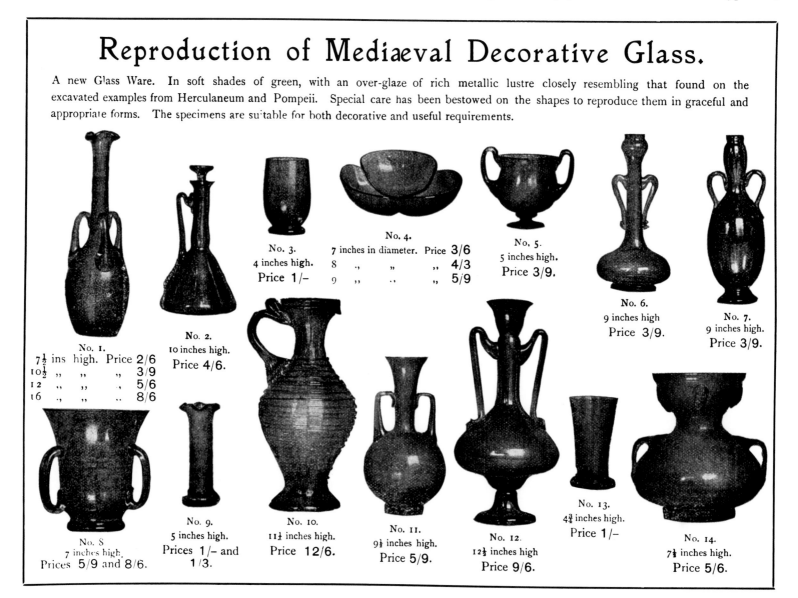

Reproduction of Mediaeval Decorative Glass.

A new Glass Ware. In soft shades of green, with an over-glaze of rich metallic lustre closely resembling that found on the excavated examples from Herculaneum and Pompeii. Special care has been bestowed on the shapes to reproduce them in graceful and appropriate forms. The specimens are suitable for both decorative and useful requirements.

No. 1.
7½ ins high. Price 2/6
10½ ,, ,, ,, 3/9
12 ,, ,, ., 5/6
16 ., ,, .. 8/6

No. 2.
10 inches high.
Price 4/6.

No. 3.
4 inches high.
Price 1/–

No. 4.
7 inches in diameter. Price 3/6
8 ,, ,, ,, 4/3
9 ,, .. ,, 5/9

No. 5.
5 inches high.
Price 3/9.

No. 6.
9 inches high
Price 3/9.

No. 7.
9 inches high.
Price 3/9.

No. 8
7 inches high.
Prices 5/9 and 8/6.

No. 9.
5 inches high.
Prices 1/– and 1/3.

No. 10.
11¼ inches high.
Price 12/6.

No. 11.
9½ inches high.
Price 5/9.

No. 12.
12½ inches high
Price 9/6.

No. 13.
4¾ inches high.
Price 1/–

No. 14.
7¼ inches high.
Price 5/6.

some Loetz glass was called 'Kreta' and Steuben used 'Tyrian' for one of their lines of iridescent glass. About 1900, Liberty's were offering a 'Reproduction of Medieval Decorative Glass' which, as they claimed with scant regard for historical consistency, had 'an over-glaze of rich metallic lustre closely resembling that found on the excavated examples from Herculaneum and Pompeii'.

The manufacturers of this glass were James Powell & Sons, the firm which from 1834 had run the ancient Whitefriars glasshouse near Fleet Street in London. During the nineteenth century they had established close links first with some of the Pre-Raphaelite painters, whose designs for stained glass they had executed, and then with Morris & Co. whom they supplied with coloured glass for their stained-glass windows. Powell's had also made the table glass designed by the architect Philip Webb which Morris & Co. retailed through their Oxford Street shop and had themselves commissioned another architect, Thomas Graham Jackson, to design a complete range of table glass. They were clearly manufacturers interested in supplying the demands of more advanced artistic taste, and they had displayed their glass alongside Clutha at the Arts and Crafts Exhibition Society. Liberty's would naturally have been glad to retail their glass, and there was another less tangible reason why Arthur Liberty should have wanted to do business with the firm. In the course of his researches into the Liberty family history there had emerged a Jonathan Richard Liberty who had worked as a glass-cutter at Whitefriars during the first half of the nineteenth century.

The 'Dewdrop' range of glass tableware, to which this hock decanter belongs, was an instant international success when it was introduced in 1899 by James Powell & Sons. Liberty's stocked the line from 1902 and the following year added several new shapes to the range.

Whether Liberty's bought the 'Reproduction of Medieval Decorative Glass' from Powell's as an existing product, or whether they instigated its design and manufacture, is not known, but the line fitted particularly well in their range. Both its medievalism and its 'soft shades of green' (as 'Yule-Tide Gifts' described its colour) complemented the Farnham pottery which also came in 'soft rich shades of green' according to an 1898 brochure. The shapes of the glass were probably designed by Harry Powell who often found inspiration in the glass vessels depicted in Old Master paintings. Some pieces, in their stark angularity, look surprisingly modern.

Powell's manufactured for Liberty's decanters and bowls in green (not iridescent) glass for mounting in Tudric pewter. A more distinguished Whitefriars product was a range of table glasses and decanters called 'Dewdrop'. This line, made in clear, colourless lead crystal, and retailed by Liberty's from 1902, had been introduced by Powell's three years earlier. The simple shapes, decorated only with drops applied to their sides, had instantly charmed the public not only in Britain but on the Continent too; examples of the glass had been illustrated in the Munich magazine *Dekorative Kunst* in 1899, and the following year more appeared in *The Studio*. Liberty's seem to have had some success with the line because they expanded the range in 1903 to include jugs, vases and decanters in new shapes.

Graphics

By 1890 LIBERTY'S had helped to create considerable interest in aesthetic style and decoration in both Britain and Europe. Displays of novel and exotic items in the shop itself and at exhibitions at home and abroad generated an enormous amount of publicity in journals, newspapers and magazines. Notably, however, Liberty's never felt the need to institute a graphic campaign of the kind commissioned by Bing at L'Art Nouveau in Paris (established in 1895) where posters advertising the gallery were designed by artists like Combaz, Vallotton and Brangwen, and where the works of Bradley and Beardsley were displayed. Meier-Graefe's department store, La Maison Moderne, also used lithographic posters which, with their thick black outlines influenced by Japanese engraving and pure flat colours, were at the very forefront of Art Nouveau graphic design. This omission may perhaps be explained by Arthur Liberty's essential ambivalence about the Art Nouveau style which he had done so much to influence in the early years.

By the mid eighteen-nineties, like several influential figures in the decorative arts in Britain, he had become suspicious of what he saw as the decadent extremes of the style as it had developed on the Continent. Nonetheless, in its first thirty years, Liberty's produced and promoted a large quantity of graphic material that was consistent with the aesthetic aims evident in other areas of the shop's work. In 1881 the first Liberty catalogue of 'Eastern Art Manufactures and Decorative Art Objects' was published. Among the clusters of press quotations extolling the virtues of the shop and its 'marvellous lovelinesses of the East' were a number of illustrations intended to appeal to the customer of artistic sensibility. Many of these designs were to reappear in the catalogues in various guises, sometimes over a period of fifteen to twenty years. The head of an exotic woman with a cloth head-dress and jewellery appeared in 1881 promoting Chinese handkerchiefs, again in 1883 in a section on Indian and Egyptian jewellery, and rather curiously with 'Select Teas and Condi-

Illustrations from J. Moyr Smith's 'Ancient Greek Female Costume', the 'Liberty Art Fabrics' catalogue of 1883. Moyr Smith provided a number of designs for Liberty catalogues and his views on dress reflected Liberty's interest in a simple aesthetic style based on historic prototypes.

This aesthetically dressed female (opposite) *first featured in the Liberty catalogue of 'Eastern Art Manufactures' of 1881 in an advertisement for hammocks. Like many of the illustrations for Liberty catalogues, it was to be reprinted in a variety of guises.*

ments' as late as 1900. Similar in the frequency of her appearances is the aesthetically dressed lady reclining in a hammock clutching a fan lettered 'Liberty & Co. Regent Street'; she is associated in 1881 with 'Indian Grass Hammocks' but more often thereafter with fans or handscreens.

While the designers of this sort of illustration were rarely acknowledged, one of the most typical vignettes, from 1883, showing a female in medieval costume leaning on a fountain, is monogrammed 'JMS'. J. Moyr Smith had trained in Dresser's studio and became known for his illustrations to Lamb's *Shakespeare for Children* (1879), as well as his book on *Ornamental Interiors Ancient and Modern* (1887). The same catalogue also includes extracts and designs from his *Ancient Greek Female Costume*. Clearly, however, illustrations for the catalogues were frequently produced by designers working for the company in other capacities, and those considered successful were used again and again. Soon, Liberty's began to present its goods in context, printing designs for room settings by Leonard Wyburd, head of the furniture department. 'Indian Furniture and Decoration' of 1883 was the first of many such designs by Wyburd, which were later to include groups of decorative objects in the 'Arabian', 'Chinese' and 'Japanese' styles and were to become a staple of the Liberty catalogues and advertisements until the end of the century. It was in the early eighteen-eighties also that colour plates illustrating Eastern textiles and decorative borders in the Arts and Crafts style first began to appear. Excerpts from M. Chevreuil's *The Principles of Harmony and Contrast of*

Colour (in the 'Art Fabrics' catalogue of 1886) and the maxims of Ruskin and Viollet-le-Duc ('Handbook of Sketches', 1889) were further enlisted to endorse the view expressed in an 1887 catalogue that 'This is truly the home of aestheticism'.

In spite of this, many of the Liberty publications of this era seem graphically rather austere. As was explained in the somewhat lacklustre jewellery catalogue of 1895: 'The illustrations on the accompanying pages unfortunately convey a most inadequate idea of the UNIQUE STOCK held'. Part of the problem, as Liberty's were at pains to point out, was the varied and ever expanding nature of their range of goods. In 1886 they had

'Cecilia' from the 'Dress and Decoration' catalogue, 1905, showing a version of a seventeenth-century evening gown; this was one of Liberty's more vibrant publications; it contained twelve colour plates signed by A. E. Howarth illustrating Liberty dress designs adapted from historic costume (other examples are illustrated on pages 70–71).

THE CHILDREN'S FROCK PARTY

U Ursula—says she has come up to town
For mother to buy her a Liberty-gown.

'U Ursula', an illustration (above) *from 'The Children's Frock Party' catalogue of 1906, perhaps the most ambitious Liberty catalogue of the period; influenced both by the work of Kate Greenaway and the fashion for children's alphabets, it was produced by Edmund Evans.*

Two postcards from the 'Susan' series of 1912 (above right); like the children's books and nursery wallpapers introduced by Liberty's at the turn of the century, such cards were intended to 'train the eye from infancy to discriminate and enjoy artistic work'.

stated that: 'Liberty & Co. are receiving almost daily bales of other Silks, which on account of their great rarity and miscellaneous nature, it is impossible to catalogue. They beg respectfully to invite a visit of inspection.' Like the 'Handbooks of Sketches' (although these were generally more elaborate in style and incorporated reproductions of watercolours showing interior designs), most of the catalogues were 'compiled to depict types of work only'. The Liberty fashion publications which began to emerge in 1894 tended on occasion to be rather more lavish. The famous 'Dress and Decoration' catalogue (1905) contained twelve colour reproductions of water-colours by A. E. Howarth, each showing a Liberty dress design inspired by historic costume. Both the vineleaf borders and the Gothic typeface on each page are reminiscent of the work of the earlier Arts and Crafts presses and give a distinct aesthetic coherence to the publication. Similar in this respect was 'The Children's Frock Party' catalogue (1906). Perhaps the outstanding Liberty catalogue of the period, it owed an enormous debt both in concept and style to the work of Kate Greenaway, and was also influenced by the contemporary vogue for children's alphabets. Although designed by Liberty's, this catalogue was entirely printed by Edmund Evans, the engraver who had revolutionized colour illustration in children's books and who had long been associated with artists like Walter Crane and Randolph Caldecott, as well as Greenaway. Here, the rather mawkish figures of fashionably attired little girls were accompanied by rhymes in the Greenaway manner with a commercial slant: 'S stands for Susan – whose Liberty-coat/Is one upon which any mother might dote'.

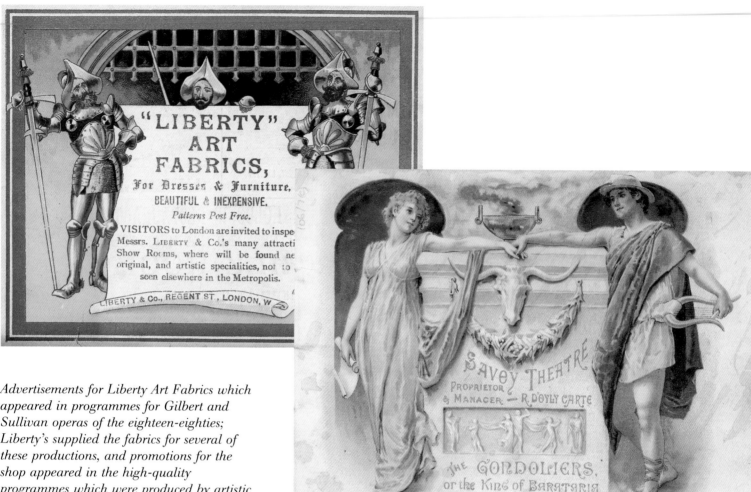

Advertisements for Liberty Art Fabrics which appeared in programmes for Gilbert and Sullivan operas of the eighteen-eighties; Liberty's supplied the fabrics for several of these productions, and promotions for the shop appeared in the high-quality programmes which were produced by artistic publishers, such as Marcus Ward and Hildescheimer & Faulkner.

Among the more unusual advertisements for Liberty's were those that appeared on theatre programmes, most often for Gilbert and Sullivan productions for which the store provided the fabrics. The programme for the 'Aesthetic Opera' *Patience, Or Bunthorne's Bride* (1881) at the Savoy included a promotion for Liberty Art Fabrics, which were also used in *Iolanthe* (1882) and *The Mikado* (1885); the Liberty name also appears on a number of other Gilbert and Sullivan programmes. These advertisements do not seem to have been devised separately, but were integral to the programme design, and Liberty's benefited from the generally high quality of these publications. One series of Savoy programmes of the eighteen-eighties was based on a pink and gold scheme with classical motifs, and with illustrations of the main characters featuring in the Liberty promotion on the back cover.

Some of these pamphlets were produced by Marcus Ward, a major figure in the field of artistic publishing, who had commissioned early work from Greenaway and Crane. An alternative series of programmes for the Savoy Theatre during this period incorporated colour lithographs signed

The title page from Kate Greenaway's
A Apple Pie *(1886); this was probably the prototype for 'The Children's Frock Party' catalogue and was advertised in Liberty's 'Yule-Tide Gifts' catalogues from about 1900 with other artistic children's books by illustrators like Caldecott and Crane. Greenaway's pictures of aesthetically attired little girls were also to provide inspiration for the Liberty costume department.*

by A. Havers, again including advertisements for Liberty's. Perhaps the most familiar of these illustrations, first seen on the back of a programme for *The Yeoman of the Guard* (1889) shows two females in classical dress with a figure of Pan. Although first associated with Liberty Art Fabrics, this image was later used to promote a number of other enterprises, among them the Savoy Hotel and the mysterious 'Harness Electropathic Belts'. This series was also issued by a prominent artistic publishing company, Hildescheimer & Faulkner.

When Liberty's introduced nursery wallpapers with illustrations by Cecil Aldin and John Hassall in the 'Liberty Bazaar' catalogue of 1898, it was explained that: 'The object is to place before children such pictures only as are well drawn and well coloured, and thus train the eye from infancy to discriminate and enjoy artistic work'. The sale of 'artistic' children's books was clearly intended to attract Liberty customers bringing up a new generation of aesthetes. Describing 'Picture Books for Children by Kate Greenaway Selected by Liberty & Co.', the catalogue noted that: 'There is so close an affinity between the work of Miss Kate Greenaway as manifested in her picture books, and the many artistic innovations of Messrs. Liberty, that those who appreciate the latter will

doubtless welcome these books now being added to Messrs. Liberty's Stock'. By the time Liberty's began to sell these works in 1900, the reputations of illustrators like Greenaway, Caldecott and Crane had been established for many years.

Kate Greenaway's *Under the Window*, printed by Edmund Evans in 1878, had marked the beginning of a long and successful collaboration between the artist and the shop; her charming if rather saccharine pictures of little girls in bonnets and high waisted dresses must have been well known to Liberty customers who had been dressing their children in versions of this costume for some time. The high quality of the illustrations, which could now be achieved by the photographic transfer of the artist's design on to woodblocks to be printed in separate planes of colour, had enabled the Liberty costume department to use the Greenaway publications almost as pattern books. Interestingly, Kate Greenaway herself seems to have anticipated later criticisms of her designs as adapted by Liberty's for long-suffering real children. In *Under the Window* 'Little Fanny wears a hat/Like her ancient grannie . . .' and a trio of girls in print dresses with frilly pinafores and straw bonnets are greeted with the taunt, 'My eye!/Three Grannies out today'. Other Greenaway books like *A Apple Pie* (undoubtedly the prototype for the 'Children's Frock Party' catalogue) and *The Marigold Garden* featured in the 'Yule-Tide Gifts' catalogues year after year. According to Liberty's they were 'aesthetic in the best sense of that oft-abused word and unconsciously train and develop the taste of the young'. Books illustrated by Aldin, Hassall, Caldecott and Crane also fell into this category, and were advertised alongside a range of nursery items like 'Three Blind Mice' tea-cosies and wastepaper baskets which were perhaps less calculated to develop sound aesthetic judgement in the young mind. Crane's *Baby's Opera* (1877) was sold by Liberty's from 1905. The original success of this book of old rhymes with music and illustration had done much to spread the decorative manner of the Pre-Raphaelites in graphic design, and had first prompted Edmund Evans to commission work in this style from Caldecott and Greenaway.

These illustrations for children were to inspire a series of 'Artistic Cards and Calendars' which Liberty's brought out in 1902. Many of them were printed from hand-coloured designs depicting 'Dutch boys and girls' and scenes from nursery rhymes, and later included calendars on Japanese paper and bookplates with Arts and Crafts borders and mottoes. While beautifully produced, this sort of material represented the perpetuation of styles that had been at the height of their influence three decades earlier. As the catalogues and books the company promoted also seem to indicate, the Liberty interest in graphic design during this period remained firmly with the Arts and Crafts and Aesthetic Movements and rarely extended to the more radical versions of Art Nouveau that now prevailed among continental designers.

Both these illustrations (opposite) *and* (right) *by Kate Greenaway appeared in the 'Liberty Art (Dress) Fabrics' catalogue of 1886; the Greenaway style was instrumental in establishing the 'Liberty look' in the public imagination.*

LITTLE baby, if I threw
This fair blossom down to you,
Would you catch it as you stand,
Holding up each tiny hand,
Looking out of those grey eyes,
Where such deep, deep wonder lies?

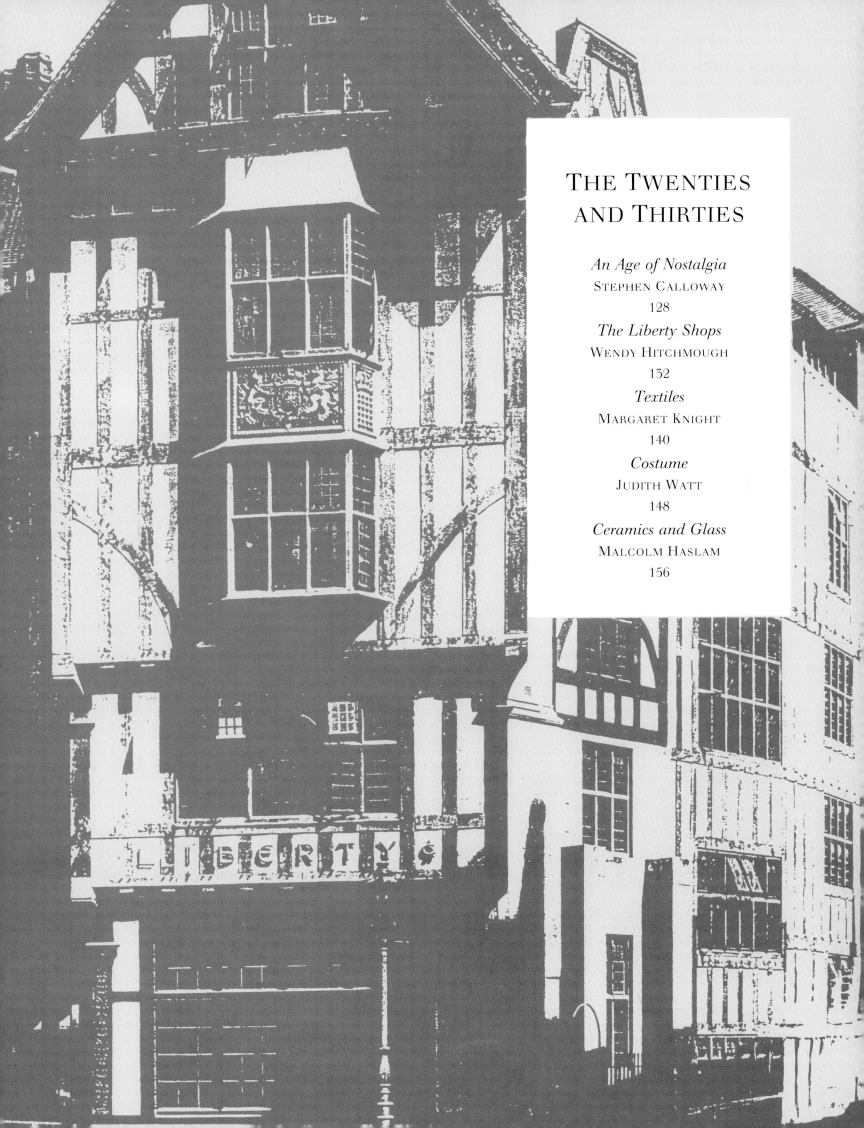

THE TWENTIES
AND THIRTIES

An Age of Nostalgia

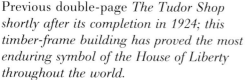

AS A REALLY CHIC STYLE, Art Nouveau was a completely dead letter by the last years of the Edwardian era. Identified to such a degree as the shop was with the style, it might be supposed that Liberty's would, especially in the great upheaval of social patterns that followed the First World War, have suffered the fate of many an enterprise that had had its day. Arthur Liberty was, however, much too astute both commercially and aesthetically to be left behind in the march of fashion, or to fail to perceive the enormous potential offered by the vast new, middle-class housing market to a well-established firm with a reputation for taste and quality.

In the immediate post-war years, at the upper levels of fashion, the avant-garde reacted strongly against both the overblown opulence of the late Edwardians and the grimness of the war years. The new vogue was for a brilliant exoticism which embraced a love of chinoiserie and a passion for the colourful Orientalism of Diaghilev's Ballets Russes. As in the days of the 'Eastern Bazaar', Liberty became the ideal hunting ground for those in search of a silk scarf in the coruscating colours of the moment or a lacquer screen. But the Bright Young Things of the twenties were a small

Previous double-page *The Tudor Shop shortly after its completion in 1924; this timber-frame building has proved the most enduring symbol of the House of Liberty throughout the world.*

This group of furnishing cretonnes (opposite) *typifies the dominant style of the shop during this period* (left *to* right): *'Floral Stripe', with lateral stripes of flowers in various colours on a drab background; 'Poppy and Bird', with flowers and leaves with baskets, and long-tailed blue birds against a green ground; 'Delphinium and Fuchsia', in pink, purple, yellow and brown on a beige background.*

These four designs (above) *date from the early part of the thirties* (left *to* right): *'Poppy and Pheasant' in shadow taffeta, with birds and flowers in pinks, blues, browns, purple and green on a greyish ground; 'Claremont' in cotton furnishing fabric, with trees, birds and leaping deer; 'Highclere' in cotton furnishing fabric, with flowers and birds in shades of pink, blue, green and yellow on a pink imitation moiré background; an example of the floral designs used on a variety of dress fabrics by Liberty's between 1932 and 1934.*

group, and their taste for exoticism was to remain a minority one; Liberty's path was to lie elsewhere.

Liberty, as has already been suggested, was from the start a supporter of the aims and ideals of the Arts and Crafts Movement. Though not without its Continental counterparts, that movement, in its second generation by the twenties, but still firmly rooted in a vision of English country life, was perceived as a distinctly solid and honourable tradition. Its tenets of honesty in design, sound workmanship and dependable, indigenous materials struck a deeply resonant chord of patriotism in a land anxious to throw out dubious foreign and theatrical styles and to get on with the great task of building homes for heroes.

In reality Britain was creating houses for bank-managers and middle-ranking civil servants in what would prove to be the greatest boom in domestic house building since the hectic days of the Georgian speculators. By far the greatest proportion of these new, suburban homes were put up in that curious hybrid style which derived in part from the work of Richard Norman Shaw and Art Nouveau architects such as Voysey, but which in reality depended for most of its styling upon an ill-digested idea of English domestic vernacular architecture of the Tudor period. No better term has ever been coined to describe the style than the, at first, derisory phrase 'Mock-Tudor'.

The interior of the Tudor Shop in the late nineteen-twenties; the arrangement of balconies around three central wells provided unique facilities for the display of carpets and textiles.

These homes were, by and large, inhabited by people who could afford to and would choose to buy new furnishings, but preferred them to be in comfortable, un-demanding and often period styles. They represented a major force in the market and their desires and needs were catered to by a great many old-established or newly-formed firms. For Liberty's this new market represented a challenge; it may well be argued that it was a challenge met with yet another burst of creative energy from the firm, but this time it was one which found its best expression not in the merchandise, but rather in the building of the great Mock-Tudor shop that still stands behind Regent Street. Remarkable and popular at the time, it remains to this day the most potent visual symbol of the Liberty enterprise.

Liberty design in these inter-war years tended towards the traditional and revivalist, but a number of new designs were still being added, for instance, to the Tudric pewter range and a number of new silver designs were introduced. The ceramics department continued to be dominated by

Moorcroft, both in the form of decorative stoneware and, more practically, in the addition of some exciting, modernistic ranges to Liberty's table-ware. The furniture department does seem to have languished at this period, but the commissioning of new textiles continued unabated – the scarf and furnishing fabric ranges being massively extended, mainly in the traditional, strongly-coloured floral designs with which Liberty was to become so closely associated in the public imagination.

A pen and ink sketch by Hanslip Fletcher of the new Tudor Shop in Great Marlborough Street (then Argyll Place), c. 1925.

The Liberty Shops

LIBERTY'S decision to build two separate shops after the First World War – an imposing Neoclassical block clad in Portland Stone fronting on to Regent Street, with a separate Tudor Shop directly behind – was characteristically individual. By the nineteen-twenties Arthur Liberty's shop had expanded into the neighbouring houses on Regent Street; the resultant warren of small rooms, although inconvenient, had a domestic intimacy and a quality of mystery which complimented the company's retailing style. Liberty had also acquired a substantial freehold site fronting on to Great Marlborough Street to the rear of the Regent Street shop, but this opportunity to rebuild brought with it a series of controversial restrictions and regulations. The Great Marlborough Street site was freehold, but the Regent Street buildings were on Crown land and Liberty's were obliged to conform to the overall pattern of Reginald Blomfield's Neoclassical designs for the rebuilding of Regent Street.

If the design for a new shop had been commissioned fifteen years earlier or ten years later, then Liberty's might have opted for an Art Nouveau store or an International Style building in Great Marlborough Street, but the years around the First World War heralded a reactionary period in British architecture and in the outlook of the Liberty board. The proposal to build in the Tudor style – and Liberty's were careful to point out that this was not 'Mock-Tudor' but an assimilation of Tudor values – was put forward before the war by John Llewellyn, one of the directors whose own house near Great Missenden was a 'Mock-Tudor' masterpiece, and the board were quick to recognize the marketing as well as the ideological and aesthetic advantages of such a choice.

Few London buildings are as instantly recognizable or as strikingly placed as the timber-frame structure of the Tudor Shop, drawing the attention of shoppers from Regent Street and along the length of Argyll

Leaded light window with stained-glass galleon; the Tudor Shop is constructed from the timbers of two great battleships, and the pioneering days of merchant adventuring are alluded to throughout the shop.

Street from Oxford Street. From a practical point of view, this plan retained the variety and intimacy of spaces that Liberty's had valued in their
original shop; the building also acts as an advertisement for the firm at a
variety of levels. Ivor Stewart-Liberty wrote in a booklet about the building
when it opened: 'The Tudor period is the most genuinely English period
of domestic architecture ... There is a glamour about the lavish and
stirring days of Henry VIII and Queen Elizabeth; while the sight of red
tiled gables and carved barge boards, of hanging balconies and leaded
casements, is essentially English, and brings to mind a picture of those bygone days when the ancient guilds of the craftsmen and the merchant
adventurers displayed, in the beautiful gabled buildings of old London,
the productions of their handicrafts and the treasures for which they sailed
so far and endured so much.'

*The Tudor Shop in Great Marlborough Street
had only one public entrance when it first
opened in 1924. Later, the display window in
the angled gable to the right was made into
a second entrance for the convenience of
Regent Street shoppers.*

The Tudor Shop is generously planned around three light wells, each suggesting the courtyard of an Elizabethan inn.

The Tudor Shop and East India House were designed by Edwin Thomas Hall and his son Edwin Stanley Hall and were completed in 1924 and 1925 respectively. Edwin Thomas Hall was a pillar of the architectural establishment, a former Vice-President of the Royal Institute of British Architects, nicknamed 'Byelaw' Hall for his assiduous attention to detail and legal matters. He designed the Tudor Shop at the height of the nineteen-twenties fashion for Tudor Revival and clearly he was given free rein to create a building worthy of its patron. The determination to make a sixteenth-century-style building which would demonstrate the craftsman's art recalled the Pre-Raphaelite values which had played such an important part in the foundation of the company and appealed strongly to Liberty's new clientele. The shop is constructed from the timbers of two nineteenth-century men-of-war battleships: H.M.S. *Impregnable* and

H.M.S. *Hindustan*; by coincidence, the Great Marlborough Street frontage is the same length as the *Hindustan* and the distance from the pavement to the eaves of the building corresponds to the height of the ship out of water. The timber framing – and there is no concealed steel structure here – is of oak and teak set in solid brickwork, while the filling between the external timbering is rendered with white Portland cement mixed with a yellow sand to achieve a natural buff colour.

Colour, light, and surface texture are subtly manipulated to add depth to the Great Marlborough Street elevation. The projecting bays with their corbelled bay windows and upper floors, connected by balconies with sturdy balustrades, cast deep shadows across the black and white façade, while the red brick twisting of the Tudor chimneys and the ridges of hand-made Loughborough roofing tiles accentuate the pitch of the gabled roof-line. Heraldry is used to add colour and interest throughout the building: the arms of Queen Elizabeth I decorate the angled gable facing Regent Street and the arms of the six wives of Henry VIII are carved into the main entrance doors on Great Marlborough Street. Inside, the shields of Ben Jonson, Sir Thomas More, Sir Philip Sidney, George Herbert, Bacon and Shakespeare decorate the roof of the eastern light well and even the air vents above the leaded light windows are pierced with heraldic motifs. The hand-worked texture of the Portland stone bastions on either side of the main entrance could only be achieved by chisel-working the blocks from the quarry face. The rough finishes of timber and stone, revealing the marks of the tools which worked them in true Arts and Crafts spirit, contrast with the fine carving around the doors and window frames and on the great barge boards. Even the lead rainwater pipes were traditionally cast and decorated.

Hall planned the Tudor Shop around three immense light wells, taking advantage of the relaxation in building regulations which at last allowed London's department stores to emulate the great atrium spaces of Bon Marché and Printemps in Paris. The simplicity of the plan, with its

Panelled display cases, decorative plaster-work and exposed ceiling beams provided traditional and, in the twenties and thirties, very fashionable, domestic settings for Liberty's merchandise.

The main entrance of the Tudor Shop in Great Marlborough Street, accentuated by massive Portland stone bastions and finely detailed with the coats of arms of the six wives of Henry VIII.

dramatic open vertical spaces flooded with natural light and accentuated by the enclosed intimacy of the surrounding wooden galleries, determines the success of the shop. The light wells give a rhythm and direction to the plan, making the identification of departments far easier than in the conventional shop. Each rectangular well has its own individual character and decoration, but only the narrower central well cuts through the full height of the building from the fourth floor down to ground level.

The range of display spaces, from the central floor areas at the base of each light well to the small rooms around the perimeter of the building allowed Liberty's to show smaller items in a domestic setting, delicate fabrics away from potentially damaging direct sunlight, and rugs and quilts could be draped over the gallery balustrades. The whole of the ground, first, and second floors and parts of the third and fourth floors were used as showrooms and Liberty's offices were on the third floor. The kitchens and dining room for a staff of 1,100 were situated on the fourth and fifth floors, and the staff cloakrooms, with a separate 'Mannequins Cloakroom', were in the basement.

Over twenty carvers worked for eighteen months on the shop frames and barge boards, the staircases, balustrades, and posts, and the quality of craftsmanship and attention to detail is exceptional throughout the building. Liberty's own studios and workshops in Highgate designed and made the traditional oak and teak panelling, and the stone fireplaces and enriched fibrous plaster work on the fourth floor must have inspired many visitors to Liberty's interior design department. The main solid oak staircase at the west end of the building has carved posts and pierced and carved panelled balustrades. The floors are made from the deck timbers of the original ships. Pictures of galleon ships appear in the stained glass of the windows and high over the Great Marlborough Street entrance a gilded model of the *Mayflower* sails above the four points of the compass.

In contrast to the idiosyncratic charm of the Tudor Shop, East India House stands formally correct in full Renaissance dress. The Portland stone pilasters so disliked by Ivor Stewart-Liberty find their place supporting the Regent Street façade, while the upper storeys sweep back in a shallow crescent divided by an Ionic colonnade surmounted by a richly carved frieze and modillioned cornice. It is here, unnoticed by most visitors to Regent Street, and in the sculpted attic storey frieze by Thomas Clapperton from which life-size figures peer down over the parapet, that the fine carving and meticulous attention to detail distinguishes the building from its Regent Street neighbours and establishes a link with the Tudor Shop behind.

Four Japanese 'Iohan', disciples of Buddha, sit on a ledge outside the first floor windows to either side of the main entrance. These same four can be seen on early photographs of Liberty's original Regent Street shop, glimpsed between the canopies, bestowing good fortune upon the busi-

Liberty's row of Georgian shops during the rebuilding programme; the Tudor Shop is complete and the new south-end bay of East India House (to the right of the photograph) is in place. On the left, the site is cleared ready for the north-end bay, but Liberty's continued to trade from their remaining Regent Street shops even when surrounded by demolition and new building work.

East India House is crowned by a life-size frieze (above) *carved by Thomas Clapperton. The same builders and craftsmen who were responsible for the Tudor Shop in 1924 went on to build East India House* (right) *the following year, applying their carving skills and meticulous attention to detail in Neoclassical stone-work. Liberty's were anxious to retain their Regent Street presence throughout the building; display cases can be seen here in front of the new building.*

ness. The basements of East India House and the Tudor Shop are joined by a subway and a three-storey bridge spanning Little Argyll Street connects the second, third, and fourth floors. This bridge, designed in the form of a Tudor archway, carries a famous clock in which George and the Dragon do battle every fifteen minutes: the figures come out and threaten one another as the clock strikes each quarter hour and every hour there is a determined fight in which George strikes the fatal blow to the dragon on the last chime of the clock.

The construction of the buildings began with the Tudor Shop so that Liberty's could continue to trade throughout the building programme. The row of Georgian shops on Regent Street continued in use until the Tudor Shop was completed, and even while East India House was under construction, Liberty's traded from their original Regent Street premises until the last possible moment, clearly viewing the removal to Great Marlborough Street with some trepidation. A progress photograph taken by Higgs and Hill, the contractors for both buildings, shows the Liberty awnings out over Regent Street well into the rebuilding programme: the south end bay of East India House is already constructed; at the north end the old buildings have already been demolished and the Georgian terrace is shored up by wooden buttressing until the second phase of East India House can be built. Even when the original premises were demolished and Liberty's were obliged to trade exclusively from the Tudor Shop until East India House was ready for occupation, they were determined not to lose their presence on Regent Street even for a few months. A row of false shop windows was set up in front of East India House shaded by the old Liberty awnings and a large sign with an arrow directed potential customers: 'Liberty's Entrance Centre of Timbered Building'.

Liberty's apprehensions about the move to Great Marlborough Street proved to be without foundation. Even before the Tudor Shop was completed, its flamboyant spirit, its structural integrity, and the quality of its finishes had captured the imaginations and the commitment of everybody associated with it. The builders and specialist craftsmen of Higgs and Hill – the same men who went on to build East India House on Regent Street – asked if they might bring their families to see the building just before it opened to the public.

East India House shortly after it opened in 1925; the bronze galleons which decorate the second floor balustrade originally carried electric lamps.

Textiles

BRITISH DESIGN between the wars was undoubtedly conservative; it had a tendency to revivalism and historicism evident in all areas from buildings to textiles. The Liberty shop reflected this trend both in its architecture – Tudor Revival – and in the design of much of its stock. Liberty textiles from the twenties and thirties were essentially traditional, with only passing reference to the Continental taste for strong colours and flat, heavily outlined, abstract patterns. The Silver Studio which was still supplying Liberty's with a high proportion of their textile designs found a request for something more contemporary sufficiently unusual to note in the diary for October 1933: 'Mr Cram (of Liberty's) actually suggested that we should send him one or two modernists'.

The taste for historically inspired patterns had its most obvious impact on the company's furnishing fabrics. There were designs which echoed the prevailing taste for Tudor, eighteenth-century or Chinese-style furniture. The shop imported Oriental *objets d'art* and rugs for which there was a tremendous demand in the twenties; there was also a marked Oriental influence in some of their fabric designs. Liberty brochures from the twenties make frequent reference to 'Many handsome designs reproduced

'Ranelagh', a design registered by Liberty's in 1928; it consisted of flowering tree, flower and pheasant motifs, mainly in shades of lilac, blue and red on a beige ground; it was marketed as a furnishing cretonne.

Two furnishing cretonnes, 'Floral Bowl'
(above) *and 'Fruit and Floral Stripe' (above*
right), *both registered in 1928; the former*
design consisted of a basket of mixed flowers,
with birds and butterflies, on a green ground;
the latter also incorporated a hanging basket,
but with multi-coloured fruit against a beige
and orange 'brick wall' background.

from old examples', 'Famous old designs', 'Rare Oriental patterns' and, most explicitly, 'Whether it be Tudor, Jacobean, Adam or some other bygone period Liberty's will gladly wait upon you.'

The success of this approach was reflected in the sales of two cretonnes, 'Peacock and Peony' and 'Pheasant', both Oriental Rococo in their inspiration, which in the late twenties and early thirties broke all previous shop records. A majority of the designs registered by the company in this period were based on natural motifs, fruit, flowers, birds and vines. There are occasional marriages of these motifs with abstract patterns; 'Fruit and Floral Stripe' from the twenties has a pattern of hanging baskets against a beige and orange 'brick' background, but such combinations are outnumbered by designs drawn from Tudor embroideries or the floral silks and Chinese papers of the eighteenth century; the registered names of these designs, 'Ranelagh' or 'Penhurst', for example, reflect their origins.

In the twenties, patterns were often set against a dark background, a combination which worked well with Oriental-style furniture and which offered an alternative to the more usual pastels. For example, the 'Stork and Peacock' cretonne of 1925 had motifs in blue, pink, yellow and tan on a very dark brown background. By the early thirties few of these darker toned fabrics were being produced and the colour schemes of Liberty's furnishing textiles were lighter and more romantic, with an increased naturalism in the depiction of floral and other motifs.

In most cases the designers responsible for the shop's textiles were not named. One exception was Frank Ormrod, who was responsible for one of the shop's few abstract prints of the thirties – an untitled pattern of stylized birds and geometric shapes inspired by a Caucasian rug. Otherwise, the

A printed silk chiffon scarf (right), *produced in 1922; the original design by Lindsay P. Butterfield of stylized poppy plants in ochre, apricot, orange and light brown, was intended for a printed furnishing fabric, c. 1901.*

'Ayesha', a printed furnishing linen and cotton union (below), *with a design of interlacing branches, flowers, blossom, birds and deer, registered by Liberty's in 1931.*

period between the wars saw no 'star' designers, equivalent to those working at the turn of the century. Lindsay Butterfield's work was revived (for scarf prints), but the designs were ones originally produced in 1901. In addition to their patterned ranges, Liberty's offered warp-printed 'Shadow' cretonnes and plain fabrics of different weaves and exciting colours – 'the brilliant colours of the Orient', as the brochure says. Their casement cloths, registered with names like 'Bagdad', 'Akbar', 'Kin-Kab' and 'Bamboo', were particularly successful and attractively priced.

At the other end of the price scale were the fabrics hand-printed at Merton in south London. Liberty's had taken over the workshops at Merton in 1904 and in 1922 they bought the freehold, ensuring that only Liberty fabrics could carry the Merton name and all its associations with craftsmanship and quality. The freehold was bought at a time when the shop was beginning to cut back on its other manufacturing commitments, an indication of the importance Liberty's attached to their textile lines.

Merton was more than a workshop, it was associated in the public mind with the best of nineteenth-century design. Liberty's well understood the publicity value of Merton; it was open to the public (by arrangement) on Wednesday and, in the thirties, the shop produced a charming booklet, *The Renaissance of Merton Abbey*, which gave an illustrated account of the complex process of hand-printing along with hints on the care of Merton fabrics. Hand-blocked textiles were produced in relatively small quantities to very high standards, which was reflected in the price (approximately double that of a machine print). Merton fabrics sold particularly well in New York at McCutcheon's at 609 Fifth Avenue. Continental modernism had a limited audience in the States, particularly in the domestic environment and the majority of design magazines advocated traditional styles. There was thus a thriving trade in European antiques on the East Coast and the Liberty fabrics were well received because they were perfectly in accord with this taste.

Designs for dress fabrics were less influenced by historicism, perhaps because clothing was seen as less of a long term investment than furnishing. Liberty's had introduced a range of dress fabrics with small scale floral prints in clear pastel colours before the First World War and these enjoyed continuing success in the twenties and thirties. The prints were well suited to the simple lines of twenties dresses and adapted equally to the more romantic mood and complex cutting of fashion in the thirties. These small florals were the most imitated of Liberty prints, perhaps the most imitated of any dress textiles of the period, but they were not the only prints produced by the company between the wars. The taste for Oriental motifs was expressed by a range of modified paisleys, often in deep, rich colours which were also produced as scarves; a number of prints with a black background were also made.

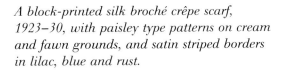

A block-printed silk broché crêpe scarf, 1923–30, with paisley type patterns on cream and fawn grounds, and satin striped borders in lilac, blue and rust.

A printed 'Sungleam' crêpe dress length (right) *in cotton and rayon, c. 1935; the design consists of a close floral repeat in green, purples and blue on a dark blue background.*

A hand block-printed linen furnishing fabric (below) *with a polychrome 'Jacobean' design on a natural ground, c. 1934.*

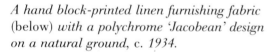

The range of fashion fabrics offered by Liberty's in this period was vast. There were cottons and linens of every weight, silks, wool and wool mixtures, velvets and a line of semi-synthetic fabrics, which became extremely successful in the thirties and were marketed under the registered name of 'Sungleam'. The most expensive of the printed ranges were produced at Merton; in 1924 the company was selling a silk gauze described as 'Tinsel silk' which was block printed with a metallic effect on rich colours and which retailed for 42s. per yard (more than a week's wages for a semi-skilled labourer at this time). More reasonably priced was a hand-printed crêpe de Chine which cost 13s.6d. in 1928. In addition to the traditional prints, Liberty's were also selling dress lengths which were hand-painted, sometimes with an overprint; each length was of course completely unique. All the fabrics, plain or patterned marketed by Liberty's were of extremely high quality and some of the weaves and textures were exclusive to the company; for example, a particular cotton lawn available only at Liberty's was registered as 'Tana' and the crêpe as 'Runis'.

Fabrics made from viscose rayon had been introduced to the textile range just after the First World War under the name 'Woodray', but it was not until the twenties that Liberty's were completely happy with a series of fabrics using synthetic yarn. 'Sungleam' was a mixture of rayon and either silk or wool, the resulting textile had the weight and drape of a purely natural material, but the rayon admixture gave durability, lower cost and scope for novel weaves and effects. The sheen peculiar to synthetic fibre combined with silk could give a finish not unlike a fine metallic gauze; combined with wool, it gave an interestingly textured surface. 'Sungleam' fabrics could be successfully printed and examples were appearing regularly in Liberty brochures by the end of the twenties. The line was so popular that the Regent Street shop gave a whole department over to it.

A sample of printed dress fabric in the type of small-scale floral design which is so firmly associated with Liberty style, 1934–38.

Overleaf *Thirties textile design at Liberty's: a selection of the 'Primrose' design* (left above); *a selection of furnishing cottons with designs inspired by Indo-Persian painting* (left below); *pattern books of the 'Sungleam' range against a background of 'Florence' cretonne* (right).

The importance of textiles to the shop is reflected in the attention and care given to the production of illustrated brochures describing the ranges, introducing new lines and giving prices. In the twenties these booklets tended to include ready-to-wear fashion, imported accessories, shawls, rugs and so on. Later they are concerned entirely with textiles. The brochures also indicate how the shop was responding to the economic climate of the thirties and the onset of the Second World War. Although the ready-to-wear clothing industry was extremely sophisticated by the middle of the decade, many women preferred to spend rather more on a good fabric and make their clothes at home from one of the many commercially produced paper patterns. In the second half of the thirties Liberty's were offering a cutting service to their customers wishing to make garments from Vogue, Butterick or McCall patterns.

By 1939 Liberty textiles no longer had a brochure to themselves, but were incorporated along with fashions, accessories and small decorative objects into a single publication. The implications of the declaration of war were recognized in a couple of sentences on the last page: because of possible 'travelling difficulties' Liberty's would be offering a mail order service, which included fabrics, to their customers.

Liberty's textile production in the twenties and thirties is often contrasted unfavourably with the great flowering of the Liberty style at the end of the nineteenth century. While it is certainly true that there was less innovation, it is clear that Liberty's understood their market very well and that their emphasis on tradition and quality was appropriate to that market. It would also be wrong to overlook the fact that their ranges of floral prints produced at this time were some of the most influential designs of the period and that they have lasted; the term 'Liberty print' evokes an immediate image of these fabrics, several of which are still in production.

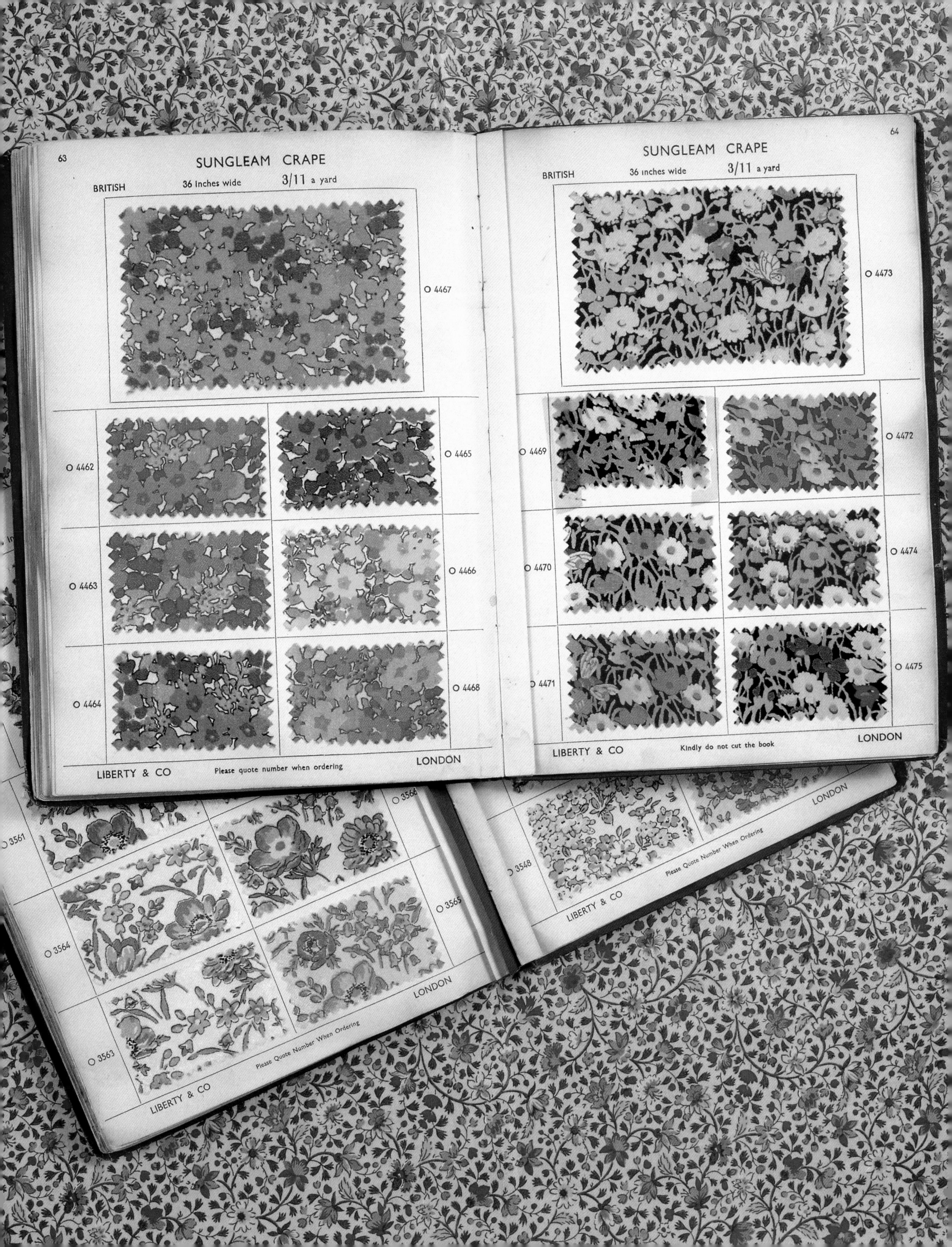

SUNGLEAM CRAPE

O 4467

O 4462

O 4465

O 4463

O 4466

O 4464

O 4468

LIBERTY & CO   Please quote number when ordering   **LONDON**

SUNGLEAM CRAPE

O 4473

O 4469

O 4472

O 4470

O 4474

O 4471

O 4475

LIBERTY & CO   Kindly do not cut the book   **LONDON**

O 3561

O 3562

O 3564

O 3565

O 3563

LIBERTY & CO   Please Quote Number When Ordering   LONDON

O 3548

LIBERTY & CO   Please Quote Number When Ordering   LONDON

Costume

DESPITE THE CHANGES IN FASHION after the First World War, Liberty's costume department maintained many of its pre-war attitudes to both design and fabric. The result was an opulence and historical decorativeness more in keeping with the Belle Epoque than the frenetic and modern atmosphere of the Jazz Age. Couturiers were now designing clothes for active women, whether dancing in nightclubs, climbing into and out of motor cars, playing golf or sunbathing. Coco Chanel brought sports clothes into everyday wear: her simple jersey jumpers and pleated skirts were the acme of chic. Liberty's costume department, however, continued to make luxurious gowns for the artistic lady of leisure.

The first spring catalogue of the twenties opened with a quote from *The Queen* magazine, praising the style of the 'array of attractive gowns and costumes ... One never ceases to marvel how these authorities continue to assimilate the vogues of the moment, and then evolve designs that are absolutely exclusive, and with that element of difference that at once hall-marks them as Liberty.' This little booklet could not be called innovative; it contained illustrations of costume department staples, as did catalogues throughout the twenties, which continued to advertise historical gowns. Indeed, it was not until the end of the decade that Liberty's began to look more in tune with the times and carried out a reorganization of the London showrooms.

An attempt at historical verisimilitude: a 'Stuart' dress (right) in brown velveteen, c. 1924, with a large white linen collar finished in lace.

A hand-painted satin cape, c. 1931, in lustrous satin in blue, red and gold (opposite left); the distressing or mottling was a finish much used by Fortuny.

A heavy, swinging 'Mandarin' cloak, (opposite right), cut with padded shoulders and velvet sleeve openings in a rich orange, brown and gold brocaded silk, c. 1930.

The spring catalogue of 1920 was divided into two sections: 'Gowns Never Out of Fashion' and 'Gowns of the New Season'. The former featured 'Tea Gowns' – by then an old fashioned term – opulent in crêpe de Chine and satin, and very similar to the Fortuny 'Delphos' dress. Four years on, the format was still the same: 'Gowns Never Out of Fashion' featured artistic ladies wearing 'Greek', 'Stuart' or 'Empire' gowns. The 'Novelty' evening gowns were on the safe side, featuring medieval-style embroidery and ladies with long hair – at a time when the bob was all the rage.

The costume department was aimed at the older woman rather than the Bright Young Thing. But by 1926, there were fashionable 'Jumper Suits' influenced by Chanel, and the evening gowns reflected the current Paris fashions: one, sumptuous in silk and metal brocade, was draped with gauze and decorated with 'handmade tinsel ornament', and cut with an asymmetrical hemline, making it perfect for dancing the Charleston. Another, heavily influenced by Lanvin in its panier skirt and ankle length, was made in Liberty's 'Ilia' satin, with an underskirt of gold lace, and embroidered in pastel shades and gold. Ready-to-wear was half price: a dress in 'Tyrian' silk, decorated with printed silk, rather than hand-

The interior of the couture department at the Maison Liberty, 3 Boulevard des Capucines, where the firm moved in the early nineteen-twenties.

embroidered was £5.19s.6d., in comparison to a similar 'couture' model at 19½ guineas.

The gowns were created by a team of in-house people, based either on standard models adapted to suit the current mode, or on the season's Paris couture. They were made up on the premises, using exclusive dyes and embroidery designs created by artists according to the specifications of the customer. Embroidery and smocking was the hallmark of the costume department, and while cotton jersey, silver lamé and man-made rayon were the fabrics most expressive of the sartorial spirit of the age, Liberty's continued to produce floral cottons and silks. Twelve workrooms made children's clothes, the most popular being the smocked frocks and little tweed coats. An employee described the embroidery workrooms: 'As well as the head lady, there were seven embroidery hands, four junior hands, and five apprentices in our workroom. Each apprentice was put to work beside a hand. Too much talking was discouraged ... We young people made twisted and plaited cords, covered small buttons and embroidered larger ones, made tassels and embroidered collars and cuffs. The materials we handled were beautiful. Mostly silk, crêpe de Chine, and Liberty's own "Tyrian" Silk, plain or patterned.'

The element of hand-embroidery attracted some illustrious names: Queen Ena of Spain, Queen Maria of Roumania, the Princess of Monaco, the Duchess of York. 'It was because Princess Mary dressed her boys in smocks that smocking became popular and gave us plenty of work,' she continues, 'We did more smocking than embroidery. Liberty smocking was much coveted because it was a speciality of the House.' In the meantime, the Paris shop continued to do a roaring trade in hand-smocked garments in the tradition of Kate Greenaway and Walter Crane.

The Maison Liberty in Paris added the cachet of the couture capital to the Liberty label. The French branch was run by Paul St George Perrot, who both designed and managed the department. In April 1926 he described in *Liberty Lamp* the Bal de la Couture: 'The gowns were sensational to a degree. One mannequin, among a bevy in evening gowns, was presumably wearing Maison Liberty, as she was "habillée entièrement en smocking".' The next year, he described the 'new look' salons at the Boulevard des Capucines, evoking their essentially French atmosphere: 'The elaborated gilded and sculptured cornice, the massive classic columns, the tall arched windows, the well-drawn lines, and above all the symmetry, all these combined to recall the past glories of eighteenth-century France. The entrance to the fitting-rooms is topped by an artistically-mounted clock, and flanked by heavy marbled columns; on either side, little recesses made an admirable background for a bright-hued mantle or gown. A little polygon-shaped salon is peculiarly charming. It has three tall windows, whose crossed curtains of creamy silk recall the period of Marie Antoinette. A vast mirror ornamented with gilt studs gives an effect of considerable perspective as the pretty mannequins pass before it.'

The dreadful economic climate of the early thirties forced Maison Liberty to close in 1932 and St George Perrot returned to London to give the costume department a long overdue face-lift. An announcement sent to customers in April 1932 read: 'On May 2nd we are inaugurating A Model Gown Department, when a fresh collection of new Models executed under the direct supervision of a Paris dress designer will be shown at extremely attractive prices and made in the well-known Liberty materials. Our workrooms and, in fact, everything to do with our dress departments are being reorganised.' The bohemian Arts and Crafts image was to be eradicated. St George Perrot invited the grand couturier Paul Poiret to design for him; he created four collections in all. Poiret fitted in with the Liberty tradition and had often used their silks, but by now he was sadly out of touch with the current mood. His own house had closed down in

Designs from a brochure of ready-to-wear Liberty dresses (right above) *in Yoru crêpe, printed cotton georgette and hand-printed Tyrian silk, c. 1930. Designs of Liberty dresses and jumpers* (right below) *in printed 'Sungleam' crêpe, 1931.*

The cover of the 'Liberty Dresses and Children's Frocks' catalogue of 1935 (below).

One of Paul Poiret's finest designs for Liberty's – the 'Calypso' evening dress of 1933 (right), *with an asymmetrically clasped bodice and a tiered, furbelowed skirt in different shades of lustrous silk. A dress with coat and hat ensuite* (far right) *made as a special order in 1928 by Liberty's for Mrs William Moorcroft to wear at her wedding; the coat is in bright blue wool over a block-printed silk dress which matches the lining of the coat and has a machine-pleated skirt; the hat is a 'cloche' trimmed with ostrich feathers.*

1929; to quote his biographer Palmer White: 'Poiret epitomised a period when a woman dressed to enhance her personal beauty ... Now women dressed to follow a career ... He felt that the new trend was only temporary, and was convinced that he could channel it back into his way of more opulent beauty. He failed to understand the irrevocability of change.' Liberty's too had been forced to become less exotic and more realistic.

An invitation to a Dress Parade held on 3, 4 and 5 October 1933 seems to indicate that the shop was seeking broader appeal: 'Whether it be the exclusive model gown for the formal occasion, or the less expensive dress for practical wear, there are pleasant surprises ... For not only do the creations of Paul Poiret gratify those who seek, above all, artistic perfection, but the models fashioned by our own expert designers and dressmakers delight those in search of elegance at a price which is, to say the least, quite discreet.' An embroidery room, a pleating room and a 'French Room' made up the dress-making workrooms. In the French Room, copies were made of various models designed that season by different couturiers; a Liberty model gown could be inspired by Vionnet, Redfern, Chanel or Schiaparelli. A chic rather than artistic image was now important. For the first time, in 1933, a photograph appeared on the cover of a catalogue; this was of a day dress which is a conventional bias-cut frock. The illustrations inside the catalogue became increasingly glamorous as the decade progressed, with heavily made-up ladies set against a backdrop of palm trees or leaning against the rail of an ocean liner. Hollywood and the cinema had an enormous effect; the illustrations were inspired by stars such as Jean Arthur and Claudette Colbert. The 'Liberty Woman' was now sophisticated and modern; the delightful heroine of 'She Bought a Liberty Scarf' is a tweed suited girl in the Nancy Mitford mould. Off on a country house weekend, and staying with a distinctly conventional Duchess, the ever versatile silk scarf helps her to catch her man: 'It's wonderful what a Liberty Scarf can do for you. Tucked inside your tweed coat, and with gloves and handbag to match ... with a Liberty Scarf you'll find you're quite all right ...'

Liberty now seemed much more open to outside influences and no longer exclusively dependent on its own vision of things. The fashion for the Tyrol during the early thirties, for instance, was reflected in sporty puffed sleeve tops in 'Blouses of Beauty and Charm'; 'Lamont' was tailored with military-style padded shoulders. Neither owed inspiration to either the historical past or concerns for health; and both were utterly fashionable. Liberty was once more a leader in popular fashion while its silks continued to be used by the top couture houses – Worth, Hardy Amies and Norman Hartnell.

A highly detailed commemorative scarf for the Coronation of King George VI and Queen Elizabeth in 1937; in block printed silk twill, the intense working of the paisley pattern recalls the cashmere shawls which were among the most characteristic of Liberty's early merchandise. The colours include black, two reds, green, pale blue and royal blue (see overleaf).

Overleaf *A perennial Liberty speciality – a selection of scarves from the nineteen-thirties, including the Coronation scarf of 1937.*

Ceramics and Glass

AFTER THE FIRST WORLD WAR the china and glass department at Liberty's presented much the same face to shoppers as it had before 1914. Moorcroft pottery appeared in the same shapes and with the same decoration. The colourful Breda-ware was still on sale. The Netherlands, where it was manufactured, had been neutral during the war and production had not been interrupted. On the other hand, the import of Loetz iridescent glass, described in pre-war catalogues as 'Austrian', had to be immediately curtailed when the Austro-Hungarian Empire became an ally of Germany. In 1922 the shop offered a line of 'Hand Made Glass' which was reminiscent of Clutha. It may have been manufactured by Richardson's, the firm of glass makers which had been running Couper's works since early in the century, or it may have been an old stock of Clutha which became available in 1922, the year that H. E. Richardson sold the Glasgow glass house. In general, during the first few years following the end of the war, there must have been a feeling of *déjà vu* about Liberty's pottery and glass.

Over the next twenty years, a small number of novelties would be introduced, but most of them expressed more than a hint of nostalgia. Nevertheless, throughout the inter-war years the shop would offer well-designed pottery and glass of good quality. Liberty's never mounted an exhibition of china and glass designed by avant-garde painters and sculptors, as Harrod's did in 1934; the directors at East India House may well have felt that they and their customers had outgrown the need for such gimmicks.

The Moorcroft pottery sold by Liberty's in the nineteen-twenties and nineteen-thirties represents well the attitude of confidence without complacency which the shop assumed in its choice of merchandise during the inter-war period. In the case of Moorcroft, such an attitude was due, no doubt, to the terms of the commercial relationship which evolved between shop and supplier. When William Moorcroft had left Macintyre's in 1912, Liberty's had loaned him much of the capital required to set up his own works in Cobridge, and by converting the loan into voting shares the shop had gained effective control of the pottery. Throughout the nineteen-twenties, Liberty's paid the workmen's wages and, although William Moorcroft was allowed artistic and commercial autonomy, the shop's orders would always have been filled quickly and efficiently, and any suggestions – whether relating to colour and shape or to supplies to other retailers – would have received ready consideration. In addition, strong personal links were forged between the Moorcroft and Liberty families. Before the war, William Moorcroft had struck up a close friendship with Aylwin Lasenby, Sir Arthur's cousin, and when Florence Moorcroft, William's wife, died in 1927 barely a year elapsed before he married his friend's sister, Hazel Lasenby. The twin bonds of commercial partnership and personal intimacy were signified by the appearance of the name 'Moorcroft' in Liberty's publicity material, one of the very rare instances when the supplier was identified, and almost as great an accolade as Moorcroft received in 1928 when he was officially appointed 'Potter to H.M. the Queen'.

The patterns used to decorate the Moorcroft pottery sold at Liberty's between the wars were little different to those which had adorned the wares before 1914. In their catalogues the designation 'Murena' was applied to several different patterns featuring pomegranates, irises, poppies, wisteria, toadstools or landscape. Some pieces were mounted in Tudric pewter, a resolutely nostalgic gesture. More innovative were the bands of geometrical Art Deco ornament which were sometimes introduced into the pattern. The development of 'flambé' glazes was of greater significance.

By 1921 Moorcroft had built a kiln for the specific purpose of making experiments with high-temperature transmutation glazes, particularly the rich red which the French, when they discovered it on Chinese ceramics, had named 'sang-de-boeuf'. From the eighteen-forties onwards, potters in Europe and America had attempted to reproduce this copper reduction glaze, and by the second decade of the twentieth century the term 'rouge flambé' had been used to describe a wide variety of more or less spectacular effects. In Staffordshire, where the glaze was usually applied to various bone china bodies rather than stoneware or porcelain, a smooth, luminous red had been developed by Bernard Moore which was exploited by Doulton's and other, smaller potteries. The version produced by Moorcroft was

The Tudor Tearooms, in the basement of Liberty's new building completed in 1924, provided an ersatz Gothic setting for the Moorcroft 'Powder Blue' china laid on the tables. First produced in 1913, the 'Powder Blue' range was modern in both its shape and decoration, reflecting twentieth-century functionalism rather than medieval romance. Note also the Riemerschmid-style chairs, sold by Liberty's from 1900.

Moorcroft continued through the nineteen-twenties and nineteen-thirties to use some of the patterns which had first been devised before the First World War. However, the wisteria painted on these two vases (above (left, c. 1935; right, c. 1920) are treated more loosely than their predecessors.

The glazes with which these pieces of 'Moorcroft Rouge Flambé' (right) have been decorated were introduced during the nineteen-twenties. The very high temperatures required in their production, and the greater number of pieces spoiled during firing, resulted in the ware being much costlier than comparable pieces that Moorcroft manufactured using conventional methods.

Moorcroft's 'Powder Blue' tableware (opposite) was manufactured from 1913 to 1963 with only a short break during the Second World War. The colour seems to have been what attracted the public; when Liberty's launched the same range glazed yellow (called 'Sunray'), the new colour made little impact on the sales of 'Powder Blue'.

allied to this, although his glaze ranged from yellow through orange and scarlet to a dark aubergine. He used different shades for the various elements in a pattern, or sometimes he covered a plain vessel with a single tone. Liberty's sold examples as 'Moorcroft Rouge Flambé', which were much more expensive than comparably sized pieces with conventional glazes. The higher prices reflected a considerable rate of wastage in production, in addition to William Moorcroft's personal involvement in the manufacture of each piece. He never divulged the secrets of his 'rouge flambé' glaze except to his son.

Liberty's continued to sell the blue-glazed tableware that Moorcroft's had introduced in 1913. The manufacturers called it 'Blue Porcelain', but in Liberty's catalogues it was dubbed 'Powder Blue Ware'. Its blue glaze, speckled with small black spots, was quite different to the colour generally known as 'powder blue' which had long been used by Wedgwood and Worcester factories. Liberty's, however, claimed that 'the colour of this pottery is similar to the Chinese Powder Blue'. Even in the nineteen-twenties it was important to the shop to invoke the aesthetic authority of the Far East whenever it could. Some of the shapes in the range of Moorcroft blue tableware had a slightly Chinese flavour, but they are more notable for their functional simplicity. The designs are not modern in the sense of Modernist, Art Deco or Streamline, but 'as "modern" as anything created now', according to Nikolaus Pevsner writing in 1937; 'undatedly perfect', he apostrophized the ware. Eighteen years later Michael Farr would assert in *Design in British Industry* that the shapes 'still look modern and undated', and 'Powder Blue' remained in production until 1963. Probably one reason for the china's timeless quality was that each piece was hand thrown (apart from odd items, such as toast-racks), and the contours reflect the naturalness of the creative process. The speckled blue glaze certainly contributed to the ware's popularity. Towards the end of the thirties, Liberty's sold a version in yellow called 'Sunray' which was much less successful.

The paradox of old and new styles at Liberty's during the inter-war period must have been very evident on a visit to the Tudor Tearooms in the basement of the new building opened in 1924. In a setting of stone walls and a beamed ceiling, with a great cowled fireplace occupying the middle of the room and huge iron-banded lanterns hanging from the beams, stood oak tables surrounded by Riemerschmid chairs and laid with Moorcroft's 'Powder Blue' china. These two icons of twentieth-century design (although the chair first appeared in 1899) contrasted vividly with the ambient bric-à-brac of historicism.

A more straightforward clash between modern and historical styles occurred in the range of Compton garden pottery, still being sold by Liberty's in the nineteen-twenties. Many of the designs harked back to the heyday of the Arts and Crafts Movement. One plant tub bore a band of Celtic ornament in relief, another was decorated with a pattern of vine leaves and bunches of grapes, which both Morris and Voysey had often used. If these must have seemed a little fusty, a third Compton tub represented a frank submission to the weight of Classical antiquity; it was moulded in the form of an Ionic capital adorned with floral festoons. In contrast, and presumably as a gesture to the Bright Young Things, was a tub decorated with widely-spaced vertical bands of chevrons. All these tubs were shown in a Liberty's catalogue issued about 1925, and they reflect the circumstances which prevailed at Compton during the years immediately after the war. The aged Mrs Watts, widow of the painter George Frederick Watts who had died in 1904, and her barely younger foreman James Nicol, ran the pottery with the help of a handful of workmen. In 1919, the thirty-six-year-old sculptor Alan Durst was introduced into the firm to supply fresh ideas. But after staying for the trial year to which he had agreed, Durst hurried off, quite unable to gain any co-operation from either Mrs Watts or Nicol. Perhaps the chevron decoration can be attributed to this brief flirtation with contemporary art.

Although the Clutha-like glass offered in the 1922 'Liberty's Gifts' catalogue made no reappearance, the shop was soon marketing a replace-

Monart glass was decorated internally with air bubbles and flakes of gold and silver, a treatment that had earlier been used on Clutha glass. But, as can be clearly seen from these two pieces of Monart, the shapes of the new glass were more traditional, often inspired by Oriental ceramics, and more suited to the artistic conservatism of the inter-war years.

Monart glass was made in Scotland by a family of Catalan craftsmen using techniques they had learnt in a French glass house. The ware epitomized the internationalism which had always inspired Sir Arthur Lasenby Liberty.

ment. Monart glass, manufactured by John Moncrieff Ltd. at the North British Glassworks in Perth, Scotland, was sold by Liberty's from about 1925 and was described in their catalogues as 'Scotch Glass'. Like Clutha it was decorated internally with more or less informal patterns of coloured glass. But Monart was different in a number of ways. First, the shapes were generally more conventional than those designed by Dresser for Clutha, although occasionally a wide undulating rim on a piece of Monart suggests that Liberty's had been holding Clutha up as an example to the Perth firm. Some Monart shapes were classical, but a greater number were inspired by Oriental ceramics. Second, the coloured decoration usually fills the walls of a Monart vessel more densely than it does an average piece of Clutha; most Monart is opaque, whereas most Clutha is transparent. Thirdly, the markings on Clutha were usually disposed at random, but on Monart the colours have often been manipulated into regular patterns. Fourth, the Monart colours are much brighter than the pink, pale green and amber that characterize Clutha. Typical colours found in Monart are orange, turquoise, black, green and red – in fact, the distinctive palette of Art Deco. Gold and silver flecks were used more liberally in Monart than they had been in Clutha.

John Moncrieff Ltd. manufactured specialist glass products for the chemical and engineering industries. In 1922, the firm took on a Catalan glass blower, Salvador Ysart, and his son Paul, who had been employed by Cochran's Glassworks in Glasgow. For the first two years after their move to Perth, the Ysarts made laboratory vessels, but production of this type of

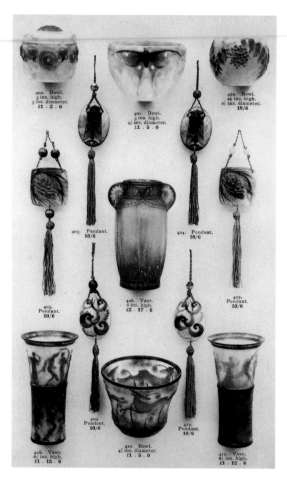

Gabriel Argy-Rousseau's pâte-de-verre *was stocked by Liberty's from 1929 to 1932. This selection of pieces* (above) *appeared in the 'Liberty Gifts' catalogue of 1929–30 under the heading 'Glass Craftsmanship'. The tasselled pendants proved to be the most popular items. Later Liberty catalogues featured them strongly, and very few other pieces were shown.*

The Japanese pottery (opposite) *shown by Liberty's in their 'Gifts' catalogue of 1934 represented the shop's response to the success in Britain of Clarice Cliff's brightly-coloured 'Bizarre' china. The stylized floral motifs, the predominant red, yellow and black, and even some of the shapes (particularly the small bowls on flange feet) closely resemble some of the Cliff designs.*

glass was suffering from the depressed economic conditions and cheap imports from the Continent. Salvador Ysart had worked for a small French glass house at Epinay-sur-Seine, just outside Paris, which had been opened in 1913 by the brothers Charles and Ernest Schneider. A range of art glass was produced there, including pieces internally decorated with streaks and clouds of colour. When Ysart found time weighing heavily on his hands at the North British Glassworks, he started to make some of this sort of glass, as presents to give to his friends. His work came to the attention of Mrs Isabel Moncrieff, the proprietor's wife, who encouraged him to develop his talents and supplied him with designs. She became the driving force behind Monart glass, and she not only designed most of the shapes but took a prominent role in marketing the new line.

In a brochure entitled 'A Friendly Talk on Monart Ware' written by Mrs Moncrieff about 1925, she echoed the sentiments expressed by Charles Eastlake half a century earlier: 'Although,' she declared, 'the standardised perfection of moulded ware cannot be secured, the skill of the workmanship is such that wonderful precision of shape and size is obtained, while to the eye of the connoisseur any trifling irregularity is but an enhancement of value.' John Llewellyn must have appreciated such an accurate reprise of Aesthetic Movement opinion. She had enunciated an important part of the creed formulated by Whistler, Rossetti and Arthur Lasenby Liberty himself, when they had preached their gospel of Orientalism back in the eighteen-seventies. Further on in the brochure, Mrs Moncrieff reaffirmed her faith. Pointing out the suitability of Monart glass for flower arrangements, she wrote: 'The single rose in its specimen-glass on the davenport of Miss 1850 has given place to the glorified ginger-jar in which the shingled Miss 1925 arranges her branches of wild cherry, catkin or prunus.' As has already been mentioned, many of the Monart shapes were of Oriental inspiration, and this aspect of the glass was underscored by Liberty's in their catalogues when they illustrated pieces standing on Chinese carved wood pot-stands.

Eventually, Salvador Ysart was joined at his work by Paul's three younger brothers, Antoine, Vincent and Augustine. Many different markings on Monart glass were developed, but two patterns are particularly notable. Both were created during the early days of production and were described by Mrs Moncrieff in her brochure. One, which she called 'Paisley Shawl', consists of a frieze of swirls in one colour over another. This pattern was used very frequently and its successful execution depended on manual dexterity as much as anything else. But the 'Cloisonné' pattern relied on expert working of the glass at the furnace. An inner layer of colour was cased in clear crystal and then rolled in crushed white enamel. Next, the piece was reheated until the white enamel fused, and then the glass was plunged into a bucket of cold water. The white outer layer cracked, and when the piece, after reheating, was blown a little larger, the white split further apart exposing the inner layer of colour through the clear crystal.

343. Bowl.
7¼ ins. diameter.
8/6

345. Box.
4½ ins. diameter.
2/6

346.
Pot Pourri Jar,
filled. 5 ins. high.
2/6

347.
Bowl, with bamboo handle.
7¼ ins. high.
3/9

348.
Pot Pourri Jar,
filled. 5 ins. high.
2/6

344. Bowl.
7¼ ins. diameter.
3/9

349. Bowl.
5 ins. diameter.
1/6

350.
Pot Pourri Jar, filled.
3½ ins. high. **1/6**

351. Bowl.
8 by 7 ins.
diameter. **4/6**

354.
Pot Pourri Jar,
filled.
3½ ins. high.
1/6

352. Bowl.
3½ by 2½ ins.
diameter.
9d.

353. Bowl.
3½ by 2½ ins.
diameter.
9d.

356. Trays.
4 ins. diameter.
1/-

Trays. 355.
4½ ins. diameter.
1/-

357. Bowls.
3 ins. diameter.
6d.

358. Biscuit Jar.
6 ins. high.
4/9

359. Bowls.
3 ins. diameter.
6d.

360. Box.
6 ins. diameter.
2/9

361. Bowl.
6 ins. diameter.
2/9

362. Bowl.
5½ ins. diameter.
1/9

363. Box.
6 ins. diameter.
2/9

As the nineteen-twenties were followed by the less prosperous nineteen-thirties, Liberty's began to promote the usefulness of Monart glass as lamp bases. This example is an appropriate shape, with its broad, heavy base offering great stability.

Sometimes a touch of iridescence was added by exposing the piece to fumes from the furnace. The skills displayed by the Ysarts, father and sons, were comparable to those found frequently among the craftsmen of Murano, and far superior to any shown by the average British glass maker.

'Now-a-days,' Mrs Moncrieff had written in her brochure, 'fashion demands that an article be useful as well as beautiful', and the stipulation became more imperative during the Depression which followed the Wall Street crash of 1929. Monart bowls and vases could be used for flowers, but such a function might be regarded as frivolous. But the glass could serve a more essential purpose as a lampstand, and it was in that role that Liberty's began to present their 'Scotch Glass'. Monart glass lampstands were illustrated in Liberty catalogues from 1930, and they were shown fitted with parchment shades painted in colours and patterns matching the base. There were also Monart lampstands made with matching glass shades, but Liberty's apparently baulked at the high price that they would have had to charge for them. Another means of presenting Monart glass as a practical item was to match the colour markings to furnishing fabrics. Mrs Moncrieff used to take samples to the glassworks and the Ysarts would try to capture the effect of the woven pattern in glass and enamel, a challenge equal, perhaps, to their virtuosity.

Glass of a very different sort to Monart was stocked by Liberty's between 1929 and 1932. The *pâte-de-verre* made in Paris by Gabriel Argy-Rousseau represented the boldest step taken by the shop's glass and china buyers in the direction of hard-core Art Deco. In an attempt to emulate the chromatic sculpture of Classical antiquity, the French artist Henri Cros had developed *pâte-de-verre* towards the end of the nineteenth century. It consists of powdered glass and water (or some other binding agent) mixed into a malleable paste which can be modelled and moulded like clay. Metal oxides are introduced to give colour, and the material is then heated enough to vitrify without the colours running into each other. The finished product may be opaque or translucent, mat or shiny, depending on the ingredients and the exact procedures taken in firing.

The clearest sort of *pâte-de-verre* is called *pâte-de-cristal*. Argy-Rousseau made both kinds. In 1921 he formed a company with Gustave-Gaston Moser-Millot who ran a large decorative art gallery in the Boulevard des Italiens, Paris. Argy-Rousseau's *pâte-de-verre* was greatly admired when it was shown at the 1925 International Exhibition of Decorative and Industrial Arts, and over the next few years a large number of items appeared in Moser-Millot's windows. The Boulevard des Italiens is the continuation eastwards of the Boulevard des Capucines where Liberty's had opened their new Paris shop in the early nineteen-twenties, so the buyers would have been aware of Argy-Rousseau's stylish glass.

By 1929, moreover, Liberty's would have been feeling pressure to respond to moves made by other London retailers in the direction of contemporary French design. An exhibition of Art Deco furniture from

France had been held the previous year at Shoolbred's in Tottenham Court Road, and Waring & Gillow had just opened a department of modern French furnishings. The 'Liberty Gifts' catalogue issued in 1929 offered several items of Argy-Rousseau's *pâte-de-verre* and *pâte-de-cristal*, most of them in a style which reflected the moderate, classical aspect of Art Deco. There was a bowl decorated with leaping deer, one of the most ubiquitous of Art Deco motifs. Tall vases bore friezes of classical figures. Geometrical flowers adorned a covered bowl, but other bowls and several pendants were decorated with plants and insects treated in a more naturalistic manner.

As the promotion of Monart glass during the years of the Depression had tended to emphasize the more functional items such as lampstands, so the bowls and vases by Argy-Rousseau disappeared from the catalogues, and the 'Liberty Christmas Gifts' for 1930 featured pendants only. But the suppliers could not contend with rising costs and falling sales, and in December 1931 Moser-Millot had to wind up the company producing Argy-Rousseau's *pâte-de-verre*, a victim of the economic constriction which was suffocating the decorative arts everywhere. Designers and manufacturers dispensed with decoration and embraced modernism which made a virtue of the unadorned. Liberty's were loath to follow this course, and in china and glass they made few concessions to the new trend. Some monochrome vases, made by the Poole pottery of Carter, Stabler & Adams and designed by Harry Trethowan, a fervent supporter of modern industrial art, were being sold by the shop towards the end of the nineteen-thirties, and that was about as far as a firm which had given its name to a style of flowery ornament was prepared to go along the road of stark modernism.

The simple shapes, prominent throwing-rings and lack of decoration found in these earthenware vases made by Carter, Stabler & Adams suggest the curious compromise that the ceramics industry made with the studio-pottery movement. Towards the end of the nineteen-thirties, Liberty's were keen to meet a growing demand for the hand-made look, but were also anxious not to exceed the prices that their customers were used to paying.

Priceless Presents —
THAT COST LESS THAN YOU THINK

THE FIFTIES
AND SIXTIES

PATRICIA BAYER

An Era of Revivals

THE HOUSE OF LIBERTY in the nineteen-fifties continued its long-standing role as a tasteful arbiter of fashionable – but never outrageous – design, offering a wide variety of fabrics and scarves in both traditional and contemporary patterns, as well as furniture, ceramics, glassware, cutlery, wooden utensils and assorted other furnishings. Some of the tried-and-true designs retailed by Liberty's before the war continued to be offered, such as Eric Ravilious's earthenware mugs and beakers featuring the jaunty 'Gardening Implements' pattern, originally designed for Wedgwood *c*. 1938. Furniture, glass and ceramics in traditional forms and designs – reproduction Georgian chairs, Staffordshire floral boxes, Victorian toile tea cosies and Whitefriars glass goblets – still formed a considerable part of the merchandise on offer.

New designs and designers were also promoted – often those associated with the more organic forms then prevalent in contemporary design. Much of this furniture, ceramics, glass and fabrics was characterized by subtle curves and simple but distinctive forms which could be nature-derived or geometric. The palette of the fifties comprised a rainbow of striking colours, used on their own as well as in tandem with each other

This simultaneously otherworldly (stars and Saturn) and down-to-earth (Scotties and bread knives) window of 1951 (right) was designed by Eric E. Lucking. The moon goddess-like figure was created by Phyllis Richards, one of Liberty's most talented model designers of the period.

Roy Gentry designed and dressed this surreal Young Liberty shop window (opposite) for the 1951 Festival of Britain; featuring flying 'Boomerang' tables by A. M. Lewis, it won first prize in the national display competition.

Previous double-page *Christmas at Liberty's: a window showing the variety of goods offered by the shop, designed by Eric E. Lucking in 1955.*

(or with black or white) – from soft greys, greens, fawns and blues to bold chartreuse and shocking pink. Figurative designs on fabrics and ceramics were often simply drawn and wittily stylized, and included smiling suns, mysterious masks, comical fish, cartoonish horses and the ubiquitous hot-air balloon. Surrealism, too, crept into some Liberty products: for instance, ceramics, metalwork and furniture designs by Piero Fornasetti. The style also asserted itself in some of Liberty's intriguing window displays by Eric E. Lucking and Roy Gentry: a prize-winning 1951 window by the latter featured mannequins amid a constellation of suspended 'Boomerang' tables, exclusively designed for Liberty by A. M. Lewis.

During this decade Liberty's began to play an important role in promoting contemporary studio craftsmen. There was the Oriental-inspired, earth-toned studio pottery of Bernard Leach and Lucie Rie, and the bold and colourful ceramics of Fausto Melotti, Marcello Fantoni and Guido Gambone. New (and soon-to-be classic) furniture designs of Robin Day, Ernest Race, Arne Jacobsen, Finn Juhl, Gio Ponti and Vico Magistretti were offered by the modern furniture department, inaugurated in 1950. Liberty's also sold the marvellously innovative, colourful glass vessels of

169

The 'Peacock Feather' (opposite) probably *expresses the spirit of Liberty's more than any other single design sold by the shop. It was originally designed by Arthur Silver in 1887 (this version can be seen in the centre of this arrangement) and then became one of Liberty's most successful revivals in a variety of colour combinations and variations in fabric and wallpaper.*

This Liberty Christmas window from 1958 (below) *is a magical doll's house in the Liberty Tudor vein.*

Liberty's Tudor Shop is close to Carnaby Street, London's world-famous thoroughfare of the 'Swinging Sixties'; this photograph (below right) *dates from 1966.*

Paolo Venini, Gino Cenedese, Archimede Seguso and Nason & Moretti, and the utilitarian and decorative glass of Kosta Boda and Orrefors in Sweden. There were also one-man shows of outstanding talents, including Leach, Ponti and the Finn Tapio Wirkkala.

In the field of commissioning and retailing fabric designs, Liberty's continued their nearly century-long pre-eminence. Many patterns created under its aegis by designers such as Lucienne Day, Marianne Straub, Althea McNish, Jacqueline Groag and Robert Stewart in the fifties were colourful, vibrant, and often whimsical, whether appearing on a place mat, sewing box, pillow cover, wastepaper basket, lady's dress, silk scarf or simple length of screen-printed cotton.

In the sixties, when the password was youth and its mecca was London, some retailing aspects of Liberty's did remain conservative, catering to a traditionally-minded clientele. But Carnaby Street, the hub of 'Swinging London', was a mere stone's throw away, literally touching on parts of the Tudor Revival building, and the shop was not immune to that fact — and its potential customers. The House of Liberty now provided many of the members of the youth explosion (as well as their fashion-conscious parents) with ranges of exciting fabrics. Many featured Art Nouveau Revival designs, their colours brightly updated, and later came various Art Deco-style patterns. Indeed, the Regent Street emporium was at the forefront of marketing these to the world, just as the two early twentieth-century styles were gaining respect in terms of design history. Pop culture was acknowledged in the 1968 'Avenger' collection of cashmere by Ballantyne of Scotland, marketed by Liberty's — women's and men's sweaters, and mini- and maxi-dresses bearing names like 'Libra', 'Scorpio', 'Mars', 'Capricorn', and 'Astra'.

Interest in the actual artifacts of the first and second decades of this century was, even in the early sixties, still the preserve of a tiny coterie of collectors, writers and museum curators. Among these enthusiasts, Philippe Jullian in France and Martin Battersby in England did much to promote an informed appreciation of not only the artists, but also the architects and designers of the turn of the century. In particular, Battersby formed a major collection of decorative arts of the period, rich in Knox pewterware and other early Liberty objects. An important sequence of exhibitions through the sixties at the Victoria and Albert Museum revealed to a new, excited and predominantly younger public the importance of several crucial figures in the decorative arts of the early part of the century: Alphonse Mucha (1963), Aubrey Beardsley (1966) and Charles Rennie Mackintosh (1968). For many, the quality of their works, most of them on view in the original for the first time in living memory, came as a revelation.

As if in direct reaction to the meanness and conventionality of so many features of post-war Britain, the sixties were a period of exuberant cultural eclecticism. Exciting visual experimentation and new approaches to design were seen as a precise counterpoint to fresh intellectual and political ideals, playing an essential part in the widespread search of 'alternative'

In 1960 Liberty's launched the 'Lotus' collection of dress fabrics, named after the shop's 'Lotus' trade-mark (which originated in the early eighteen-eighties). The patterns were redrawn and at times recoloured versions of Art Nouveau-era furnishing fabrics, and the resultant silk and wool chiffons and organza were widely embraced by European couturiers, especially the Fontana sisters of Rome, two of whose creations are seen here.

The 1967 'Tango' range of fabrics, created by Bernard Nevill, was inspired by the Art Deco nineteen-twenties, this window dating from its launch; called 'Liberty's enfant terrible' *by an approving* Women's Wear Daily *in June 1966, Nevill especially captivated American audiences who viewed his contemporary creations as a confirmation of Liberty's front-line position in fabric design.*

lifestyles. To some degree at least, the art and artifacts of the nineties and, later, the twenties struck an intriguing and essentially anti-Establishment note, making a statement which appealed not only to the young, but to many who were old enough and sufficiently affluent to indulge their tastes in collecting and decorating.

It was during the nineteen-sixties that dress became a crucial indicator of the wearer's ideals and fashionable allegiances. Extravagance and excess played an important part in 'the Look' for men and women. For women long and flowing dresses in rich patterned fabrics on heavy velvets in deep, saturated colours echoed both the paintings of the Pre-Raphaelites and the exaggerated elegance of day and evening wear of the opulent nineties and the Edwardian era. Meanwhile, for the first time in a century, the male peacock re-emerged, making gorgeousness of attire an aim, and reviving the languid, dandified pose of the aesthetes of the nineties as his chosen manner of self-presentation.

In many decorative schemes of the period and in the design of record covers and the independent or 'underground' magazines which proliferated during the period, original designs of the nineties were often mingled with a variety of Eastern influences brought back by hippy travellers, most notable of which were strong and vibrantly contrasted colours and a sort of

*The Crush Bar of the Royal Opera House was
the setting for this 1960 photograph of models
(right) wearing couture dresses made of
fabrics from the Art Nouveau Revival 'Lotus'
collection.*

*'Patience', designed by J. Scarratt Rigby in
1897 (opposite above left) was one of the
many Art Nouveau-era fabrics revived by
Liberty's in the nineteen-sixties.*

*Liberty's original 'Tana Lawn' fabric
(opposite above right), a perennial best-seller
for the shop, dated from around 1930 and
was created by William Haynes Dorell (its
name derived from Tana Lake in Sudan, the
origin of its yarn); the 'Tana Lawn' shown
was created by Blair Pride in 1960.*

*Bernard Nevill's 1969 'Renaissance' range
(opposite below) was a reaction against
Space Age patterns and fashions and
coincided with the revival of Gilbert and
Sullivan's operetta* Patience *by the Sadler's
Wells Opera Company. Yves Saint Laurent
was one of the couturiers who worked with
Nevill's wool challis fabrics in this range,
converting them from damask weave
tapestry patterns.*

generalized mysticism based on traditional religious imagery. The sinuous
forms of Art Nouveau, along with its love of bizarre lettering forms, were
rapidly assimilated into a new graphic idiom. Many old designs were
plagiarised and adapted to the creation of an all-embracing and essentially
anti-modern, anti-rationalist aesthetic. For many, the terms 'Art Nouveau'
and 'Psychedelic' became near enough synonymous.

The year 1958 was significant for Liberty's, for it was then that William
Poole, assistant to Gustav Weiner in Liberty's Merton Abbey printworks,
viewed a small exhibition of Art Nouveau in Paris. The show inspired him
to revive about a dozen of Liberty's *fin-de-siècle* furnishing fabrics and to

adapt them for the silk-screening process. The resultant dress-fabrics – wool chiffon, silk chiffon, silk foulard and organza – were both in the original (largely subdued and earthy) shades and in a bright new palette. The 'Lotus' collection was launched in 1960, with swirling turn-of-the-century florals by Harry Napper and J. Scarratt Rigby; it was an immediate success with many of the world's top couturiers. A host of exciting collaborative efforts between premier fashion designers and Liberty's continued for a whole decade, encompassing Art Deco-style, updated paisley, exotic Indian and Islamic, peasant, ethnic and other fabric designs unveiled each year by Liberty's. From London to Paris, and from Rome to New York, designers both established and fledgling adapted Liberty fabrics to their tastes: Tuffin & Foale, Jean Muir, Mary Quant, Victor Stiebel, Bill Blass, Halston, Arnold Scassi, Cacharel, Daniel Hechter and Yves Saint Laurent.

Arnold Scassi, promoted as 'one of young America's most avant-garde designers', photographed with a model wearing his Liberty dress in 1961; the fabric pattern was inspired by the Art Nouveau period, but the design of the dress was bold and ultra-modern.

Two dress fabrics from the 'Lotus' range: Harry Napper's c. 1900 'Aubrena' (above), a printed silk chiffon, and an untitled design (above right), *possibly by J. Scarratt Rigby.*

Close on the heels of the Art Nouveau Revival was the resurgence of interest in Art Deco. Actually, there were two stages of the Art Deco Revival in terms of Liberty fabrics, the first appearing in 1961 in the guise of Martin Battersby's six dress fabrics in the 'Bakst/Poiret' range, inspired by the costumes and sets of the Ballets Russes (Diaghilev's company itself being a forerunner to the original Deco style) and the costumes of couturier Paul Poiret. Battersby also looked to the later coloured *pochoirs* (fashion plates) of George Barbier and Georges Lepape for his inspiration, and the resultant fabrics were likewise used by top couturiers.

The second (and better-known) stage of Art Deco-inspired fabrics did not occur until the second half of the sixties, under the guiding hand of Bernard Nevill, who was named colour design consultant and fabric designer upon William Poole's departure to the United States in 1962. First produced were his 'Verve' (1963) and tiny paisley 'Cravat' (1964) ranges, followed by the exotic 'Islamic' and 'Scheherazade' (both 1965). Then came the tour-de-force, the Deco-inspired 'Jazz' and 'Tango', 1965–67, coinciding with the 1966 Paris exhibition, 'Les Années "25"'. These were

Martin Battersby's 'Bakst/Poiret' designs of 1961 (above), *such as this pattern with stylized blossoms, were early examples of the Art Deco Revival.*

followed by the formalized 'Landscape' in 1968, another distinct nod to the bygone decade (termed 'Bo Peep arcadia' by *Vogue*). His work continued with the Klimt-inspired, experimental 'Sequins' range and the part-classical, part-psychedelic 'Renaissance' in 1969 and culminated in the brazenly geometric 'Chameleon' of 1970 (Nevill's last range for Liberty's before he left in 1971).

Nevill's influences were eclectic and at times highly esoteric, from Britain's Omega Workshops and Vorticism, to Islamic tiles and Indian paisleys, to the set designs of Erté and the paintings of Gustav Klimt, to the English country garden and the skyscrapers of Manhattan. But he also acknowledged the spirit of the time in which he was living, updating many of the traditional motifs he borrowed by enlivening them with electric hues or energizing them with exaggerated swirls.

This late nineteen-sixties photograph (right) *shows models wearing dresses in various Liberty fabrics, including Bernard Nevill's 1969 'Landscape' range, whose stylized-landscape patterns* (opposite above and below) *were evocative of the Art Deco period; comprising horizontal patterns of conventionalized landscapes, the designer himself considered them 'a retreat into artificiality'.*

Textiles

AS IN PREVIOUS DECADES, in the fifties and sixties Liberty's continued to play a familiar world-wide role in the commissioning and retailing of contemporary textiles, including furnishing and dress fabrics and, to a lesser extent, floor coverings. Indeed, Liberty's acknowledged the singular importance of this aspect of their empire in the setting up of a powerful Advisory Design Committee in the early nineteen-fifties to concern itself with Liberty fabrics, and to ensure their success in domestic and foreign markets. No doubt the firm was well aware of the fact that the market had become highly competitive. But it did not need to worry too much about at least one overseas market: American customers spent hundreds of thousand of dollars a year on Liberty goods, and the more traditional the styles and patterns (such as the 'Peacock', 'Peony' and 'Pheasant' cretonnes), the more successful they were. For, during that decade, in terms of originality and innovation, Liberty's were at the international forefront once again, with the revival of its Art Nouveau-period patterns and the subsequent foray into Art Deco-style designs.

Throughout the fifties and sixties, however, traditional furnishing and fashion fabrics in cotton, silk, wool and linen continued to be produced in great numbers and successfully sold by Liberty's to a great many of its customers. These included the likes of Victorian florals and bird-and-berry designs, some of them authentic period patterns and others contemporary

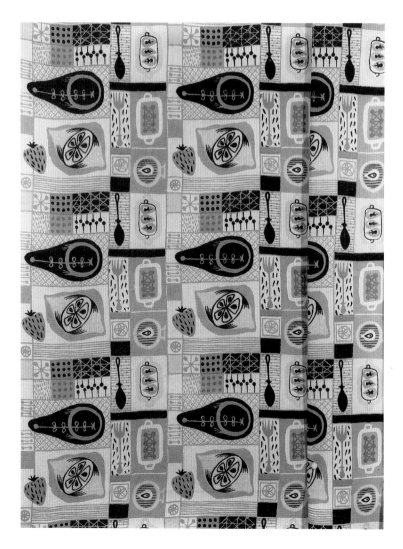

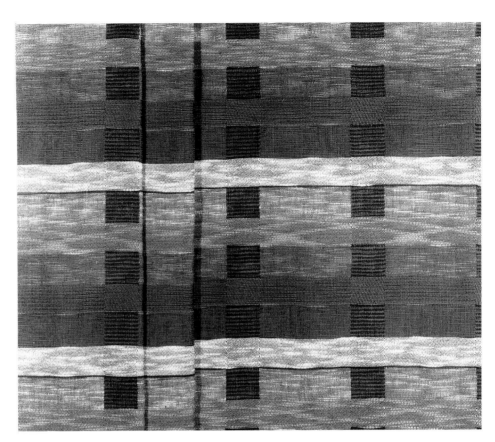

The Swiss-born, Bauhaus-influenced weaver Marianne Straub, who also designed extensively for industry, created 'Aleppo' (right) for Liberty's in 1954; this Jacquard furnishing fabric in cotton wool and spun rayon was woven by Warner & Sons Ltd and featured textured stripes in black, brown, white and dull red. Straub's all-too-often anonymous designs had a great influence on the texture of modern woven fabrics and are considered classics of the nineteen-fifties and sixties.

Robert Stewart designed 'Fruit Delight' (opposite left), a hand-block printed furnishing fabric, in 1952; its fruit and cutlery pattern, punctuated with quasi-scientific ball-and-rod motifs (inspired by atoms and crystal structures), is a typical bold fifties pattern, and the vivid red, bottle green and yellow hues, coupled with grey and set on a white ground, is a palette often found in the period.

The delicate pattern of Colleen Farr's 'Bamboo' (opposite right), a screen-printed cotton furnishing fabric from 1954, is subtly rendered in two shades of yellow, tan and charcoal grey, all on a white ground.

creations in a traditional style, as well as the popular 'Tana Lawn', the so-called 'little floral' dress fabric which originated in the nineteen-thirties.

Alongside such traditional designs were vibrant, often vividly hued contemporary patterns. Many of these modern delights were sold as anonymous 'in-house' designs, but others were created by well-known independent designers and duly acknowledged. Among the notable figures employed were Lucienne Day, Hilda Durkin, Jacqueline Groag, Anthony Levett-Prinsep, Althea McNish, Robert Stewart (who also created ceramics) and Marianne Straub. Their myriad creations ranged from typical fifties patterns characterized by geometric forms, incorporating stylized fruit and parabolic shapes, to more timeless, generally floral designs, such as an allover pattern of fern leaves in several two-colour combinations on a white ground dating from 1952; others in this category include 'Cineraria', Pat Albeck's 1954 screen-printed cotton furnishing fabric with red, pink and grey-blue flowers on a pale blue ground, Colleen Farr's 'Bamboo', another screen-printed cotton in two shades of yellow, tan and charcoal grey on white, and Althea McNish's 'Bousada', a late nineteen-fifties dress cotton featuring sketchy shocking pink blossoms with red pistils on a blue ground.

Fifties furnishing fabrics ran the gamut of hues, ranging from pale shades of grey, faun, taupe and various pastels, to bold reds, oranges, yellows and greens. Their designs, too, varied widely, but generally were as daring and vivid as many of their colours. 'Fruit Delight', Robert

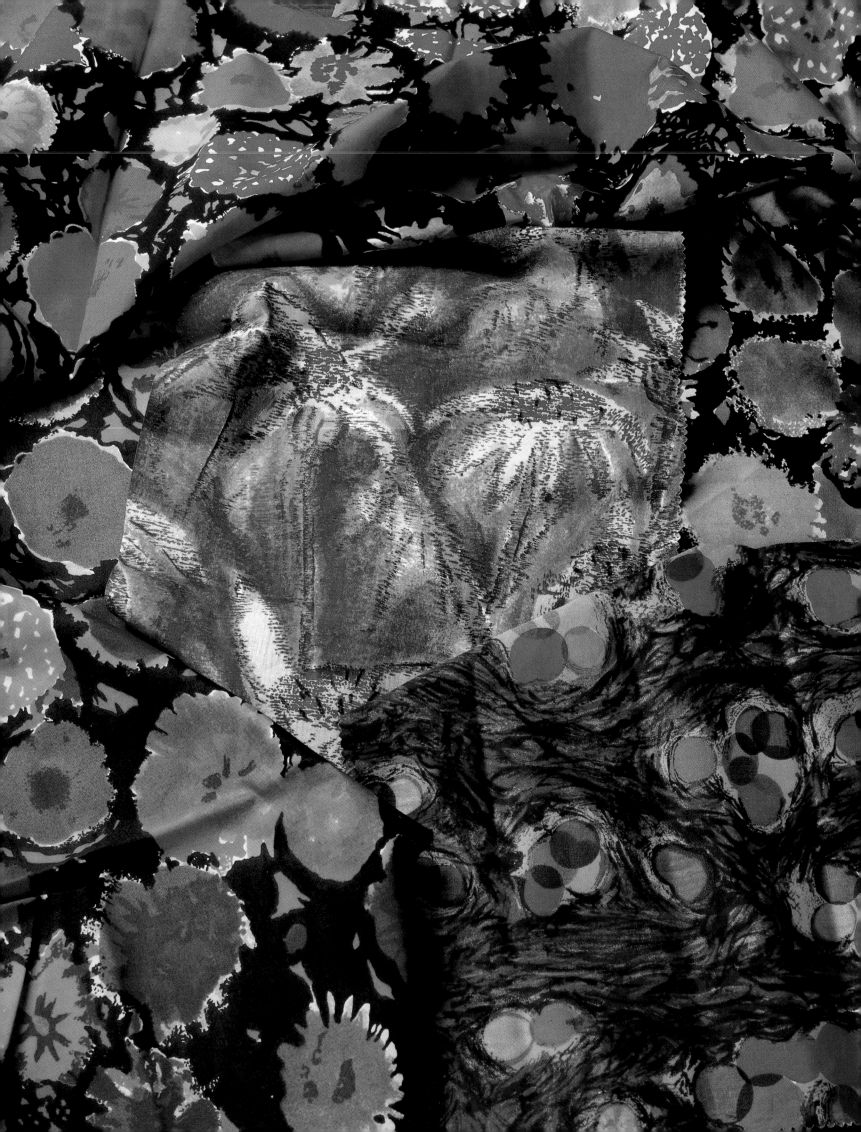

Previous double-page A selection of textile designs by Althea McNish (left): 'Bousada', 1958 (centre), 'Cascade', 1959 (upper left) and 'Midsummer', 1960 (upper right). Designs on 'Lotus' cloth (page 183) from the early nineteen-sixties (above): 'Osiris' (right) and two designs from the 'Bakst/Poiret' range by Martin Battersby (left and centre). Samples of dress fabric designs (below) by Bernard Nevill from the 'Jazz' (1965), and 'Tango' (1967), ranges.

Stewart's 1952 hand-blocked-printed linen, lived up to its name and was enough to enliven any kitchen with its busy pattern of fruit, cutlery and dishes combined with such modern motifs as the ubiquitous 'molecular' ball-and-rod (though here it might well represent a clove!); its colours, too, were bright and cheerful: bottle-green, red, yellow and grey on a white ground. Lucienne Day's 1954 linen 'Fritillary', screen-printed in almost exactly the same palette as Stewart's design, mingled horizontal rows of stylized butterflies with abstract, triangular-based shapes. Jacqueline Groag's 1954 'Books', another screen-printed linen, depicted tiers of simply rendered shelved volumes in cool shades of blue, black and grey on a pale blue ground, while Anthony Levett-Prinsep's 1956 'Denarii', a screen-printed cotton, could be a nod to Fornasetti with its overall pattern of sand and blue ancient coins on a dark blue and mottled white ground.

New patterns were introduced every season by Liberty's, some of them experiencing great success with customers. Several designs were ear-marked 'Young Liberty' and sold in the shop's eponymous department, which had been set up in 1949. One such furnishing fabric was Hilda Durkin's 1955 'Kon-Tiki', with its somewhat mysterious multi-coloured abstract design (perhaps representing rafts akin to Thor Heyerdahl's *Kon-Tiki*, which had sailed the Pacific some eight years earlier) roller-printed on a lilac ground. Equally appealing for its primeval qualities was Martin Bradley's brightly-hued 'Tampico', a screen-printed cotton furnishing fabric of the same year: black and orange on a jade green ground, it was awash with fetishistic objects and tiny equestrian figures.

Two screen-printed linen designs of 1954: 'Fritillary' by Lucienne Day (below left) and 'Books' by Jacqueline Groag (below right).

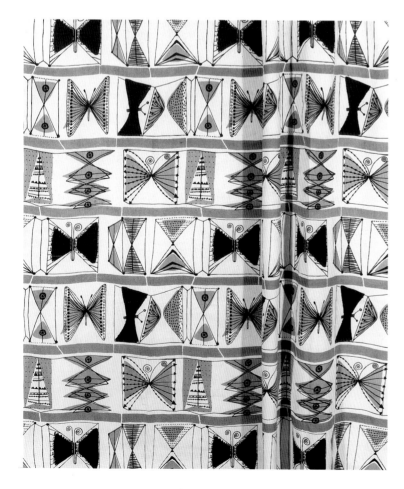

The export of 'Tana Lawn' fabrics was widespread, as this 1960 Liberty window shows (right)*: this perennial favourite, comprising dense 'little floral' patterns, originated in the nineteen-thirties and was updated in the nineteen-sixties by Blair Pride; its early wearers included the young princesses Elizabeth and Margaret, and in its later incarnations it was popular with the chic French design houses of Cacharel and Daniel Hechter.*

Bernard Nevill's designs were not the only ones being produced in great numbers by Liberty's in the sixties, though indeed they received the loudest praise. As in other decades, designers both established and youthful, credited and anonymous, created traditional and contemporary furnishing and dress fabrics for the House of Liberty. One of them was Blair Pride, who updated the 'Tana Lawn' dress fabric in around 1960 and was, in the words of Bernard Nevill's successor, Susan Collier, 'the holder of the Liberty conscience' (until his untimely death in 1971). There was also Althea McNish, already active in the nineteen-fifties, whose bright and breezy big florals, such as 'Akarana' (c. 1961) (a hand-printed cotton-satin available with orange, purple or lemon poppies), provided a nice contrast to 'Tana Lawn' with its tiny blossoms, trees and garlands combined together in dense patterns. Not so the brazenly coloured 'Auleika' (c. 1967), a screenprint on plain cotton; this featured a conventionalized floral design very much in the modern mode.

A highly conventional, yet brand-new furnishing fabric collection, called 'Mace', was unveiled in 1966; available in chintz and linen, it was based on original designs found on Dutch, English and French marquetry furniture of the seventeenth century. Another traditional pattern appeared in 1963–64 as well: 'Paradise', a glazed cotton American screenprint with an exotic bird, berry and leaf motif. It is interesting to note that the origin of non-British, exclusive-to-Liberty fabrics was now being acknowledged by Liberty's, meaning the firm was having textiles custom-made in other countries, including France and the United States.

The Liberty Scarf

The range of Liberty scarves was further extended in the nineteen-fifties and nineteen-sixties; this selection (opposite) is mainly by Robert Stewart, one of the few Liberty designers to sign his own work alongside that of the company.

Robert Stewart designed the bold 'Moon' scarf (below) for Liberty's c. 1954. The printed silk square featured a mask in shocking pink, blue, black and purple on an orange ground (a 'Sun' scarf was also created at the same time). Liberty scarves, longtime favourite items with faithful customers, kept abreast of the times, as this abstract, painterly design in the most vivid of hues shows.

NO DISCUSSION of Liberty textiles of any period could be complete without a mention of the Liberty scarf, described in a 1960 brochure as 'Legendary beauty ... captured in a few square inches'. Indeed, the Liberty scarf was – and still is – a fashion institution which has been known, and sold, in numerous countries for decades. As with furnishing and dress fabrics, the nineteen-fifties and nineteen-sixties Liberty scarf, usually a hand-printed silk square but also made of wool and chiffon and sometimes even rectangular-shaped, took on a variety of traditional and contemporary guises.

Numerous and diverse as well were the breezy seasonal brochures which sang the praises of the Liberty scarf. Many nineteen-fifties versions were of the concertina type, with tall, vertical motifs simply drawn on both sides in black and white, notably an Egyptian obelisk, London's Wellington Monument, the tree in the Garden of Eden, a giraffe's neck – all cheery cartoon images around which an array of full-colour scarves (photographs, not drawings) were tied. In the nineteen-sixties the brochures became more sophisticated and often featured head shots of real models wearing the brightly coloured scarves. A few lines were invariably appended to all the brochures on the tradition, timelessness and beauty of the Liberty scarf – one even emphasized their appeal to collectors. Earlier brochures were generally straightforward in terms of describing the scarves, but later ones waxed rhapsodically on their appeal, describing the hues in which they were available: 'Scylla' blue, 'Tuscan' gold, lettuce green, peat brown and, of course, shocking pink. A 1956 scarf brochure bestowed Christian (and some non-Christian) names on all the scarves (from 'Agneta' and 'Gisella' to 'Kyle' and 'Omar'), but this habit seems not to have continued, with the scarves' appellations usually consisting of a mix of Christian names, place names, flower types, simple descriptions (such as 'Sun' or 'Kites') and abstract words like 'Hoopla', 'Inspiration' and 'Magic'.

A scarf brochure c. 1960 described the various motifs depicted on the scarves quite succinctly, taking in their wide range of images: 'Neat geometry, lavish flowers, bizarre modern abstracts, demure Victoriana, Art Nouveau, romantic scenes'. To that list could be added a gamut of paisleys, as well as hunting scenes, smiling suns, 'little florals', Neoclassical subjects, magical landscapes and even city scenes. Throughout the years the colours and colour combinations both went with the tide of fashion (subdued pastel hues with occasional shocks of colour in the nineteen-fifties; fluorescent pinks, blues, yellows and greens in the sixties) and against it (plain pastel or earth-tone combinations).

There were even designer scarves in the nineteen-fifties and nineteen-sixties – something taken for granted in more recent times, with Liberty's offering designs by Balmain and Givenchy. Not surprisingly, couturiers' names were the only ones to appear next to scarf designs, but Liberty scarves, like the fabrics, were also designed by in-house and free-lance designers, including familiar names such as Robert Stewart.

Furniture

Liberty's continued to offer an extensive range of traditional, reproduction furniture to its customers in the nineteen-fifties and nineteen-sixties. Indeed, such designs – of bed-, sitting-, dining- and even board-room suites, of individual chairs, tables, settees, sideboards, desks and so on – comprised the bulk of furniture sales. Examples of the many ranges available were shown in Liberty's antique and reproduction furniture department, which was refurbished and enlarged in 1969, though its inventory remained as it had for decades, featuring Tudor, Georgian, Regency, Victorian and other period-style furniture.

Numerous British manufacturers provided Liberty's with traditional, tasteful, impeccably crafted 'antique' furniture, including Titchmarsh and Goodwin, W. W. Harkins and Dickson of Ipswich (the Suffolk town was, according to a Titchmarsh and Goodwin brochure, 'the home of reproduction furniture'), as well as Mines and West Ltd. of High Wycombe, H. J. Berry and Sons Ltd. of Preston and Thomas F. Walker and Hawes and Murray of East London.

But to the House of Liberty 'tasteful' did not always have to go hand in hand with traditional English, and 'classical' did not always mean in the style of the eighteenth or nineteenth century. Numerous Liberty catalogues from the nineteen-fifties and early sixties illustrate a healthy blend of reproduction and modern English and contemporary Continental furniture. It is interesting to note, however, that in most of these nineteen-fifties and nineteen-sixties catalogues – just as in house publications of nearly a century earlier – individual designer's names are few and far between (this despite a 1975 Liberty press release which stated that, 'At the time of the Festival of Britain, Liberty's broke their habitual practice of not acknowledging the authorship of designs, and since this time, they publicise their artists').

Unless the designer was a well-known, respected, marketable or exclusive-to-Liberty entity (such as the Swede Stig Lindberg and the Italians Paolo Venini, Piero Fornasetti and Gio Ponti, the latter of whose designs were featured in a one-man show at Liberty in 1957), the name of the country was the only proper noun – and sometimes not even *that* was listed – preceding an object: 'Swedish chair with sea-grass seat', 'teak dining table from Denmark', 'Finnish breakfast cup'.

A clever brochure of the nineteen-fifties which opened in a concertina fashion to show on each side a long 'spread' of furniture and objects, featured a Danish settee-bed, a Fornasetti coffee table, a Scandinavian teak stacking chair, a Danish teak chair, a Chiavari chair (modelled on the Italian classic made in the eponymous Italian village) in the style of Ponti, a Robin Day chair with metal legs and 'nylon fur' upholstery, a nest of four Danish coffee tables and a bar stool with metal legs and wicker seat by Terence Conran. These were all illustrated cheek-by-jowl with reproduction pieces, including a plush Victorian settee, an eighteenth-century-style, hide-covered, winged chair, a Regency chair and a miniature yew

The 'Antelope' chair (above) was designed by Ernest Race for the Festival of Britain in 1951. Its creator, who had trained as an architect, stated that 'there is a Race chair for everyone', and Liberty stock books of the nineteen-fifties list a variety of Race rocking, swing and easy chairs.

tallboy, also in eighteenth-century style. As jarring as this combination of objects may sound, they nicely conjoined to present a handsome mélange of what Liberty's considered and pronounced to the public as good taste: nothing too loud, too ornate or too outrageous for its regular clientele. Indeed, with this and others of its brochures and catalogues, Liberty's were making it acceptable to blend periods in an interior: a bit of Georgian here, some contemporary Scandinavian there, a smattering of modern fabrics used as coverings for furniture and pillows.

This tasteful blending of the old-new and new-new aside, of greatest interest is the contemporary British, Scandinavian and Continental furniture that was offered by Liberty's to customers in the modern furniture department. For it was with so many of these pieces, by such designers as Jacobsen, Day, Fornasetti, Ponti and others, that the House of Liberty exerted its influence as a tastemaker.

A surprisingly large number of British firms provided furniture in the contemporary taste to Liberty's in the post-war decades. These included Race Furniture, Morris of Glasgow, H.K. Furniture, S. Hille & Co., William Plunkett, R.S. Stevens, Peter Brunn Workshop, Terence Conran, the relatively long-established Gordon Russell, Parker Knoll, O.M.K. Design and Finmar.

The London firm of Ernest Race Ltd (later Race Furniture) was co-founded in 1945 by Ernest Race, who had trained as an architect, and a tool-and-die maker, both of whom wanted to produce furniture along modern engineering principles. Race's 1945 cast-aluminium 'BA' chair, intended to be produced from salvaged aircraft wreckage, is a modern British classic (it won a Gold Medal at the 1954 Milan Triennale). But Race's company also made more conventional pieces; one advertisement from the early nineteen-fifties claimed 'there is a Race chair for everyone'. Race rocking chairs, upholstered settees, wing and easy chairs all

A 1957 exhibition of the work of Gio Ponti featured a window display by the talented Italian designer: his slim and elegant classic, the 'Superleggera' chair (designed in 1955, made by Cassina from 1957 and sold by Liberty's) can be seen at left in the photograph, along with an assortment of metal and ceramic objects.

Ernest Race's 'BA' chair (below), *designed in 1945 and originally intended to be made from aluminium salvaged from aeroplane wrecks, has become a British design classic.*

appeared in Liberty's stock books in the nineteen-fifties. Liberty's also sold Race's thoroughly modern 'Antelope' chair, comprising a painted steel-rod frame and plywood seat, which was first produced as an outdoor chair for the 1951 Festival of Britain.

H.K. Furniture, much of whose output was created by its founder Howard B. Keith, produced seating furniture sold by Liberty's. Though their names were somewhat exotic – such as the 'Aruna' and 'Simplon' settees and the 'Calypso', 'Comet' and 'Intruder' chairs – their shapes were basic and unremarkable. Indeed, their main attraction seemed to be their comfortable upholstery, which would easily fit in with any décor.

S. Hille & Co. Ltd., located in Chigwell, Essex, benefited for many years from the talents of Robin Day who, during his long association with the company, designed a wide range of seating and case furniture, including many pieces which were sold by Liberty's. Moulded plywood and steel frames were used in many of Day's chairs for Hille, while his handsome veneered cabinets (simple rectangular units from the Hilleplan range) were as fine as any Scandinavian designs. Especially handsome were Day's stacking chairs of ebonized beech and a natural beech table with a top of black Warerite (a synthetic material similar to Formica), which featured in a Liberty interior reproduced in the 1955–56 edition of *Decorative Art, The Studio Year Book of Furnishing & Decoration*. Also available were Hille's plush 'Telesettee' and 'Telechairs', obviously intended to appeal to the owners of Britain's first television sets.

The name of Terence Conran appears frequently as a supplier in Liberty's stock book in the fifties and sixties. Indeed, before opening his own retail store, Habitat, in 1964, the young Conran sold furniture of his own design and of others, including Gio Ponti, and designs such as the 'Tripolina' chair, the ubiquitous classic also known as the 'Butterfly' chair, through

Two Liberty-furnished living rooms of the nineteen-fifties, both illustrated in the English design annual, Decorative Art, The Studio Year Book of Furnishing & Decoration, *exude a no-nonsense yet inviting warmth with their light-hued furniture, organic forms and cheerful fabrics. In the 1951–52 interior (opposite left), the natural birch wall desk is from Finmar Ltd., the Windsor armchair is by The Furniture Industries Ltd., the upholstered chair was designed by Howard B. Keith and made by H.K. Furniture Ltd., and the Chilean rauli and birch tray-top table was by Ronald Harford and Henry Long. The 1955– 56 living room (opposite right) has cork flooring, upholstered chairs by H.K. Furniture, and ebonized beech stacking chairs and a natural beech table with black Warerite top by Robin Day; the 'Macrahanih' draperies at left were designed by Robert Stewart, while the 'Philodendron' curtains at right were created by Helen Close.*

Finnish architect Alvar Aalto's bent plywood chairs (above right), which epitomized Organic Modern Scandinavian furniture of the nineteen-fifties, were provided to Liberty's by the London-based company Finmar; the dining room table was originally designed by Finmar in 1933–5 and the stacking chairs by Alvar Aalto in 1929 (below).

Liberty's and other established outlets. Although this method of selling was later deemed a failure (in part precipitating the opening of Habitat), it nonetheless made the public aware of the young designer, for his name was one of the few credited individually in Liberty catalogues (for instance, for the sleek cane-seated, black-metal-legged bar stool mentioned above).

Since the thirties, the London-based company Finmar had supplied Finnish bent plywood furniture, notably to the designs of Alvar Aalto, to the English market. Through Liberty's (and other outlets) it provided nineteen-fifties Britain with sleek, handsome Scandinavian tables and

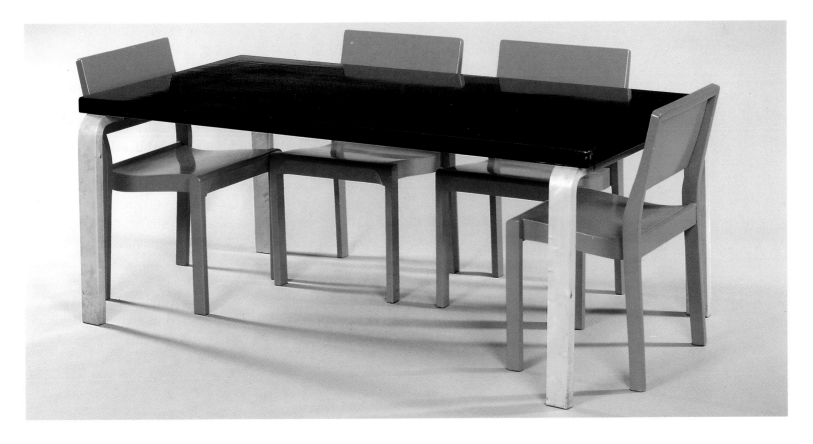

Liberty

Liberty's live up to their reputation for matchless quality and design with their contemporary collection of price-controlled English, Scottish and Scandinavian furniture . . . Swedish glass . . . modern light fittings . . . and their own Liberty-designed occasional pieces and hand-printed furnishing fabrics.

of Regent Street

This advertisement for nineteen-fifties furniture and objects offered by Liberty's appeared in the 1951–52 issue of Decorative Art, The Studio Year Book of Furnishing & Decoration.

chairs of teak, beech and maple, as well as plywood, mostly marketed under its own name (not that of the designer). It also sold some domestic furniture and, like Hille, made concessions to the dawning age of television, with its 'Tee Vee' chairs.

Liberty's also commissioned individuals to create exclusive furniture designs for the shop, which were marketed under the Liberty name. Two of the most striking, quintessentially nineteen-fifties designs were the twelve-inch-high 'Boomerang' table and the 'Nimbus' table. The former, designed by A. M. Lewis, was available in oak, walnut and mahogany, and comprised a boomerang-shaped top on three legs, which could snugly fit around a chair or settee corner. The 'Nimbus' coffee table, designed by Lewis and K. McAvoy, had a symmetrical four-cornered cloud shape and, as illustrated in the 1952–53 *Studio Year Book*, came equipped with four of its own 'Boomerang' tables, which could neatly be stored under the 'cloud'.

The gently curving or unseverely rectilinear chairs, settees, tables and other furniture designed and made in Denmark, Finland and Sweden from the nineteen-fifties were logical successors to the 'Scandinavian Modern' pieces first marketed in the nineteen-thirties. Indeed, several designers from the earlier period, such as Bruno Matthson and Alvar Aalto, continued to create classic furniture in the post-war period. Liberty's singled out Aalto's designs by featuring them in a special exhibition in the store in the early nineteen-fifties.

Handsome yet practical, comfortable without being overstuffed, innovative in its materials, method of manufacture and lack of decoration, this Scandinavian furniture held an immense appeal to the young families of the post-war period, who wanted both to assert their own uncomplicated, relatively streamlined tastes and break with the overdecorated, hand-me-down furniture most of them had grown up with, either in the form of authentic antiques or faithful reproductions.

Besides Matthson and Aalto, two other Scandinavian designers whose furniture was sold by Liberty's were the Danes Arne Jacobsen and Finn Juhl. The former, an architect, created handsome, often stackable plywood and steel seating furniture, as well as extremely comfortable cushioned chairs, such as the 'Egg' and 'Swan', both from 1957 which enveloped the sitter in their upholstered foam-rubber seats and arms. The '3107' chair, also from 1957, was made by Fritz Hansen's Danish company and sold by Liberty's. Its chromium-plated, steel-tube frame supported a sleek seat and back of moulded teak-veneer plywood. Like much furniture design of the day, the chair was both ergonomically correct in the way that it properly supported the body and aesthetically pleasing, its nicely curving back resembling a smooth-edged fishtail poised above the waterline before submerging.

Less overtly functional and more sculptural were the finely crafted furniture pieces designed by Finn Juhl, who favoured such woods as teak

Finmar Ltd., the London-based company which imported Finnish, Danish and other Scandinavian furniture and objects, provided a multitude of tables and chairs to Liberty's; illustrated here is the Arne Jacobsen section of a 1959 Finmar exhibition at the shop, featuring furniture, cutlery, ceramics and glass; note the Danish designer's swivel-seated, womb-like 'Egg' chair of 1957, made by Fritz Hansen.

and maple – alone or in combination – and leather upholstery (some of his seats seemed to 'levitate', though in reality they were suspended on the chair's crossbars). From the late nineteen-thirties through the nineteen-forties many of Juhl's creations were hand-crafted. But by the nineteen-fifties, when Liberty's and other retailers began to sell Juhl's designs, they were mass-produced by several firms in Europe and the United States. In autumn 1957, Liberty's presented an exhibition of Scandinavian design arranged by Finmar, which featured not only furniture by Juhl and Jacobsen, but also the Danish metal- and woodworker Kay Bojesen and the Finnish glass artists Tapio Wirkkala and Kaj Franck. A Liberty publication of the period praised the objects on display for their 'elegant Scandinavian simplicity' and for 'finding their beauty solely in their clean lines and fine materials'.

The House of Liberty showed considerable prescience and taste when it took note of and began to market contemporary Italian furniture in the nineteen-fifties. The creations of two of the most significant Italian furniture designers of the day, Gio Ponti and Piero Fornasetti, were sold from that decade. The creations of the other Italian notables, including Vico Magistretti, were also marketed (though not always properly credited to their designers) by the firm.

Besides having his designs regularly sold at the emporium, Gio Ponti, architect, designer, writer and publisher (of the Italian periodical *Domus*), was honoured with a one-man exhibition at Liberty's in spring 1957. Not only was there furniture on display, but also paintings, ceramics, glass, rugs and metalwork. Arguably the best-known Ponti classic offered by Liberty's was his 'Superleggera' ('Superlight') 699 chair, designed around 1955 and manufactured from 1957 by Cassina of Milan. Based on a traditional chair type made in Chiavari, Italy, the 'Superleggera' was available in a variety of materials: the body could be ash, rosewood, walnut or black- or white-lacquered wood, the seat could be woven cane, plaited cellophane or fabric-, vinyl- or leather-covered rubber. Other Ponti furniture sold by Liberty's included a simple, angular desk (shown accompanying the 'Superleggera' chair in a Liberty window of Ponti's own design) and a smart low, round table with a metal top.

Piero Fornasetti was a designer remarkable for both his prolific output (including furniture, ceramics and metalwork) and for his distinctive style, a striking vision – part Neoclassical, part Surrealist – which, remarkably, characterized his massive *oeuvre* for some four decades. His aim was to make everyday objects of a high artistic level, but at a moderate price, using contemporary materials and manufacturing techniques. Fornasetti himself said, 'For an object to be useful is not enough. Each object should have a kind of poetry. The object's true value lies in its spirit'.

Fornasetti's spirit was most strikingly evident in his huge screens and cabinets, many of them *trompe l'oeil* tour-de-forces drawing on the design of classical buildings (intact or in ruins), Renaissance landscapes, cities (not houses) of cards and other lofty subjects. His smaller furnishings, too, such as umbrella stands, magazine racks and wastepaper baskets, which Liberty's sold in large numbers, were covered with classic Fornasetti images, like the row of black umbrellas and riding crops against a bright red ground adorning a cylindrical umbrella stand. Liberty's also sold a simple rectangular coffee table by Fornasetti; covered all over with a design of old coins, a popular motif of the designer which appeared as well on ashtrays and other objects, it retailed for a hefty £50 in the nineteen-fifties (in comparison, a set of four nesting teak tables from Denmark cost £19).

The creations of the Italian architect, urban planner and furniture designer Vico Magistretti were also offered by Liberty's. His 'Carimate' chair of *c.* 1959, originally designed for the eponymous Italian golf club, was illustrated in an early nineteen-sixties catalogue. Made from 1963 by Cassina (who called it simply 'Armchair 892'), the beechwood chair was available with walnut or natural stain, or with a red or white glossy finish; its seat could be made of woven grass, cane or leather. The Liberty catalogue pictured the red, cane-seated version, describing it simply as 'Chair from the real Italian countryside, lacquered red with rush seat'. As with so much other furniture, the designer remained anonymous, though the chair's country of origin is mentioned.

A cupboard by Piero Fornasetti (opposite) in his familiar whimsical style; this piece, which dates from c. 1955, is typical of the larger furniture produced by the Milan designer. The relationship between Liberty's and Fornasetti still continues.

Ceramics

THE MYRIAD ceramics sold at Liberty's in the nineteen-fifties and sixties fell into one of three categories: mass-produced utilitarian tableware (porcelain and earthenware available in either contemporary designs or traditional, mainly English patterns); innovative studio pottery, emanating largely from English and Italian kilns; and decorative, mostly mass-produced objects, from Fornasetti ashtrays and Wedgwood floral-motif cigarette boxes to 'Portuguese swans' and Porcelaine de Paris Marmite jars!

Liberty's offered a wide range of British ceramics, from one-off examples of studio pottery to mass-manufactured tableware. The studio potter Bernard Leach was heavily promoted by the shop, not only by being singled out for a one-man exhibition there but even somewhat more mundanely by featuring in the store catalogues. A 1956 edition illustrated a two-pint Bernard Leach casserole for 16s.9d. (17s.5d. with handle) and another fifties publication illustrated a pottery bowl, 9 inches in diameter, by Leach (for 16s.9d.); a 1961 Christmas catalogue offered individual casseroles at 10s. each. Likewise, Liberty's sold works by the German-born potter Lucie Rie, who had arrived in Britain as a refugee in 1938; a stoneware bowl of hers was pictured (and credited to her) in a 1960 Christmas catalogue.

Liberty's carried the output of several larger potteries as well, including piggy banks, figurines, painted dishes and sweet dishes by the Chelsea, Guernsey and Rye potteries. There were also stoneware coffee and spice jars and handsome tiles designed by Robert Stewart (who also provided Liberty's with fabric designs). Assorted decorative objects, such as chic pink-and-black candleholders and plates decorated with Edwardian couples, came from Foley China in Staffordshire.

This lemonade set, comprising a jug with matching mugs, was designed by Richard Guyatt and made for Liberty's by Wedgwood & Sons Ltd., c. 1953. Wedgwood designer Guyatt received the commission from Arthur Stewart-Liberty, and his brief was to depict views of old London churches. The result was this set, made of white earthenware and transfer-printed and colour-washed with the nursery rhyme 'Oranges and Lemons'.

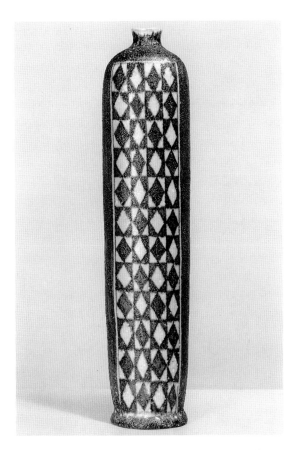

Among the many studio artists whose work was sold by Liberty's in the nineteen-fifties was Guido Gambone, who created this earthenware vase c. 1954 (above). The Italian's studio pottery was among his country's most expressive fifties creations, and featured whimsical animals as well as painterly motifs that could be either geometric, organic or abstract.

Giovanni Gariboldi, the artistic director of the Società Ceramica Richard-Ginori of Milan, designed this elegant, etiolated porcelain coffee service in 1955 (right); its white body was simply decorated with narrow bands of grey and gilt.

However, it was the long-established factory names which dominated the inventory of English porcelain and ceramics sold at Liberty's. Wedgwood, Royal Doulton, John Aynsley, Spode-Copeland, Royal Staffordshire and Royal Worcester, among others, provided dinnerware, tea and coffee services, and decorative objects to the shop, in traditional as well as contemporary patterns. In addition to the classic, fairly conservative designs, there was Wedgwood's white earthenware transfer-printed and colour-washed 'Oranges and Lemons' lemonade set of *c.* 1953, designed by Richard Guyatt. Guyatt received this commission from Arthur Stewart-Liberty, then chairman of the store, who requested a beaker and jug whose motifs would include views of old London churches.

Fine contemporary Italian porcelain was sold at Liberty's, such as elegant (largely undecorated) soft-hued coffee and tea services designed by Giovanni Gariboldi and made by Società Ceramica Richard-Ginori of Milan (for whom Gariboldi was Artistic Director). But the firm was more daring, inventive and prescient in promoting ceramics designed by Piero Fornasetti and studio pottery by some of the country's foremost talents, including Marcello Fantoni, Guido Gambone, Fausto Melotti and Urbano Zaccagnini of Ceramiche Zaccagnini-Manifattura. Gambone's work perhaps best expressed the new spirit of the nineteen-fifties: strong painterly motifs – geometric, organic and abstract forms alike, as well as occasional flights of whimsy, such as a comical cow (his signature was in fact a donkey) – decorated, subtly curving, organic forms whose colourful glazes were largely prepared by Gambone himself. During the fifties he managed an autonomous department within the huge Cantagalli Manufactory in Florence, where he created one-off pieces as well as supervising the production of a number of series.

A major ceramics supplier to Liberty's has long been Rörstrand in Stockholm, a selection of whose fifties wares is seen here (above). Their popular 1956 'Picknick' range is represented here by a stoneware casserole and cheeseboard (below right).

The Finnish firm Arabia AB, part of Oy Wärtsilä AB since 1940, created fine porcelain that was exported widely throughout Europe. The 'Northern Lights' coffee service of 1956 (below) was created by Arabia's design department head, Kaj Franck.

Piero Fornasetti's largest output was arguably his ceramic production: myriad plates, platters, cups, ice buckets, ashtrays, figurines and other utilitarian and decorative pieces decorated with motifs from his vast Neoclassical-Surrealist repertoire. Among the pieces sold by Liberty's were an ice bucket decorated with hot-air balloons, ashtrays adorned with vintage-coin and chequerboard motifs, a set of six little 'cocktail dishes' featuring drinks recipes and a series of plates whose decoration (faces formed from fruits and vegetables) he borrowed from the paintings of the Milanese Mannerist Archimboldo.

The Rosenthal ceramics factory, founded in Selb, Bavaria, in 1879, produced fine porcelain in the fifties and sixties, including many artist-decorated pieces. Among its wares sold at Liberty's were whimsical organic-shaped ashtrays painted with cartoon fish. No doubt Rosenthal pieces, and those of other factories, were included in the mid-fifties exhibition of German furniture, sculpture, ceramics and fabrics organized by Liberty's as well.

Scandinavian ceramics, like those countries' furniture, was much admired and sought after in the post-war decades and Liberty's became a major promoter in Britain. Although neither the names of individual designers nor those of factories were publicized in the catalogues, the countries themselves were generally acknowledged, as in, for example, 'Swedish green cutting tile' or 'Finnish spice jar'. Three of the largest suppliers were the long-established Swedish firms, Rörstrand and Gustavsberg, and the Finnish company Arabia (the former were later to merge with Oy Wärtsilä AB, to which Arabia had belonged since 1940).

From the late nineteen-thirties Arabia AB led all of Europe in terms of sheer numbers of its porcelain output, which was overseen by design

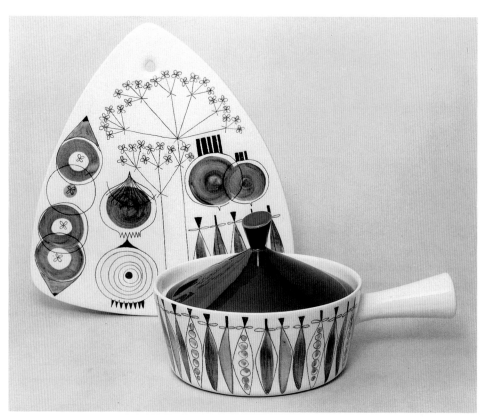

The 'Garden Implements' lemonade set c. 1938, by Eric Ravilious for Wedgwood, was produced in 'Queensware', printed in sepia and painted by hand in at least two coloured versions, pink lustre and green lustre. Liberty's sold it through the fifties.

department head, Kaj Franck, from 1945 to 1973. Not only were its utilitarian wares of high quality, but many of them showed as much inventiveness and contemporary good taste as Scandinavian furniture. From Franck's 'Northern Lights' porcelain coffee service of 1956, with a stylish geometric design, to the whimsical animal-decorated 'Zoo' child's mug and plate, created by Anja Juwrikkola in 1957, Arabia produced a wide variety of wares to please its international customers.

Likewise, Rörstrand and Gustavsberg produced many handsome pieces which catered to contemporary taste and were offered by Liberty's. These included ceramics such as Rörstrand's 'Picknick' range of oven- and tableware, designed in 1956 by Marianne Westman, which included casseroles, covered pots, cheeseboard, cutting boards, and cups and saucers, all awash with a jaunty motif of hand-painted vegetables on a white ground. Noted multi-media designer and teacher Stig Lindberg was associated with Gustavsberg from 1937 to 1957, and his earthenware, stoneware and bone china designs for the firm's tableware, vases and other pieces were especially elegant.

Glass

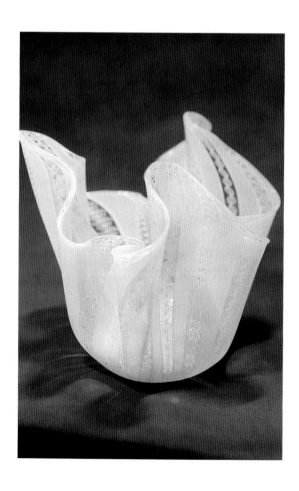

THE FIFTIES marked the start of an exciting era in glass design, with the Italian factories at Murano leading the way in terms of bright colours, new techniques and bold forms. Liberty's sold a great deal of the Italian wares, but it also offered handsome Scandinavian pieces, notably by Orrefors and Kosta Boda, and traditional modern pieces by established English, French and Dutch glass factories.

The Murano factory of Paolo Venini was especially heavily promoted by Liberty's: there was an exhibition devoted to its output in the nineteen-fifties, its name appeared frequently in virtually every Liberty catalogue of the period and some Venini creations became closely identified with the shop, such as the renowned, now-classic 'Handkerchief' vases, a pastel-coloured range of which featured (along with the name Liberty) in the 1954–55 *Studio Year Book*. In addition to these sculptural pieces, Liberty's also sold a great deal of utilitarian Venini glass, including vases, decanters, jars and bottles. For the more conservative customer, there were traditionally shaped vessels of grey, green, brown and clear glass, but for the more daring there were the 'Handkerchief' vases, which were in fact created by Fulvio Bianconi at Venini, and bottles in turquoise, yellow, pink and other vivid hues.

Although their names were not generally publicized in the catalogues, Liberty's also sold a great deal of Italian glass by other important makers. The stock book from the late fifties to the early sixties included Barview & Toso, Gino Cenedese, Nason & Moretti, Salviati & Co. and Archimede Seguso. These comprised a litany of esteemed Italian glass makers of the time who, like Venini, were both reviving traditional techniques and inventing new ones, imbuing so many of the resultant pieces with a distinctive, modern flavour.

The Swedish firms Orrefors and Kosta Boda, which had long been names to reckon with in terms of fine-quality, innovative Scandinavian glass, continued to produce outstanding utilitarian (and some purely sculptural) pieces which were sold by Liberty's during this period. A 1958 home-furnishing booklet, for instance, illustrated a chic (but uncredited) Boda bottle, its top 'sliced off' on the diagonal, its added spout like a beak; Liberty's called it a 'Swedish martini mixer', and sold it, along with eight glasses for £4.17s. A 14-inch-high teardrop-shaped Orrefors decanter, on the other hand, sold for a substantial £5.1s.

Glass, as well as other objects in other media designed by the talented Finn Tapio Wirkkala, was sold by Liberty's in the fifties and sixties. Wirk-kala designed for Iittala, the huge Finnish glass factory, as well as Venini in Murano, from 1959, and the German firm Rosenthal (which produced glass as well as ceramics). Additional Scandinavian glass sold by Liberty's included vases, bowls and other pieces by the Swedish factories Gullaskruf Glasbruk and Ströbergshyttan and the Norwegian Hadelands Glassverk.

Glass by Baccarat, Lalique and Daum was sold by Liberty's in the nineteen-fifties and nineteen-sixties, with the latter's modern art glass

much promoted. Contemporary Lalique designs, including Marc Lalique's fifties jardinières, 'Bermudes' and 'Champs-Elysées', were available, as were more 'traditional' designs of the nineteen-twenties and thirties created by Marc's father, René. These included the (empty) perfume bottle 'Clairfontaine' and the bookends 'Hirondelles' ('Swallows'), not to mention the hugely successful (but at the time uncredited) flacons containing the Worth scents 'Je Reviens' and 'Dans la Nuit'.

Traditional cut-glass forms reigned in terms of domestic products, with familiar names like Whitefriars, Brierley and Waterford heading the list of Liberty suppliers (actually, the latter Irish firm had only begun production of its wares in 1951 – the original Waterford Glass closed down a century earlier). Among the many types of traditional glass vessels offered by Liberty's were brandy balloons, claret glasses and of course vases. Modern domestic pieces included a footed vase sporting two 'uneven' handles. Credited to Constance Spry (a much-admired floral arranger and cookery writer of the time), the vase was offered in a late fifties Christmas catalogue for 13s.; the same publication featured Spry's highly sculptural 'Ice Island', designed for flower arrangements, but a fascinating work of abstract art in itself.

One-off 'Unica' glass created by the Royal Dutch Glass Works at Leerdam was sold at Liberty's, as well as non-limited-edition pieces, such as a fairly abstract, frosted-glass Madonna figure.

The Swedish glass firm, Orrefors, provided Liberty's with an assortment of utilitarian and art glass in the fifties and sixties, of which this c. 1948 engraved glass vase (above), *designed by Nils Landberg, is a fine example. Finmar, the London firm which imported Scandinavian objects and furniture, sponsored at least three annual design exhibitions at the emporium in the late fifties. This display of utilitarian glassware* (right) *is from the 1958 show. In the nineteen-fifties Liberty's began to sell innovative Italian glass, of which the 1954 'Handkerchief' vase* (opposite), *designed by Fulvio Bianconi at Venini, is now considered a classic. This particular example is in clear glass with white latticino decoration.*

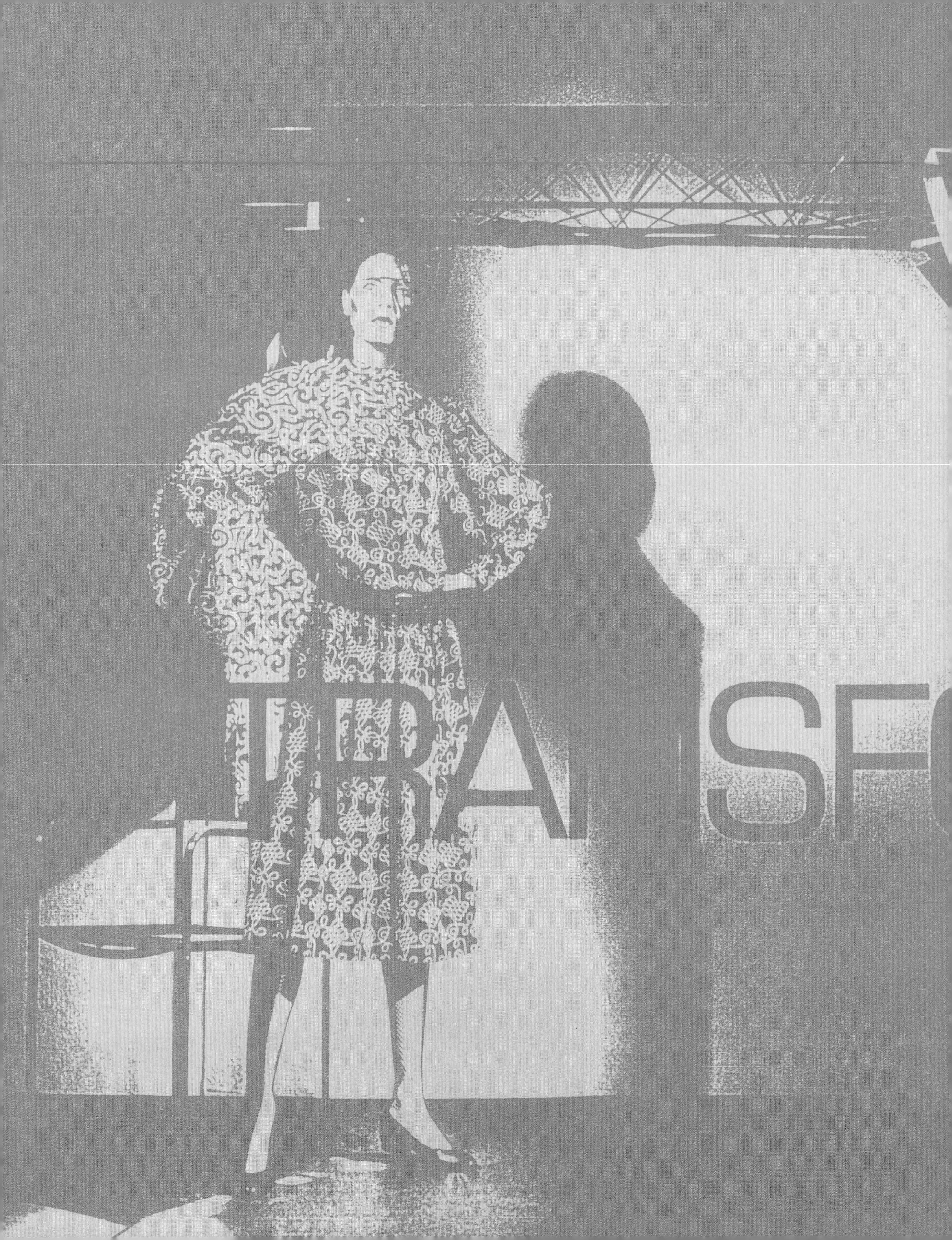

LIBERTY'S NOW

FAY SWEET

The New Internationalism

URING THE POST-WAR PERIOD and, in particular, in the last ten or fifteen years, we have witnessed a silent, but nonetheless far-reaching revolution in merchandising. Great shifts in the display and presentation of goods, in advertising and even in the very social patterns of shopping have brought about a profound alteration to the ways in which the trade, especially in luxury goods, is carried on. In the past two decades we have seen in Britain, America and Europe the demise of many of the great department stores of the earlier part of the century. Seen by many as dinosaurs, ill-fitted for the sudden ice ages and rapid thaws of the modern financial world, they have given way to other, often shorter-lived and certainly less stylish forms of retailing.

In the same way many older-established but smaller firms whose natural constituency lay in what has long been known as the 'carriage trade' have found it difficult to adapt to changing social patterns and to find their new place in the market. Of those older firms, both large and small, which have survived, the most successful have tended to be those who have held to the best of their own traditions, but presented them in a way which appeals to the customers of today.

One of the windows (opposite) *celebrating the 1975 Centenary Exhibition; this was a pivotal point in the shop's modern history, raising Liberty's distinctive, high-quality profile. This display incorporates a picture of suffragettes breaking the windows of the shop. The Liberty style is unmistakable and timeless* (right): *a sample of the 1984 autumn fashion collection in richly coloured 'Varuna' wool and 'Jubilee' fabrics, featuring the ever-popular paisley patterns and other motifs derived from Celtic ornament.*

Previous double-page A minimalist window designed by Paul Muller for 'The Year of Just Black and White', 1983–84.

Few shops on the scale of Liberty's have been able to avoid a dilution of their house style or to maintain so strong a sense of their own identity. Leaving others to be complacent in times of prosperity and panicky and gimmicky in leaner years, the House of Liberty has consistently demonstrated a certain calm. But this sense of poise and approachable grandeur has – and here lies a major reason for the firm's success – always been spiced by a touch of mystery and imagination, as befits an enterprise whose origins lay in the excitement and exoticism of the East.

Liberty's Now

A NY ACCOUNT of the shape of Liberty's now should perhaps begin in 1975, when the company commemorated one hundred years of trading. A large centenary exhibition was held at the Victoria and Albert Museum in South Kensington, together with celebrations in the Regent Street and Great Marlborough Street shops. Both venues displayed objects sold throughout the store's history, including many of the finest furniture, ceramics, metalwork and textiles commissioned during the Arts and Crafts and Art Nouveau period. There were vases and jars by William Moorcroft, fabrics by Walter Crane, Lewis Day, Arthur Silver, C. F. A. Voysey and Christopher Dresser, pewter and silverware by Archibald Knox and Bernard Cuzner, and furniture by Leonard Wyburd and E. G. Punnett. A centenary mug, designed by William Adams and made by Wedgwood, was produced for the exhibition. The pretty turquoise, terra-cotta and yellow bird-and-flower design was so popular that it still continues to be produced. A range of furniture was specially commissioned from John Makepeace, including a curious table which stood on feet in the form of horses' hooves and wall-cupboards with knot-shaped holes cut from the doors.

The retrospective exhibitions confirmed Liberty's outstanding place in the history of design and decoration during the past hundred years. They confirmed the strength of its past and also helped to crystallize ideas on the shop's future as an emporium of the finest goods from around the world. Plans were also made to revive the shop's pioneering role in commissioning the best of contemporary design, building on its success in recycling its magnificent design archive in the revivals of Art Nouveau and Art Deco.

Entering the latter quarter of the century, the shop has continued to enjoy a reputation for particular types of merchandise – glorious fabrics, either by the yard or made into scarves, ties, clothing, bags and countless gifts; high quality accessories – luggage, leather belts and gloves; and then there are the Persian rugs and Turkish kelims, the antiques, the toiletries,

and the great basement bazaar stuffed with all manner of pots and bowls and trinket boxes, silks, jewellery, small sculptures and paintings gathered from workshops around the globe. Regular visitors still know that Liberty's is an excellent hunting ground for unusual wallpapers, fine bed and table linens, contemporary furniture, entire modern kitchens and bathrooms, classic and contemporary crockery, cutlery and glassware and English crafts. In the summer of 1991 the stylish Japanese Muji store opened as an adjunct to the main Liberty shop, selling to the most fashion-conscious customer items such as clothing, bags, kitchenware and stationery.

One notable characteristic of Liberty's trading in the early seventies was the strengthening of traditional lines of Oriental goods. The Republic of China had just joined the United Nations and had begun to open up as a source of new and exciting merchandise. In 1974 Liberty's began to take delivery of some of the most superb textiles, items of furniture, ceramics, pieces of jewellery, antiques and paintings Britain had seen for decades. The objects, ancient and modern, ranged from modestly priced ceramic bowls to exquisite jade jewellery.

The re-establishment of the shop's trading links with the East has continued to exercise strong influence on retailing policy; for example, popular annual exhibitions of Chinese jewellery were held through the remainder of the nineteen-seventies, and important links with Japan have led to successful marketing there of Liberty goods and the opening of Muji.

At the same time as these developments in the retailing side of Liberty's were taking place, its creative design arm, Liberty of London Prints, was also undergoing profound changes. One of the most powerful influences on Liberty's fabric design during the decade was the design consultant Susan Collier. An admirer of such artists as Sonia Delaunay (who in the past had been commissioned to design Liberty fabrics), Matisse and the Fauves, Collier's approach to textile design was characterized by geometrical shapes combined in a distinctive, painterly style. She injected great freshness into the Liberty studio, based in an old laundry in Wandsworth in south-west London, and was responsible for producing between 300 and 400 new designs each year.

The early nineteen-seventies witnessed a great revival of interest in the designs of the nineteen-thirties; this was an ideal opportunity to celebrate the work of the Bauhaus designers and Collier produced the abstract, geometric, patchwork-like design called 'Bauhaus'. First produced in 1972, it challenged the public's preconceptions of Liberty fabrics and became an instant success. Old designs were also adapted and revived, including the geometric patterns created in the nineteen-twenties by Claud Lovat Fraser. Zigzags, chevrons, crosses and stripes in the boldest of primary colours all exploded on to Liberty's shelves alongside the traditional paisleys and floral prints. Japanese design was also reinterpreted as Liberty prints. With names such as 'Fuji', 'Koaoi' and 'Choki', these prints depicted

A Chinese charm necklace from the 'Chinese Jewellery' exhibition of 1979; Liberty's buyers were among the first to enter China when it reopened international trading in the nineteen-seventies.

stylized Japanese landscape, chrysanthemums and intricate, geometrical patterns. In the mid seventies the purchase of a printing plant in France unearthed a spectacular find when a parcel of original designs by Raoul Dufy was discovered. The designs were transformed by the studio in Wandsworth into the 1978 Dufy Collection of prints with such evocative names as 'Nuances', 'Hortensias' and 'Tulipes'.

Other departments of the company also found the seventies a time for reinvigoration. Rosalind Christie began commissioning exciting jewellery from designers such as Mick Milligan, Jacqueline Mina, Mario Saba and David Watkins, who subsequently became head of jewellery design at London's Royal College of Art. The jewellery department became one of the store's greatest strengths during the decade, even surpassing the revenue generated by the ever-popular scarves department.

However, the major opportunity for commissioning contemporary work came at the end of the decade with the opening of the One Off shop. After

'Geometric' textile design by Bernard Nevill, 1969, an indication of the increasingly wide range of patterns to be marketed by Liberty's during the seventies.

considerable remodelling of the London shop's interior, this new venture was opened in the basement. The space, resembling a gallery setting, was given over to the work of various craftsmen who would take part in a series of one-man and group exhibitions over the following decade. The potter Lucie Rie, who had previously sold many objects to Liberty's, staged a successful show of her delicate pots and vases with their distinctive broad, flat rims. Pauline Solven's inventive and brightly coloured glassware found an eager public, as did David Pye with his large show of wooden, marble and iron bowls. And such was the enthusiasm for Quentin Bell's boldly coloured and patterned ceramics that he was invited back to exhibit three times.

Liberty's modern history as one of Britain's most distinctive shops can be plotted by the numerous special exhibitions it hosted through the nineteen-seventies and nineteen-eighties, beginning in September 1971, when Ringo Starr, the ex-Beatle, and his designer partner Robin Cruickshank were invited to stage a show of their new furniture in the London store. The centrepiece was an object very much of its time – a five-feet-long stainless steel table, supported at either end by a pair of Rolls Royce automobile radiators. Also distinctively of the nineteen-seventies were the

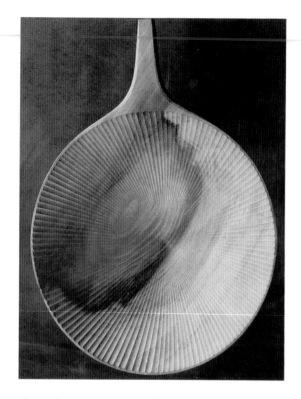

Carved wooden bowl (above) *by David Pye, 1980, shown in the newly-established One Off shop; Pye's work became a regular feature in the exhibition calendar.*

Ceramics by Quentin Bell (right) *exhibited in 1985; the bright colours and bold designs of Quentin Bell's work made striking displays in the One Off shop at a time of great public interest in the work of the Bloomsbury group.*

Previous double-page The discovery of designs by Raoul Dufy at Liberty's French textile factory led to the creation of the Dufy Collection in 1978; illustrated (left above) *are:* 'Tulipes' (upper left), 'Hortensias' (upper right), 'Nuances' (centre left), 'Liserons' (centre right) *and* 'Anémones' (lower left to right). *In the mid nineteen-seventies Liberty's produced a number of Oriental designs in the* 'Fuji' *and* 'Choki' *textile ranges* (left below) *derived from Japanese motifs. Two examples of present-day artwork for textile designs* (right above), *with the original turn-of-the-century patterns from which they are derived. Colourful designs by Alison Wootton* (right below): 'Les Demoiselles' (left) *and* 'Tourbillon' (right) *date from 1984.*

Ringo Starr's 'Rolls-Royce' table, 1971; in one of Liberty's most extraordinary shows Ringo Starr, Robin Cruickshank and British Steel combined to produce a range of steel furniture, displayed to great effect under spotlights in a black-painted room.

'cylinder of sound' circular tower hi-fi unit with a pair of steel drum speaker cabinets, the television set cased in stainless steel, and a circular storage tower with hinged doors. Most stylish of all the forty or so objects was a circular fireplace surround designed for Ringo's house.

While the designs have hardly survived as modern classics, the exhibition was quite unlike anything Liberty's had ever staged before and marked an important stage in the shop's history. As Penny Radford remarked in *The Times*: 'It is a double celebration. Not only does it herald a mammoth new collection of furniture from ROR, but the opening – or drastic revamping – of a large section of Liberty's modern furniture department.' Liberty's had in fact taken a radical step and painted an entire room jet black and spotlit the steel objects – the idea was to make them look like planets against the sky.

Furniture was not, however, one of Liberty's major strengths in the seventies. The post-war attempts at introducing modern styling from Scandinavia enjoyed a brief success, but had dwindled during the sixties. The English Arts and Crafts – 'Liberty Style' – did continue as a perennial favourite with customers and so too did reproduction pieces, especially in Regency styles.

Late in the seventies, however, the furniture department began to display its harvest from visits to Italy, where strong links were forged with many manufacturers of international stature. Among the most interesting and prestigious suppliers were Arteluce, Artemide, Flos, Arflex, B&B and, of course, Cassina which produced innovative and startlingly simple furniture designed by the likes of Gio Ponti, Mario Bellini and Vico Magistretti. Indeed, Magistretti's famous 'Maralunga' sofa, with its articulated arms and back, became the best selling item of furniture at Liberty's from the late seventies through to the mid eighties.

The mounting of large in-store extravaganzas, begun in the nineteen-seventies, became a permanent feature of the shop's activities. In the spring of 1980 the hugely successful 'Japan at Liberty' show was staged; by the end of the first evening the entire range of specially imported contemporary ceramics had been sold. The shop had, by this time, become expert at bringing a sense of drama to retailing, characterized by Paul Muller's stunning window displays and such visual devices as the scaled-down red pagoda he placed over the main Regent Street entrance. Like many subsequent exhibitions, 'Japan at Liberty' was linked to an exhibition on the same theme at the Victoria and Albert Museum. However, while the museum exhibits were shown in glass cases, Liberty's placed exactly the same exhibits in the shop for sale. There were fans, ceramics, paintings, examples of calligraphy, decorative screens, kitchenware, paper lanterns, masks, cast iron kettles, kimonos, and even plastic replica food.

Pagoda-style entrance (above), *1980; at the 'Japan at Liberty' exhibition customers were able to buy the Japanese goods which were also displayed at the concurrent Victoria and Albert Museum exhibition.*

'Memphis Meets Liberty', 1983; the shop took the avant-garde furniture, ceramics and glass fresh from the Boilerhouse Gallery's exhibition of Memphis design and sold the whole collection within a few days. A special collection of scarves (right), *reflecting the Memphis palette, was produced to coincide with the exhibition.*

Howard Hodgkin's room (opposite above) *in the 'Four Rooms' exhibition, 1984.*

The 'Plastics Age' exhibition (opposite below) *of 1990 was to coincide with a similar event at the Victoria and Albert Museum, another example of Liberty's combination of commercial promotion and up-to-date cultural awareness.*

At the Regent Street and Great Marlborough Street shops the grand set-piece exhibitions followed each other with increasing rapidity. Among the finest shows of the early nineteen-eighties was '21 Years – 21 Chairs' which set the pace for the rest of the decade; all the manufacturers and designs featured in the show became firm favourites with Liberty customers. Among the most popular were Bellini's straight-backed leather and steel 'Corium 1' chair and several of Magistretti's designs, including the 'Selene' all-plastic chair, the 'Maralunga' sofa and, later, the plush leather 'Veranda' folding and extendable chair. This heralded the arrival at Liberty's of the latest smooth, sculpted designs from leading furniture producers. Then, in spring 1982, there was 'Little India', for which the shop imported a huge collection of dhurries, shawls, rubies from Rajasthan, brass pots and woks, silks, chapati boards and even saffron ice cream. This coincided with major London exhibitions at both the Victoria and Albert Museum and the Hayward Gallery.

The skill of linking commercial enterprise with the most exciting elements in modern design was never better displayed than in the selling exhibition featuring the Italian group Memphis. The Boilerhouse, the short-lived modern design gallery at the Victoria and Albert Museum, invited the Italian group to display its furniture, ceramics and glass there for the first time in Britain; Liberty's then agreed with Memphis and the Boilerhouse to sell the goods afterwards. The brightly coloured and geometrically eccentric furniture and objects attracted huge attention in the exhibition and at the shop; the Regent Street windows were ablaze with day-glo colours, neon flashing sign, jukeboxes, fluorescent clothes and dazzling printed fabrics.

The most contentious exhibition of the decade at Liberty's came in 1984 – 'Four Rooms'. During the quietest time of the year, February, it was visited by approximately 50,000 people. 'Four Rooms' was in fact a touring Arts Council exhibition devised by four contemporary artists: Howard Hodgkin, Marc Camille Chaimowicz, Richard Hamilton and Anthony Caro. Each was invited to design a room interior.

The show occupied two large rooms on the shop's fourth floor where Hodgkin's room, cosy and filled with bright patches of paint on walls and furniture, soft furnishings and bronze lamps, stood in stark contrast to Richard Hamilton's oddly disturbing hospital-like room, with grilles as windows and a television monitor showing a continuous-loop video of Margaret Thatcher, then Prime Minister. The plastic bucket placed by the bed was continually being taken away by the cleaners and eventually had to be nailed to the floor. This space was, in Hamilton's words, 'inspired by the bleak, disinterested, seedily clinical style of the establishment institution'. In contrast, the ascetic, minimalist and beautiful detailed apartment interior by Chaimowicz was designed to be an anonymous part of an imaginary city. Again this contrasted strongly with Caro's 'Child Tower Room'. This latter space was filled with a Cubist-inspired, oak sculpture

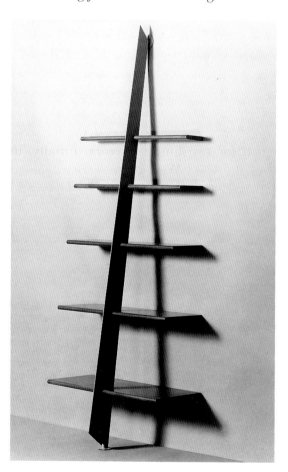

This shelving unit was featured in the 'Negative Positive' exhibition of 1985; the exhibits were selected by Andrée Putman. Following close on the heels of an Arts and Crafts retrospective, the exhibition was proof once again of Liberty's commitment to the most exciting forces in modern design.

Russian-style embellishments over Liberty's Regent Street entrance announced the 'Russian Christmas' theme inside, 1989. The shop responded rapidly to the spirit of glasnost *in the late nineteen-eighties by importing a wide range of arts and crafts from the Ukraine.*

resembling a crashed space rocket and which had a stairway leading up to an upper look-out room.

The 'Four Rooms' exhibition highlighted a problem constantly faced by the late twentieth-century Liberty's: whether to be associated principally with the marketing of nostalgia or with innovation, finding the balance between selling antiques and classic prints or commissioning and buying in modern work. In the event, the store has found itself in the unique position of being able to promote both sides of its character successfully.

After the success of 'Four Rooms', in the following year Liberty's displayed its dual nature: the 110th anniversary saw the store filled with important Arts and Crafts objects, from furniture to jewellery and silverware. The exhibits, many of them originally commissioned by the store, were all for sale and included metalwork by Archibald Knox, E. W. Godwin and Bruce Talbert, chairs by Ambrose Heal, a seven-piece bedroom set by E. G. Punnett and tiled washstand by Leonard Wyburd. This return to the past was immediately countered by 'Negative Positive', a show selected by the modernist French architect Andrée Putman on the theme of black, white and chrome furniture and furnishings. The show was a reminder of the great early modernist skills of Eileen Gray and introduced Philippe Stark's angular chairs and high-tech desk lamps by Mario Fortuny.

Liberty's quickly took advantage of the newly improved relations between the Soviet Union and the West. In 1989 some of the most unusual and beautiful objects ever seen in the store were put on sale in the context of a 'Russian Christmas'. The arts and crafts of the Ukraine formed the bulk of the goods, many of which had rarely been seen outside their areas of production. Along with the traditional nesting dolls – containing up to twelve dolls, each painted to reveal an unfolding story – there were Kosova ceramics painted with naive pictures of peasants, animals and flowers, intricately woven multi-coloured hats, flat-weave Ukrainian rugs, amber jewellery and richly decorated samovar tea urns. The most expensive and bizarre item to have been imported was a briefcase on sale for £1,000. This was fashioned from Russian reindeer hide recovered from a shipwrecked boat which had lain on the seabed for two hundred years. Finally, in keeping with the rapid thawing of the Cold War, there were copies of watches produced in Russia for Pravda bearing red faces, hammer and sickle hands and the word 'Perestroika'.

An important exhibition in early 1990 of the history, development and uses of plastics at the Victoria and Albert Museum prompted Liberty's to run a parallel exhibition. The best modern furniture in plastic included designs by Philippe Starck whose recent work for the manufacturer Kartell consisted of round and square topped tables on bulbous stems, together with stacking chairs distinguished by curved tubular backs. Kartell's classic cylindrical and curved plastic storage unit systems, originally produced in the nineteen-seventies, were also shown. Theatrical costumiers Morris Angel loaned a collection of nineteen-sixties and nineteen-seventies plastic

Sofas by Jipang exhibited at Liberty's in 1984.

The logo of the Muji shop, opened on the Liberty premises in 1991, is a strong reminder of Liberty's trading links with Japan.

無印良品
NO BRAND GOODS
MUJI

clothing which could be seen alongside raincoats, umbrellas and shoes, all for sale. One of the most colourful sections of the store was in the basement bathroom and kitchens area where an explosion of brightly coloured objects stole the show. Here were swing-top bins, dust pans with slot-in brushes, watering cans, wine glasses, dishes and plates, see-through weighing scales, black frilly washing-up gloves, fluorescent hot water bottles, inflatable sharks, books with plastic pages and, of course, a bathroom duck.

Liberty's is now arguably closer in style to the great emporium envisaged by its founder than it has been for several decades. Regular buying trips around the world have brought a brilliant eclecticism to the company's approach to design and retailing. Prints are forging ahead with contemporary designs, some even on modern fabrics such as Lycra; trading links with Japan have become increasingly strong; and there has been a return to commissioning and producing Liberty's own furniture. The link with Japan, a traditional source of goods for Liberty's, was further strengthened with the opening of the Japanese Muji shop. Liberty's founder would surely have admired the Japanese devotion to good quality and design, from basic classic clothing (black polo-neck sweaters, T-shirts and tracksuit pants), nylon travel bags and stationery, to galvanized metal and wooden storage boxes, chopsticks, bowls and seaweed-flavoured crisps. Liberty's return to its traditional market links was further emphasized by its massive commitment to the 'Festival of Japan' in the same year when, for a period, virtually every department in the store exhibited and sold Japanese artefacts.

In 1991, for the first time in more than eighty years, Liberty's revived the tradition of commissioning and producing own-label furniture. The designer chosen was Hélène Tiedermann. The new collection – called

'Liberty 1', a new collection of furniture designed by Hélène Tiedermann, 1991; after a break of more than eighty years, Liberty's revived the tradition of commissioning and producing its own-label furniture. Tiedermann's designs included an appropriate dash of Arts and Crafts style blended with modern discipline.

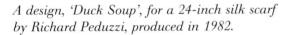

A design, 'Duck Soup', for a 24-inch silk scarf by Richard Peduzzi, produced in 1982.

'Liberty 1' – evolved in response to an increasing demand for good quality contemporary furniture. Nothing suitable was available on the market, so Liberty's commissioned its own. Tiedermann's designs were given unmistakable Arts and Crafts styling – with swooping lines, tapering shapes, gently curved legs and simple copper clasps – but with a refined, modern air. The 'Liberty 1' range, British made and produced in cherry wood, consisted of around a dozen pieces including a large dining table, coffee table, dining chairs upholstered in Liberty fabric and horizontal and vertical sideboards. The pieces were given names such as the 'Cornelian' storage unit and 'Topaz' chair, reflecting the original Arts and Crafts fascination with semi-precious gemstones.

Liberty of London Prints, meanwhile, was preparing a series of themed collections which met with instant public approval. Despite the fact that the Punk and post-Punk era left fashion with a taste for black clothing and plain fabrics, the distinctive prints held their own in the market. Among the most distinguished was the 'Celtic' range, launched in 1982. With names including 'Cassiopeia', 'Eugenia', 'Gydeld' and 'Dokkum', the designs were inspired by medieval illuminated manuscripts at the British Museum. Other medieval-style designs were commissioned from Richard Peduzzi, who subsequently became head of the Paris School of Decorative Arts. Inspiration from eighteenth-century prints then provided the studio with its 'Transformer' collection in 1983. The complex, geometric patterns were simplified and sharpened up for contemporary use and produced prints reminiscent of knot gardens, mazes, stained glass and ancient calligraphy. More recently, John Laflin, the design director of Liberty of London Prints, has commissioned a series of designs from The Cloth, a group of Scottish textile designers, on the theme of checks and squares in various colour combinations.

Acknowledgments and Contributors

The editor and publishers of the book would like to extend their thanks to the chairman, directors and staff of both Liberty Retail Ltd and Liberty of London Prints Ltd for the help they have given in its preparation. Especial thanks is due to the chairman, Harry Weblin, for his co-operation and enthusiasm in the early steps of the project and also to the following: Alastair Baldry, Heather Casimir, Ali Edney, John Laflin, Paul Muller, Tracey Norton, Lee St. Clair, Oliver Stewart-Liberty and Richard Stewart-Liberty. Thanks is also due to: Roy Gentry, formerly display manager at Liberty's; Alison Kenney of Westminster City Archives, Victoria Library, London; Isabelle Sinden and other members of staff in the Picture Library of the Victoria and Albert Museum, and Kenneth Wootton, formerly antiques buyer at Liberty's.

ALISON ADBURGHAM is an expert on the history of retailing in the nineteenth and twentieth centuries and its relationship to developments in taste and style; she is, notably, the author of *Shops and Shopping 1800–1914* (1964), *Liberty's, a Biography of a Shop* (1975) and *Shopping in Style* (1979).

STEPHEN ASTLEY is a member of the curatorial staff at the Victoria and Albert Museum, London; he has worked in the Department of Furniture and Interior Design and now works in the Department of Designs, Prints and Drawings, specializing in the decorative arts and interior design.

PATRICIA BAYER has written extensively on twentieth-century decorative arts; she is the author of *Art Deco Interiors* (1990) and *Art Deco Architecture* (1992).

CATHERINE BINDMAN is a member of the curatorial staff of the Department of Designs, Prints and Drawings of the Victoria and Albert Museum, London.

MALCOLM HASLAM has written on many aspects of the decorative arts of the first half of the twentieth century; his many publications include *English Art Pottery 1865–1915* (1975), *In the Nouveau Style* (1989) and *Arts and Crafts Carpets* (1991).

JENNIFER HARRIS is the curator of textiles and deputy director of the Whitworth Art Gallery, University of Manchester.

WENDY HITCHMOUGH specializes in the architectural history of notable twentieth-century buildings; her publications include books on *The Michelin Building* (1987) and *The Hoover Factory* (1992).

MARGARET KNIGHT is a member of the staff of the Department of Education at the Victoria and Albert Museum, London, specializing in modern applied arts.

FAY SWEET is a journalist and photographer who specializes in contemporary design and architecture; she is a frequent contributor to reviews and newspapers, notably *The Independent*.

ERIC TURNER is a member of the curatorial staff of the Department of Metalwork at the Victoria and Albert Museum, London, specializing in late nineteenth- and early twentieth-century domestic ware.

JUDITH WATT is a costume historian and exhibition consultant; she contributes frequently on the subject to a number of leading fashion journals, including *GQ*.

Illustration Credits

G.P. & J. Baker 55*r*, 59*b*.

Gawthorpe Hall, Lancashire, Rachel Kay-Shuttleworth Collection 148*l*.

Glasgow Art Gallery and Museum 99.

Liberty Archive, Westminster City Archives, London 8, 9*l*, 25, 27, 32*a*, 33, 34, 41, 42*a & b*, 44, 70, 71*l & r*, 106, 116, 118, 119*l & r*, 120, 122*al & ar*, 150, 151*l & ar & br*, 162, 163, 168, 169, 174, 175*ar & b*, 176, 178*a & b*, 179*a & b*, 189, 205, 206, 208, 209, 212*a & b*, 213, 214*a*, 216.

Liberty of London Prints Limited 10–11, 66–7, 146–7, 154–5, 171, 182–3, 187, 207, 210–11, 219*b*.

Liberty Retail Limited 2, 6*l*, 6–7, 14, 15, 82*a*, 83, 86, 87, 95, 108*l*, 109, 129*r*, 142*a*, 143, 144*a & b*, 145, 177*l & r*, 186.

London: British Architectural Library, RIBA 76*al*.

National Portrait Gallery 36*a*.

By courtesy of the Board of Trustees of the Victoria and Albert Museum 9*r*, 23, 24, 28*a & b*, 38, 43, 49, 57, 60, 63*r*, 64, 68, 72*a*, 78*b*, 89*a*, 100, 101, 104, 105*l*, 110, 114*al*, 115*l & c*, 121*l & r*, 128*l & c & r*, 129*l & cl & cr*, 140, 141*l & r*, 142*b*, 149, 152*c*, 153, 164, 165, 180*l & r*, 181, 184*l & r*, 196, 197*a & b*, 198*bl & br*, 200, 201*a*.

Manchester: The Gallery of English Costume, Platt Hall (Manchester City Art Galleries) 152*l*.

Whitworth Art Gallery, University of Manchester 22, 55*l*, 56, 58*b*, 59*a*, 62, 65.

New York: Collection, The Museum of Modern Art: gift of Liberty & Co. Ltd, London 77.

Private Collection 50, 51, 63*l*, 72*b*, 73*l & r*, 75, 76*ac & ar*, 80*a*, 82*b*, 84*b*, 88, 90*a & b*, 91*a & b*, 92, 93, 94*a & b*, 97*l & r*, 98, 102*l & c & r*, 103, 105*r*, 108*r*, 111, 112*a & b*, 114*ar & b*, 115*r*, 117, 148*r*, 160, 161, 191*a & b*, 195.

Race 189*a*.

Totnes, Devonshire Collection of Period Costume: loan from Mrs Quintin Morris 69.

Trondheim, Nordenfjeldske Kunstindustrimuseum 54, 58*a*.

Trustees of the Wedgwood Museum, Barlaston, Staffordshire, England 199.

PHOTOGRAPHIC ACKNOWLEDGMENTS

Courtesy Alison Adburgham 18–19, 20, 21, 29, 30*b*, 31, 45, 74, 122*b*, 131, 175*al*.

Associated Press 170*r*.

Richard Dennis 107, 157, 158*a & b*, 159.

Fiell 190*b*.

Courtesy Roy Gentry 16, 166–7, 170*l*, 172, 173, 185, 193, 198*a*, 201*b*, 204.

Courtesy Higgs & Hill PLC 126–7, 130, 132, 133, 134, 135, 136, 137, 138*l & r*, 139.

Dennis Hooker 189*a*.

Ken Jackson and Philip de Bay 103.

Edgar Jones Photography 61, 78*a*, 80*b*, 81, 85.

John Kaine 10–11, 66–7, 146–7, 154–5, 171, 182–3, 187, 207, 210–11.

Bibliographical Note

Description of the designs and designers of the early years at Liberty's can be found in most histories of the decorative arts in Britain. *Victorian and Edwardian Furniture and Interiors* by Jeremy Cooper (1987) is particularly helpful in its description of Liberty's in the context of the Arts and Crafts Movement. Two major sources of information about the Liberty shops and design studios are the Liberty Archive held by Westminster City Archives at the Victoria Library, 160 Buckingham Palace Road, London SW1, and the collection of Liberty catalogues held in the Victoria and Albert Museum Library, which runs from 1881 to 1949. Recent publications on Liberty's have tended to concentrate exclusively on the Arts and Crafts period of the firm or on some individual aspect of its activities. The Centenary Exhibition of 1975 did, however, produce two notable general works: *Liberty's 1875–1975* (London, 1975, the catalogue of the exhibition) and *Liberty's A Biography of a Shop* by Alison Adburgham (London, 1975). The following titles should also be noted:

Arwas, Victor, *Liberty Style*, Tokyo, 1983;
Levy, Mervyn, *Liberty Style, The Classic Years: 1898–1910*, London, 1986;
Morris, Barbara, *Liberty Design 1874–1914*, London, 1989;
Tilbrook, A. J. joint editor with House, Gordon, *The Designs of Archibald Knox for Liberty & Co*, London, 1976;
Watkins, Charmian, *Decorating with Fabric Liberty Style*, London, 1987.

Liberty Outlets

The following directory includes a list of Liberty shops in the United Kingdom and outlets in other major countries where Liberty designs may be found. While every effort has been made to include as many addresses as possible, this list should not be regarded as exhaustive. Every effort has been made to ensure that all the information given is correct, but the editor and publishers cannot be held responsible for any unintentional inaccuracies.

UNITED KINGDOM
Regent Street, London, W1R 6AH
12 New Bond Street, Bath, BA1 1BE
Rackhams Ltd, Box 132, Corporation Street, Birmingham, B2 5JS
16–18 East Street, Brighton, BN1 1HP
10 Trinity Street, Cambridge, CB2 1SU
44 Burgate, Canterbury, Kent, C21 2HW
86 The Promenade, Cheltenham, GL50 1NB
30 Bridge Street, Chester, CH1 1NQ
47 George Street, Edinburgh, EH2 2HT
127 Buchanan Street, Glasgow, G1 1JA
Army & Navy, 105–111 High Street, Guildford, Surrey, GU1 3DU
De Gruchy, King Street, St. Helier, Jersey, Channel Islands
21 Church Street, Kingston-upon-Thames, Surrey, KT1 1RW
16–18 King Street, Manchester, M2 6AG
35 London Steet, Norwich, NR2 1HU
115 High Street, Oxford, OX1 4BX
23 Catherine Street, Salisbury, Wilts, SP1 2DQ
Russell & Dorrell, 9–12 High Street, Worcester, WR1 2QT
15 Davygate, York, YO1 2RQ

AUSTRALIA
David Jones, Elizabeth Street, Sydney, New South Wales
Georges, 162 Collins Street, Melbourne, Victoria
That Special Look, 610 Stuart Street, Ballarat, Victoria
Wardlaw Pty Ltd, 230–232 Auburn Road, Hawthorn, Victoria

BELGIUM
Donald Thiriar SPRL, 610 Chaussée d'Ansemberg, 1180 Brussels

FRANCE
Bouchara, 54 blvd. Haussmann, Paris 8; 57 rue de Passy, Paris 16; 8–10 avenue des Ternes, Paris 17
Chez Peinture, 18 rue du Pré-aux-Clercs, Paris 7
Editions du Nopal, 3 rue Jacob, Paris 6
Fanny le Varlet/Mauve, 14 rue des Elus, Reims
Frères d'Emile Bloch, 31 rue Grand-Pont, Rouen
Maison Georges Havel, place Bellevue, BP11, Biarritz

GERMANY
Alsterhaus, Jungfernstieg 16–20, Hamburg 36
Breuninger, Markstrasse 3, Stuttgart
Deutsche Werkstätten, Weissegasse 8, Dresden
Jean Pitteroff, Marientorgraben 13, Nuremberg
KDW, Tauenziehnstrasse 21–24, Berlin 30
Lammfromm & Bogel, Hohenzollerndamm 12, Berlin 31
Oliver Heal Textil GmbH, Stuttgart 10
Schildknecht & Rall & Gerber, Stuttgart 10
Vieille Provence, Am Roemerberg 8–10, Frankfurt-am-Main
Walter Diehm GmbH, Hanauerstrasse 66, Aschaffenburg

ITALY
Bianzino SAS, Piazza San Giovanni 11R, Florence
Caliber, Via Fleming 55, Rome
Clerici Paolo SAS, Via Dante 4, Milan
Mazzoni SRL, Via Orsanmichele 14R, Florence
Principe di Doni, Via Strozzi 21R–29R, Florence
Telerie Ghidoli Due, Via Gonzaga 5, Milan

THE NETHERLANDS
Metz & Co, Keizergracht 455, Amsterdam

NEW ZEALAND
Ballantynes, City Mall, Christchurch
Kirkcaldie & Stains Ltd, Lambton Quay, Wellington

Limited Editions, 262–264 Thornton Quay, Wellington

Smith & Caughey, Queen Street, Auckland

Wardlaw New Zealand Ltd, Newmarket, Auckland

UNITED STATES

Liberty of London, 630 Fifth Avenue, 51st Street, New York, NY 10020

Liberty of London, 845 N. Michigan Avenue, Chicago, IL 60611

Alabama

Peanut Butter & Jelly Kids, 3607 Old Shell Road, Mobile, AL 36608

Arizona

Couture Fabrics, 7172 E. 1st Avenue, Scottsdale, AZ 85251

Fabric Gallery, 5050 N. 7th Steet, Phoenix, AZ 85014

California

Betty's Fabrics, 1627 Broadway, Santa Maria, CA 93454

Britex Fabrics, 146 Geary Street, San Francisco, CA 94148

Carole's Calico Corner, 2529 East Bluff Drive, Newport Beach, CA 92660

Cotton Bale, The, 3692 The Barnyard, Carmel, CA 93923

F & S Fabrics, 10682 West Pico Blvd, Los Angeles, CA 90064

The Handloomed Fabric Store, 1502 Walnut Street, Berkley, CA 94709

Int'l Silks & Woollens, 8347 Beverly Blvd, Los Angeles, CA 90048

Satin Moon Fabrics, 32 Clement Street, San Francisco, CA 94118

Sweet Child of Mine, 3720 Miramesa Court, Santa Clara, CA 95051

Colorado

D'Leas Fabric Affair, 2620 East Third Avenue, Denver, CO 80206

Elfriede's Fine Fabrics, 1936 14th Street, Boulder, CO 80302

Wilhelmina's, 528 North Tejon, Colorado Springs, CO 80903

Connecticut

Pine Stone Stitchery, 888 Main Street, Willimantic, CT 06226

Florida

Capitol Imports, 2518 Cathay Court, Tallahassee, FL 32308

Fabric Boutique, 31 Cross Roads S/C, Sarasota, FL 34239

Fabricsworld, 7931 SW 40th Street, Miami, FL 33155

Heirloom Stitchery, 906 Park Avenue, Sisters Village Shop Centre, Orange Park, FL 32073

High Cotton of Jacksonville, 5639 Beach Blvd, Jacksonville, FL 32207

Warp & Weft, 939 4th Avenue, Naples, FL 33940

Georgia

Gallery of Fabrics, 3161 Maple Drive, Atlanta, GA 30326

Irene's, 120 South Street, Thomasville, GA 31792

Sew Magnifique, 3220 Paces Ferry Place NW, Atlanta, GA 30305

Sewing Gallery, 362-D Furys Ferry Blvd, Augusta, GA 30907

Idaho

The Yardstick, 5th & Washington, Ketchum, ID 83340

Illinois

Fishman's, 1101–43 S. Des Plaines, Chicago, IL 60643

Hagenbring's, Campbell at Vail, 105 W. Campbell, Arlington Heights, IL 60005

Joy's Vogue Fabrics, 68 Central Park West, Jacksonville, IL 62650

Quilted Stuffing, The, 65 North River Lane, Geneva, IL 60134

Sewing Studio, 1503 E. College Avenue, Normal, IL 61761

Stitches-n-Stuffing, 790 Royal St. George Drive, Naperville, IL 60540

Iowa

Kalona Kountry Kreations, 2134 560th Street SW, Kalona, IA 52247

Kansas

Osage County Quilt Factory, 400 Walnut, Overbrook, KS 66524

Sarah's Fabrics, 925 Massachusetts, Lawrence, KS 66044

Kentucky

Baer Fabrics, 515 East Market Street, Louisville, KY 40202

Smocking Shop, 3829 Staebler, Louisville, KY 40207

Maine

Design Cotton, 399 Fore Street, Portland, OR 04104

Waterwitch, Maine Street, Castene, ME 04421

Maryland

G Street Fabrics, 11854 Rockville Pike, Rockville, MD 20852

Manor House, Corner Maryland Avenue, & State Circle, Annapolis, MD 21401

Massachusetts

Sportswear Store, A Fabric Place, 136 Howard Street, Framingham, MA 01701

Michigan

Whole Cloth, 206 S. 4th Street, Royal Oak, MI 48067

Minnesota

General Textiles, 6130 Olson Memorial Highway, Minneapolis, MN 55422

Ginny's Fine Fabrics, 220 Broadway, Rochester, MN 55904

Treadle Yard Goods, 1338 Grand Avenue, Saint Paul, MN 55105

Missouri

Eunice Farmer Fabrics, 9814 Clayton Road, St. Louis, MO 63124

Jackman's Fabrics, 1221 Andes Blvd, St. Louis, MO 63132

Kaplan's Fabrics, 438 Ward Parkway, Kansas City, MO 64112

Provence Boutique, 9757 Clayton Road, St. Louis, MO 63124

Silks & More Fine Fabrics, 1017 E. Broadway, Columbia, MO 65201

Women's Exchange, 9213 Clayton Road, St. Louis, MO 63124

Nebraska

J & J Fabrics, 13059 W. Center Road, Omaha, NE 68144

New Hampshire

Keene Mill End, 55 Talston Street, Keene, NH 03431

New Jersey

Van EPS, 494 Prospect Avenue, Little Silver, NJ 07739

White Cottage, 327 Franklin Avenue, Wycoff, NJ 07481

New Mexico

Sew Natural, 500 Montezuma, Suite 111, Santa Fe, NM 87501

New York

B & J Fabrics, 263 W. 40th Street, New York, NY 10018

Counterpoint Fabrics, 410 Elmwood Avenue, Buffalo, NY 14222

Maxine Fabrics, 62 W. 39th Street, New York, NY 10018

Knight's Designer Fabrics, Mid City Shopping Center, 100 Broadway-Menands, Albany, NY 12204

Paron Fabrics, 60 W. 57th Street, New York, NY 10019

North Carolina

Barbee Fabrics, PO Box 4235—HWY 87, Glen Raven, NC 27215

Cotton Boll, The, 91 S. Elliot Road, Chapel Hill, NC 27514

Fabric Center, Inc, 1301 National Highway, Thomasville, NC 27360

House of Fabrics, 214 Merrimon Avenue, Asheville, NC 28810

Margaret Christies, 4616 Market Street, Greensboro, NC 27407

Mulberry Silks & Fine Fabrics, 200 North Greensboro Street, Carrsboro, NC 27510

Quilters Gallery, The, 1329 E. Boulevard, Charlotte, NC 28203

South Fork Cloth Shop, 3911 Country Club Road, Winston-Salem, NC 27104

Waechter's Silk Shop, 94 Charlotte Street,

Index

Numerals in italics refer to illustrations